The *Skeptical Inquirer* is a featured journal in InfoTrac® College Edition

Clear Thinking with Psychology

SEPARATING SENSE FROM NONSENSE

JOHN RUSCIO
Elizabethtown College

WADSWORTH

THOMSON LEARNING™

Australia • Canada • Mexico • Singapore • Spain • United Kingdom • United States

Sponsoring Editor: *Marianne Taflinger*
Marketing Manager: *Joanne Terhaar*
Editorial Assistant: *Stacy Green*
Production Editor: *Mary Vezilich*
Production Service: *Shepherd Inc.*
Manuscript Editor: *Patterson Lamb*

Permissions Editor: *Sue Ewing*
Cover Design: *Roger Knox*
Print Buyer: *Jessica Reed*
Typesetting: *Shepherd Inc.*
Printing and Binding: *Webcom Ltd.*

For more information about this or any other Wadsworth product, contact:
WADSWORTH
511 Forest Lodge Road
Pacific Grove, CA 93950 USA
www.wadsworth.com
1-800-423-0563 (Thomson Learning Academic Resource Center)

For permission to use material from this work, contact us by
web: www.thomsonrights.com
fax: 1-800-730-2215
phone: 1-800-730-2214

Printed in Canada

10 9 8 7 6 5 4 3 2 1

Library of Congress Cataloging-in-Publication Data

Ruscio, John.
   Clear thinking with psychology : separating sense from nonsense / John Ruscio
     p. cm.
   Includes bibliographical references and index.
   ISBN 0-534-53659-X (alk. paper)
    1. Psychology—Study and teaching (Higher) I. Title.

BF77 .R87 2001
150'.7'2—dc21
                                       2001035583

To my parents, John and Janis Ruscio

Related Titles of Interest

To order any of these texts go to http://psychology.wadsworth.com.

Contents

Chapter 1

Introduction: Pseudoscience and the Need for Clear Thinking   1

Part One

DECEPTION

Chapter 2

Language: Misleading and Evasive Tactics   16

Chapter 3

Magic: The Allure of Exotic Rituals, Fantasy, and Mysticism   *30*

Chapter 4

Authority: Appeals to Blind Obedience   *42*

Part Two

SELF-DECEPTION

Chapter 5

Experience: The Limitations of Testimonials as Evidence   *56*

Chapter 8

Science: Evaluating Claims to Knowledge   92

Part Three

PSYCHOLOGICAL TRICKS

Chapter 9

Risk: Biased Perceptions and the Media Paradox   106

Chapter 10

*Belief: Confirmation Bias, Post-Hockery,
and Overconfidence   115*

Part Four

DECISION MAKING AND ETHICS

Chapter 13

Assessment: Classical Decision Theory   152

Chapter 14

Decisions: Clinical Versus Statistical Approaches   165

Chapter 15

Ethics: The Use and Promotion of Unverified Treatments   179

Chapter 16

Tools: Suggestions for Clear Thinking   192

References   203

Index   217

Preface

In 1973, David Rosenhan published a provocative study entitled "On Being Sane in Insane Places." Eight mentally healthy individuals—including Rosenhan himself—presented themselves to different mental hospitals, requesting admission based on a complaint of distressing auditory hallucinations. All of these "pseudopatients" were admitted to the hospitals. One individual was diagnosed with manic depression; the rest were diagnosed with schizophrenia. Once admitted, the pseudopatients stopped faking their symptoms. Aside from extensive note-taking for the purpose of data collection, the pseudopatients acted normally to determine whether the staff would discover their "sanity" and release them. After an average stay of 19 days, each pseudopatient was eventually discharged; most were given a revised diagnosis of "schizophrenia in remission."

It appeared that mental health professionals could not tell the "sane" from the "insane." Sounds outrageous, right? In fact, Rosenhan's study caused quite a stir in the field. "Something must be done about our hospitals!" But hold on a moment: Let's consider the alternative explanations and think critically about the research.

CHALLENGING WIDELY ACCEPTED CLAIMS

In a 1975 special section of the *Journal of Abnormal Psychology,* a number of psychological scientists considered Rosenhan's study and found that he had used seriously flawed methodology, ignored relevant data, and reached unsound conclusions. Throughout the special section, as well as in an elaborated critique by Spitzer (1976), many problems were identified:

- The study was fraught with the potential for *confirmation bias.* Because Rosenhan and his fellow pseudopatients had prior knowledge of the study's hypotheses, they may have selectively observed and recorded

information that confirmed rather than refuted these hypotheses or
acted in ways that brought about expected results through self-fulfilling
prophecies.

- Some of Rosenhan's key arguments ignored relevant *empirical data.*
  While making simplistic overgeneralizations about diagnoses, Rosenhan
  failed to acknowledge the evidence that diagnoses are generally not only
  quite reliable and valid, but that they also help to connect people with
  appropriate treatments.

- Similarly, Rosenhan used *faulty logic* when arguing that diagnoses were
  invalid because the pseudopatients were in fact mentally healthy. Given
  (1) the sole presenting complaint of auditory hallucinations, (2) the
  reasonable assumption that individuals would seek voluntary admission
  to a mental hospital only if they were quite distressed, and (3) the
  further assumption that there was no good reason to suspect that people
  were not faking, the diagnosis of the greatest likely validity *is*
  schizophrenia. That all but one pseudopatient received this diagnosis is
  actually evidence of impressive diagnostic agreement across hospitals in
  reaching the most valid judgment.

- Other assertions were based on *insufficient evidence.* Rosenhan
  presented no compelling support for his bold claims about the negative
  effects of labeling. The only suggestion that the staff viewed the
  pseudopatients in a biased way was several nurses' observation that
  "patients engaged in writing behavior." This purely factual note has no
  pathological overtones and is meager evidence indeed of the alleged
  biasing effects of labels on perception and interpretation.

- While condemning labels, Rosenhan consistently mistook the *name* of a
  condition for the *behaviors* it denotes. That is, he failed to consider the
  possibility that it is not labels, per se, that may influence people's
  attitudes toward the mentally ill, but rather the unpredictable and
  sometimes threatening behaviors that are associated with the disorders
  themselves.

- Rosenhan used *deceptive language.* The terms *sane* and *insane* are not
  used in psychological discourse or psychiatric diagnosis. They are purely
  legal constructions regarding a criminal defendant's ability to tell right
  from wrong. As a professor of psychology and law, Rosenhan surely knew
  this when he used irrelevant language, most likely as an attention-
  grabbing device.

- Finally, Rosenhan presented no *comparative data* to support his primary
  conclusion that the staff could not tell the difference between mentally
  healthy and unhealthy individuals. To make such an argument, Rosenhan
  would have to have shown us that the staff treated the pseudopatients
  just as they did true schizophrenic inpatients. However, compared with
  patients who do suffer from schizophrenia, the pseudopatients had

notably *short* stays on the psychiatric wards (few individuals suffering a schizophrenic episode are released in just a matter of weeks) and were released with an extremely *uncommon* diagnosis (schizophrenics are virtually never diagnosed "in remission" at discharge). Thus, Rosenhan's own data provide the strongest counterargument against his claims. The staff were indeed quite sensitive to the unusual nature of the pseudopatients, who were clearly *not* mistaken for ordinary patients.

EMPOWERING STUDENTS TO EVALUATE CLAIMS FOR THEMSELVES

Reports of Rosenhan's general procedure and conclusions are repeated *uncritically* in many (if not most) psychology textbooks. I have discussed that controversial study to illustrate what this book is all about: carefully evaluating all claims—even those that are widely accepted or personally satisfying—using logical analysis informed by empirical research. To empower students to think for themselves, this book employs four interrelated pedagogical strategies identified below.

1. Distinguishing Science from Pseudoscience

In each of the courses that I teach, I place a strong emphasis on the distinction between science and pseudoscience. To do so requires the careful balance of two complementary modes of thought long advocated by Carl Sagan: wonder and skepticism. This book encourages an open-minded approach to all subjects, so that all claims are seriously entertained. At the same time, this approach is coupled with an even-handed insistence that sufficient evidence be presented to merit belief. The benefit of this dual approach is that all ideas are given a fair hearing, but only those that are adequately supported are retained.

2. Teaching Scientific Reasoning Skills

Clear thinking is presented as a set of skills that is free to anyone wishing to reason more deliberately and carefully. These skills are presented with a respect for readers' capacity to make personally satisfying decisions. I suggest not *what* readers should believe, but *how* they can arrive at truly informed choices that are most consistent with their own values. By spotting the reasoning fallacies of others and avoiding their own, readers will be better prepared to avoid persuasive appeals that are not in their best interest, acquire and maintain more accurate beliefs, and formulate more cogent, rational arguments in support of their beliefs.

3. Using Memorable Examples

Throughout the book, vivid examples are used to help students retain and apply the principles they are learning. For example, the introductory chapter starts with the remarkable case of Patricia Burgus, whose anxiety and depression were transformed into a diagnosis of multiple personality disorder and the conviction that she was the High Priestess of a satanic cult. Similarly, the chapter on self-deception and testimonials opens with the story of a woman proclaiming the amazing curative powers of urine therapy. A host of memorable examples make the material come alive.

4. Exploring Material Relevant to Many Courses

In selecting examples, I have drawn material from a diverse array of substantive areas within and beyond psychology to show that scientific reasoning is not limited to any one sphere of our lives. Students in introductory psychology, research methods, experimental psychology, or other courses might benefit from this book as a supplementary text that introduces scientific reasoning skills. The large number of examples drawn from pseudoscientific physical and mental health practices would also make this book suitable for courses in health, abnormal, or clinical psychology, as well as courses organized around pseudoscience or critical thinking. I have even used selected chapters from the book for courses in statistics and psychological assessment.

BROAD COVERAGE IS COMPLEMENTED BY ELECTRONIC RESOURCES

This book has four major sections emphasizing unique aspects of clear thinking that apply to the evaluation of claims. The first section, "Deception," introduces the ways by which others may try to mislead us, including such strategies as linguistic tricks and appeals to magical thinking or authority. The second section, "Self-Deception," deals with the ways we unknowingly mislead ourselves, including our tendency to overinterpret the value of personal experience and to ignore the implausibility of and lack of evidence in support of some beliefs. The third section, "Psychological Tricks," presents a variety of mental shortcuts that often serve us well yet require us to trade some accuracy for efficiency. For example, we often misjudge the frequency or probability of an event based on how easily imaginable it is. The fourth and final section, "Decision Making and Ethics," reviews ways through which we can improve the accuracy of our everyday and professional judgments while reaching decisions that are more consistent with sound ethical principles.

To support the exploration of these topics and the application of reasoning skills to new domains, students will have access to Infotrac College Edition. This is one of the most extensive online databases available, with full-text access to over 900 scholarly journals and periodicals including *Skeptical Inquirer* and many other outstanding publications. InfoTrac College Edition keywords are provided in each chapter of the book to allow students to search for additional information on topics of particular interest to them.

ACKNOWLEDGMENTS

I am grateful to the countless individuals who have clarified my thinking through the years. My high school physics teacher, Dennis Gilbert, sparked my interest in science by bringing it to life through witty teaching and demonstrations. During college, Ronnie Janoff-Bulman was a role model who inspired me to specialize in social psychology. Both of my graduate advisers, Teresa Amabile and Joan Tucker, provided a wonderful mix of encouragement, sage advice, and incalculably constructive criticism. In the process of finding my own scholarly niche, three psychological scientists have had a particularly strong and positive influence on me: Paul Meehl, David Faust, and Robyn Dawes. Through discussions and reading of their exemplary research, they have fostered my intellectual growth and development more than they could possibly know. My colleagues at Elizabethtown College have also helped me approach psychological issues in a logical and empirical way. I thank Del Ellsworth, in particular, for reading and discussing an early draft of this book. I would also like to thank these reviewers for their helpful suggestions: Bette Ackerman, Rhodes College; Heinz Fischer, Long Beach City College; Ronald Fisher, Florida International University; Travis Langley, Henderson State University; and Michael Vasey, Ohio State University.

Of course, none of this would have been possible without the sustained faith and nurturance of my parents, John and Janis Ruscio. They have always stressed the value of a good education, maintaining an extraordinary trust in my abilities and respect for my decisions even when we all feared that a degree in psychology might qualify me for little more than pumping gas! Finally, I owe my deepest thanks to my wife and research collaborator, Ayelet Meron Ruscio. Coming from a family of particularly talented and compassionate individuals, Ayelet embodies everything that I aspire to be. Her kindheartedness and intelligence will one day be legendary, but for now you will simply have to take my word for it. Thanks so much to all of you.

ABOUT THE AUTHOR

John Ruscio is an assistant professor of psychology at Elizabethtown College in Lancaster County, Pennsylvania. He earned his bachelor's degree in psychology from the University of Massachusetts at Amherst and then pursued graduate study at Brandeis University in suburban Boston. After completing his doctoral work in social psychology, John joined the faculty at Elizabethtown. He currently follows a picturesque 56-mile route along the Juniata and Susquehanna Rivers to reach Etown from the tiny community of Thompsontown, Pennsylvania.

John teaches a number of courses related to scholarly passions he developed in graduate school, including courses in the psychology of judgment and decision making, research methods, psychological statistics, and tests and measurements. One stream of his research explores factors influencing the accuracy of and confidence in our predictions; another focuses on the classification of psychopathology, including studies of basic diagnostic entities as well as methods for improving psychological assessment. John's published research appears in psychological journals such as *Teaching of Psychology*, *Journal of Consulting and Clinical Psychology*, *Journal of Abnormal Psychology*, and *American Psychologist*, as well as cross-disciplinary scientific outlets such as *Child Maltreatment* and *Skeptical Inquirer*. In moments away from teaching, conducting research, and commuting, he enjoys spending time with his wife or—as vastly inferior alternatives—his electric guitar and tropical fish.

Evaluating Sources Whether in Print or on the World Wide Web

In October 1999, the results of an experimental investigation of the potential healing power of prayer were published in a premier medical journal, the *Archives of Internal Medicine* (Harris et al., 1999). This well-controlled experiment received considerable media attention, often with tantalizing headlines:

- "Heart Patients Fared Better after Secret Prayers"—*Toronto Star*, 10/26/99
- "Prayer's 'Medicinal' Value Gets an Amen from Study"—San Diego *Union-Tribune*, 11/3/99
- "Scientists 'Prove the Power of Prayer'"—London *Daily Telegraph*, 11/11/99

This landmark study captivated a large audience. On radio and television, in newspapers and magazines, on web sites and mailing lists, the message was clear and consistent: Scientific data support the effectiveness of prayer as health care. Perhaps because many previous studies of the relationship between prayer and health were plagued by serious methodological flaws, this one was widely touted as the strongest available evidence in support of prayer. But what actually *were* the results of this study?

The researchers studied 990 patients in a coronary care unit. About one-half of the patients (466) were randomly assigned to receive prayers for their swift recovery, whereas the remaining patients (524) were not. Thirty-five health outcomes were recorded for all patients, including pneumonia, major surgery, cardiac arrest, or death. However, out of the 35 statistical comparisons between groups, only *one* statistically significant difference favored patients in the prayer condition: "Swan-Ganz catheter" ratings. The obvious question is, Why would prayers improve only the "Swan-Ganz catheter" ratings of patients and not other, more beneficial health outcomes among the remaining 34 that were tested? This question is particularly important because, due to the conventions used in statistical testing, we would expect 1 out of every 20 tests to reveal a statistically significant difference *based purely on chance alone*. In this study, only 1 of 35 tests showed a difference between groups, which is *worse* than would be expected by chance! Finally, in addition to these disappointing results, there was no difference in the length of stay of patients in the two groups.

Despite the lack of differences between groups, the researchers constructed composite "course scores" that served to obscure the fact that 34 out of 35 measured health outcomes argued against the efficacy of prayer. For a study that has been widely cited and heavily publicized as providing the best empirical support for prayer, this is paltry evidence indeed. Though the authors themselves are careful to state that "we have not proven that God answers prayer or that God even exists" (Harris et al., 1999, p. 2277), the headlines quoted above show that the media generally disregarded this warning and proclaimed prayer to be an effective remedy for disease.

SHARPENING AND LEVELING

Clearly, the actual results of this experiment have been dramatically distorted—particularly at the level of the headline, beyond which only a small percentage of people read. This example therefore illustrates the ways in which second-hand sources often alter information. When people repeat information, their goals and intentions shape their narratives. Gilovich (1991) describes two processes by which we tend to distort an account in our own attempt to be more entertaining or informative. We *sharpen*—or emphasize—elements of the story that are consistent with our beliefs, theories, or biases, whereas we *level*—or deemphasize—elements of the story that are inconsistent. Each step away from primary source data introduces additional opportunities for sharpening and leveling, leading to increasing distortion of information.

For example, because many people believe in the efficacy of prayer regardless of the research data, it should come as no surprise that the results of the Harris et al. (1999) study have been so selectively filtered at each stage of reporting. First, Harris et al. reported their data in tables, but *interpreted* those data through their beliefs and expectations. They inflated the importance of scraps of evidence that corroborated beliefs in the efficacy of prayer while ignoring voluminous evidence that refuted these beliefs. Second, the press release that summarized this study no doubt sharpened elements of the study favorable to prayer and leveled elements unfavorable to prayer to make the study more "newsworthy." Third, reporters—many of whom may have read only the press release—had another opportunity to filter the results of the study, motivated by the desire to craft a "good story" that would appeal to the public. Fourth, if—like many people—you learned of this study from a friend who heard or read about it in the news, you were yet another step removed from the data.

The distortion of Harris and colleagues' (1999) results shows how important it is to seek primary source data and examine it for yourself. When you allow intermediaries to sharpen and level the available information to fit their stated or unstated assumptions, the trustworthiness of their conclusions may be severely compromised. There are a number of ways to evaluate the quality of informational sources, and these will be described below.

CRITERIA FOR EVALUATING THE QUALITY OF SOURCES

Pretend that you are a patron in a world library that contains everything ever written—from cave inscriptions to web pages. Faced with such an overwhelming array of material, how would you organize your search for suitable reading? What criteria would you establish? Suppose you set aside separate blocks of time for reading that is either entertaining or informative, though some exceptional writing may achieve both goals. How would you select readings for yourself within these two realms? Choosing completely at random would obviously be a foolish strategy, because you would need some criteria to distinguish witty, insightful, and trustworthy prose from writing that is dull, uninspired, and biased. Think for a moment about how you might approach this task. I propose that useful criteria for ranking the quality of sources would differ dramatically depending on whether you were selecting readings primarily for entertainment or for information.

Popularity

In order to be widely read, writing needs to appeal to its audience. For example, if a book is designed to amuse, it will usually become popular only if it is in fact amusing. Thus, the relative popularity of entertainment-oriented works will provide you with a reasonable sense for the extent to which you, too, might enjoy reading them. Some gauges of popularity might include ratings made by readers, book sales figures, awards that the books received, and so forth. Although you might wish to obtain a more personalized list of recommended reading based on the rough categories of comedies, romances, dramas, thrillers, and so on, you would still want to rely on popularity-based rankings of readings within categories that appeal most to you. Thus, though imperfect, the criterion of popularity may be the best gauge of entertainment value.

On the other hand, popularity is not necessarily a good gauge of the *quality* of information. For reasons that are explained below, the most trustworthy sources of factual information are peer-reviewed academic journals and scholarly books. The authors of these publications strive to document their evidence meticulously, to explain clearly the logic of their arguments, and reach conclusions based on research evidence. Unfortunately, these hallmarks of scholarly integrity are not a recipe for commercial success! The readership of scholarly journals and books is far eclipsed by that of many other, less reliable, sources. For example, stroll through any book store. What do you see? Nearly all of the books in the "psychology" section are really "self-help" manuals written by self-proclaimed experts with little or no knowledge of the science of psychology. Such books seldom make reference to psychological research, but instead assert their feel-good ideas for the best way to improve your self-esteem, save your marriage, and be successful in your work. There typically are considerably fewer books on the shelves of the "science" section—if the store even has one—than there are books on occult subjects such as UFOs and alien abductions, extrasensory perception and psychokinesis, ghosts and poltergeists, and so forth. Across the board, books that become popular tend to involve anecdotal reports of compelling personal stories and/or promises of an easy path to health, wealth, or love. These books are seldom based on anything more than the author's personal experiences, with little or no documentation of evidence in support of the author's claims. Thus, although it may be a good way to pick reading to wile away an afternoon, popularity is often a very poor gauge of the reliability, quality, or veracity of information.

Reviews

Perhaps you would like to incorporate favorable and unfavorable reviews into your reading selection process. This seems a wise strategy, though it raises difficult issues. How do you decide which reviews to read? How do you determine whether a reviewer shares your perspective? How do you reconcile contradictory reviews? In fact, it requires considerable effort to establish which reviewers—if any—tend to agree with your tastes, and the time that you spend educating yourself about reviewers would surely not be entertaining. Reviewers are often inconsistent with each other and may even contradict their own previous opinions; after all, aesthetic judgments are extremely subjective. Thus, reading reviews may provide only an inefficient aid to your selection of entertaining sources.

By contrast, you can take advantage of reviews in a far more powerful way in the realm of *informational* writing. All scholarly disciplines have an internal system of peer review that operates behind the scenes to maintain quality control of published information. For example, when a scholar submits a manuscript for publication, the prospective publisher typically obtains anonymous reviews of the manuscript from experts in the field. These peer reviewers critically evaluate the comprehensiveness and relevance of the evidence that is presented and inspect the logic of the argument—including each stated or unstated assumption—that the author has made. Based on these considerations, each reviewer makes a recommendation regarding the suitability of the work for publication. Under the protection of anonymity, peer reviewers adopt

a skeptical attitude and provide brutally frank feedback. Most academic journals and book publishers accept for publication only manuscripts that receive the endorsement of these critical peer reviewers. As a result, the task of evaluating the quality of a source is greatly simplified for the reader.

Within any academic discipline, there is a clearly established hierarchy of sources that indicates to readers the standards against which manuscripts were evaluated. The "top-tier" academic journals and scholarly books have the tightest standards and therefore provide the most trustworthy and reliable information; "second-tier" publishers have more lax standards, and so forth. In comparison, many other sources—such as magazines, newspapers, and the internet—maintain little or no quality control. As a reader, you can take advantage of quality control wielded by the scholarly peer review process by focusing your informational reading on peer-reviewed publications and by seeking top-tier publications rather than lower-ranked publications that employ few or no standards of quality control.

THE INTERNET AS A RESEARCH TOOL

As the foregoing discussion suggests, information provided on-line is ordinarily not critically reviewed by independent sources and must therefore be approached with considerable caution. One of the greatest virtues of the internet is also one of its vices: Just about anyone can post just about anything on the web. There is thus a tension between the internet's unparalleled freedom of expression and the desire for quality control. To date, universal access and unrestricted information exchange have been the prevailing values guiding the development of the internet. Because there are very few pockets of peer-reviewed information, you will have to use your own judgment to assess the reliability and quality of information posted on the web.

The Content of Web Sites

There are several questions you can ask to help evaluate the trustworthiness of an on-line source. Most of these questions are relevant for other informational sources as well.

- Is the site maintained for commercial purposes? Do advertisements appear on the site? If so, consider any potential conflicts of interest that may compromise the reliability of posted information.
- Who is accountable for the accuracy of the information? Who posted it? Is contact information provided for these individuals so you can challenge the information, provide feedback, or request additional information? Be suspicious of anonymous postings and sites that are unresponsive to feedback.

- When was the information posted, and how often is it updated? Think twice about conclusions that are drawn on the basis of potentially outdated information.
- Is the information well documented through references to scientific evidence? Be conscious of the number of steps that have been taken from the primary source to the source you are reading. Distrust uncheckable references that involve irrelevant qualifications (e.g., "As seen on *Oprah*!") or unnamed sources (e.g., "Leading scientists agree that . . ."). Look for references to scientific studies that allow you to check the conclusions and interpretations that are offered.
- Does the information contain quantitative information about the size of effects or the likelihood that they are flukes? Check to see that the author is not exaggerating trivial differences between groups or findings that could easily result from chance.
- Is there a discussion of the consistency of available evidence or acknowledgment of alternative interpretations? Consider as many possible interpretations as you can of the information to determine how strong the proffered argument actually is. A trustworthy source will acknowledge controversy and will discuss the strengths and weaknesses of evidence from all sides of an issue.
- Does the site refer you to additional information from respectable sources? Be wary of sites with predominantly self-referential links (e.g., pages within a site link only to other pages within the same site) or with hidden links (e.g., links disguised as buttons or other graphics).

For additional tips on evaluating the quality of health-related web sites, see Levi (2000) and the "Quackwatch" site (www.quackwatch.com) maintained by Dr. Stephen Barrett.

Internet Searches

In addition to this guide to evaluating web sites, some cautionary notes regarding internet searching are in order. Web-based search engines can provide you with many promising leads—in fact, you may quickly uncover more leads than you can possibly pursue. However, do not make the mistake of believing that this is a thorough search. First, internet search engines do not literally search the entire web for your subject. Rather, each search engine operates within a portion of web sites that it has catalogued. Because this catalogue contains only a small segment of the entire web, a given search engine will *miss* the majority of pages that contain information relevant to your topic of interest. A recent study of the 11 most popular search engines showed, for example, that they cover from 2.2% to 16.0% of the web ("Search Engines Fall Short," 1999). Even when all 11 engines were used, the combined results covered only

42% of the web! Second, search engines are extremely sensitive to your search terms. For example, consider how you might search for information on the efficacy of prayer. A search for "prayer" and "health" will locate a subset of potentially relevant pages, but it will miss sites that debate the alleged "healing" effects of prayer but do not happen to use the word "health." Third, and most important, internet searches are not linked to the most reliable sources of information: academic journals and scholarly books. A search of the internet will point you toward few, if any, primary sources.

THINKING FOR YOURSELF

Although there is little quality control on-line, there are many web-based tools that allow you to search databases of high-quality scholarly work. For example, as a reader of this book you have access to the InfoTrac College Edition database. InfoTrac College Edition allows you not only to search for information, but also to view full-text copies of the articles you find. You may also have free access to many other search tools through your library or its web page.

Many controversial issues will be discussed in this book, and you are encouraged to read further about any that catch your interest by following the references to primary sources. In addition, InfoTrac College Edition keyword search terms are provided at the end of each chapter to help you find articles on the topics covered in this book and to help you gain additional perspectives on hotly debated issues. For example, many of the subjects explored in this book have been discussed in the *Skeptical Inquirer*, a publication included in InfoTrac College Edition that is devoted solely to the careful evaluation of supernatural claims through the application of science and reason. This emphasis on clear thinking and careful reasoning is the overriding theme of this book, and it is your best bet when you embark on a search for information. The only way to protect yourself against misleading information, biased interpretations, and foolish beliefs is to review and critically evaluate original data. It is the goal of this book to provide you with the skills necessary to accomplish this task, enabling you to make informed decisions that are well reasoned and are consistent with your own values and goals.

INTRODUCTION

Pseudoscience and the Need for Clear Thinking

Patricia Burgus was not always a High Priestess of an international satanic cult. After nearly dying while giving birth to her second child in April 1982, she entered psychotherapy for relief from postpartum depression. Over the course of many months, Patricia made little progress in therapy with a psychiatric social worker. When a neighboring therapist began treating a patient for multiple personality disorder (MPD), Patricia's therapist wondered whether she might be suffering from this as well. Together, Patricia and her therapist discussed this possibility for months. Patricia had known that she was highly hypnotizable, readily able to lose herself in waking trances, and her therapist made frequent use of hypnotism. Patricia closely examined mood swings and searched for memory blanks that might suggest the existence of alter personalities. Three years into her therapy, to her therapist's relief, Patricia began to assume the role of "Kathy Love," an 11-year-old girl.

> "When I took on a different personality, it wasn't as if I was trying to deceive anyone but it was more of a release," [Patricia] explains of the experience. "In the beginning it was like a pressure valve. When I was another personality, I didn't have to be responsible for anything I said. I didn't have to be this mom who had been through this horrible delivery and had problems at work. I didn't have to be the person who was responsible for two kids and keeping this huge Victorian home clean. If I wanted to be a sweet eleven-year-old girl, I could. I kind of got hooked on the escape." (Ofshe & Watters, 1996, pp. 228–229)

Up to this point, Patricia had managed to keep her job and take care of her children despite making little therapeutic progress. Once she was diagnosed with MPD, however, Patricia's condition rapidly deteriorated. She sought inpatient psychiatric care for her disorder, and in March 1986, she was admitted under the care of Dr. Bennett Braun to the Dissociative Disorders Unit at Rush Presbyterian Hospital in Chicago. Upon admission, Braun asked her whether she had been sexually abused as a child. In addition to her postpartum depression, Patricia identified the suicide of a neighbor and her sister's early death as the causes of her psychological problems, but assured him that

1

she had never been abused. Braun was not interested in any of this, and told her that although she may not remember it, she *must* have been abused. Despite Patricia's persistent denials, Braun and his colleagues helped Patricia fashion "memories" of abuse through the use of hypnotism, psychiatric drugs, suggestive and highly leading questions, and lengthy "abreaction" sessions during which Patricia was physically restrained and forced to endure physically and emotionally painful "memory work."

Isolated from her family and friends, and exposed only to the coercive techniques of the hospital staff, Patricia's original depression intensified. Desperate to regain control of her life, she quickly learned that the key to survival in this environment was to tell the doctors what they wanted to hear. Braun believed not only that all MPD patients were sexually abused as children but that all human societies have been plagued by a transgenerational, international cult of satanists. Patricia, like many other patients, began to corroborate his bizarre fantasies. In the coming months, under the influence of the heavy-handed techniques of her doctors, Patricia would "recover" allegedly repressed memories of being repeatedly raped and participating in satanic rituals that included the murder of adults and babies, gruesome acts of cannibalism, and countless other atrocities. Despite her family's insistence that this was all nonsense, Braun and others convinced Patricia that she was a High Priestess in the cult, masterminding cult activities in an entire nine-state region.

> Even as she described the stories of her participation in the cult, [Patricia] realized that they were inconsistent, contradictory, and often bordered on the impossible. While reliving specific scenes, characters and settings would often change in a dreamlike fashion. She described lit torches used as sexual devices, burial for days at a time, and having to eat parts of two thousand people a year. . . . Her job as High Priestess, which she believed included frequent trips to other states, was supposedly managed without her husband's knowledge.
>
> According to [Patricia], Braun continually helped her explain away the improbable nature of her new beliefs. . . . For details too fantastic to explain away, Braun would simply reassure her that given enough time, the facts would all make sense. (Ofshe & Watters, 1996, p. 237)

Braun's fantasy involved an international conspiracy among satanists, American Telephone and Telegraph (AT&T), Hallmark Greeting Cards, the Central Intelligence Agency (CIA), FTD Florists, and—after it found no evidence to support any of Braun's claims—the Federal Bureau of Investigation (FBI). Another of Braun's colleagues used a hypnotic technique to regress Patricia to her past lives, in which she was supposedly a young British girl who died in a fire and Catherine the Great. Oddly, it may have been the very deterioration in Patricia's psychological functioning that ultimately saved her from this "treatment." After trying to start a fire, she was transferred to an acute care unit and then to another psychiatric ward on which she assumed one of her young girl alter personalities. When she refused to regain her adult personality, the staff punished her by sending her to a unit where she was treated like other patients. She received no special attention, was not regarded as a High Priestess, and underwent no memory work. Her sense of normalcy returned as she began to question the reality of her new beliefs. In December 1990, Patricia stopped taking all psychiatric drugs, cold turkey. In the summer of 1992, Patricia confronted Braun and told him that she no longer believed any of the stories that had emerged during therapy. " 'I told him that was bullshit. I told him that the problems I had were because of the hospital,' Patricia says emphatically. 'I told him that he had done a terrible thing to me and my family'" (Ofshe & Watters, 1996, p. 245).

Patricia Burgus lost an entire decade of her life to misguided therapy. Clearly suffering from depression—a common disorder for which several effective treatments are available—Patricia was nonetheless given a controversial diagnosis (MPD), coerced into recovering memories through questionable techniques, and "treated" using untested methods. Although Patricia's case is extreme, these practices are not rare. It is an example of what may happen when zealous proponents adhere to fundamentally flawed presuppositions for which there is no support in the scientific research literature. In short, Patricia was a victim of pseudoscience.

SEPARATING SENSE FROM NONSENSE

This book is intended to serve the dual purpose of teaching skills and demonstrating their application. One of its overarching goals is to help you spot and (perhaps more important) avoid the seductive traps of faulty reasoning. These are the skills that will be emphasized to help you separate sense from nonsense. The second goal is to apply these skills to an evaluation of some of the pseudosciences of our time. In order to master a set of new skills, you need to practice them, and pseudosciences provide a golden opportunity to try out these skills. The reasoning of those who promote pseudoscience is often flawed, and we can learn a lot by examining it closely.

Studying Human Reasoning

To understand our reasoning, we must first know something about how it can be studied scientifically. Our goal is to explore the psychology of human judgment and decision making, including the mental shortcuts that we take advantage of every day—but how can we learn about these shortcuts? We can take the same approach as researchers who study sensation and perception: Look for common mistakes, and infer the systematic biases in our normal

FIGURE 1

In this Frazer Spiral, the pattern of black and white stripes within each concentric circle creates the illusion of a connected spiral.

functioning that lead to these mistakes. For example, vision researchers now have an impressive understanding of how we translate light energy into perceptions of color, shape, distance, motion, and so forth. One of the chief methods by which they have achieved such remarkable progress is by investigating visual illusions. By noting how our visual system is fooled, they can infer the way it normally works. For example, look at the picture in Figure 1. What do you see? Most people report seeing a connected, spiral pattern. But take a closer look. Do the spirals actually connect to one another? No, they don't! The carefully constructed black and white stripes within each concentric circle create an illusion of a spiral. What can we infer from this? Our visual system must be responsive to edges or boundaries. Throughout this picture, each of the black and white stripes appears to trace the edge of a form originating in the middle of the figure. Thus, our brain registers a spiral. An illusion as simple as this allows us to make a powerful inference about our visual processing.

Systematic Errors Reveal Our Mental Shortcuts

The same research strategy is often useful in the study of reasoning. We can learn about mental shortcuts by looking for systematic mistakes that people often make and inferring their common cause. For example, formulate your best-guess solution to the following simple problem in just *five seconds:*

$$1 \times 2 \times 3 \times 4 \times 5 \times 6 \times 7 \times 8 = ?$$

What is your estimate? If you're like the students in an experiment by Tversky and Kahneman (1974), you probably guessed a solution close to their average estimate of 512. This is not only seriously in error, but wrong in a predictable way. However, when the same problem was written backward ($8 \times 7 \times 6 \times 5 \times 4 \times 3 \times 2 \times 1$), students' estimates were much higher, averaging 2,250. What can we infer from this discrepancy? It appears that human beings solve this kind of problem by performing a partial calculation. We multiply the first few numbers in the series and, as time rapidly expires, we *anchor* on this initial solution and make an upward *adjustment* to account for the remaining numbers in the series. People who are presented with higher numbers first ($8 \times 7 \times 6 \times$ . . .) form higher anchors than those who begin with lower numbers ($1 \times 2 \times 3 \times$ . . .). Moreover, it seems that our adjustments tend to be too small. This is apparent because almost everyone severely underestimates the correct answer for this problem, which is 40,320. In this way, a common judgment error as simple as this allows us to make several important inferences about our reasoning. Psychologists refer to this mental shortcut as the "anchoring and adjustment" heuristic: In situations that call for quick solutions to complex problems, we rely on an anchor and typically fail to adjust it sufficiently (Tversky & Kahneman, 1974).

The Pros and Cons of Relying on Shortcuts

Because we are all bombarded with an overwhelming amount of information in our daily lives, we rely on shortcuts such as this to help focus our limited attention and mental effort on what we perceive to be most important. Most of the time, we reach fairly accurate judgments and acceptable decisions. However, our efficiency comes with a price: There is a trade-off between efficiency and accuracy. The down side to the shortcuts that we utilize is that they sometimes simplify our thinking in a way that yields predictable mistakes. Understanding the nature of these mistakes can alert us to problems in our own reasoning or that of others, suggesting the need to override these shortcuts and process information in a more deliberate and thorough manner.

Thinking Clearly

Each chapter of this book will delve into some of our mental shortcuts, presenting them in terms of classic and contemporary research that shows how profoundly they can impact our judgments and decisions. You will see how to recognize the flawed reasoning that can result from an overreliance on shortcuts and learn when to override these shortcuts and think more clearly.

By spotting others' reasoning fallacies and avoiding your own, you will be better prepared to avoid persuasive appeals that are not in your best interest; acquire and maintain more accurate beliefs; and formulate more cogent, rational arguments. Clear thinking is empowering.

Applying the Tools of Clear Thinking

The best way to learn a new skill is to apply it. To this end, lessons learned from the study of human reasoning will be applied through examination of pseudoscientific beliefs and practices. Almost every science has one or more pseudosciences to deal with. For example, astronomy has astrology; chemistry has alchemy; evolutionary biology has "creation science"; historical science has Holocaust denial; medicine has "alternative" medicine; and psychology has repressed memories, the treatment of MPD, "thought field therapy," and others. Because of their enormous potential for direct personal harm, pseudosciences in the realm of physical and mental health will receive considerable attention in this book.

Throughout history, people have been deceived by individuals who have claimed expertise they did not have, who hawked products or services by making remarkable promises they could not fulfill. In most pseudosciences, there is a surface plausibility to the claims that are made. Scratching the surface, though, will often expose the flawed reasoning and lack of sound evidence. Because an obvious motive of these claims is to take advantage of you, a certain measure of healthy skepticism is appropriate. This is why all the psychological principles discussed throughout this book will be applied through a close inspection of the arguments offered by proponents of pseudosciences.

Ten Characteristics of Pseudoscience

Pseudoscience is perhaps best defined by its contrast with science. Science is a method for coming to know reality, a process for sorting truth from fiction, a way of thinking that helps us make tough choices in an informed manner. Pseudoscience, on the other hand, lacks the fundamental respect for research evidence that is the hallmark of any true science. It is a sham, masquerading as science in order to garner respectability without delivering the observable results of a true science. Although the line between science and pseudoscience is not always crystal clear, there are many ways to distinguish them. The ten characteristics of pseudosciences listed below constitute an interrelated set of warning signs that indicate a heightened need for clear thinking.

1. Outward Appearance of Science

Pseudoscientists may use language that sounds scientific, but they cannot back up this language with substance. Scientists' "jargon" is actually a concise language that facilitates communication among experts. Pseudosciences, on the other hand, employ vague and obtuse language to mystify or to evade scrutiny.

For example, whereas a physicist can provide a clear definition of "energy" and demonstrate its conservation in countless, precise ways, an acupuncturist uses the term "energy" in a vague, imprecise way. By taking on an outward appearance of science, pseudoscience gains the credibility and legitimacy associated with science without following the rigorous procedures that gained public trust of science in the first place.

2. Absence of Skeptical Peer Review

Both sciences and pseudosciences confer degrees, hold conferences, and publish journals. In all these activities, scientists exercise a degree of skepticism that often surprises nonscientists. When an article is submitted for publication in a scientific journal, for example, it undergoes rigorous scrutiny by several anonymous scientists whose job is to find mistakes. Are the hypotheses grounded in theory? Were the data collected without bias, using a sound methodology? Was the analysis conducted properly? Can the results be interpreted in other ways? Peer review is often a painful process for an author to undergo; the comments can be brutally frank, and when an article has serious flaws, the reviewers often recommend that it not be published. Not only is this process tolerated, but it is actively encouraged. Scientists are no more masochistic than anyone else. However, they do recognize that by screening all research in this tough-minded manner, only those articles that make a genuine contribution to accumulating knowledge will survive into the literature. Healthy skepticism is likewise exercised at scientific conferences and in the oral examinations of candidates for scientific degrees. By contrast, although there are journals, conferences, and degrees in pseudosciences, there is only token or nonexistent skepticism. Any idea—no matter how foolish, unsubstantiated, and invalid—can be embraced by pseudoscience because it lacks the corrective, error-checking machinery of science.

3. Reliance on Personal Experience

Science is based on systematic empiricism. This means that scientists conduct controlled studies to test the observable consequences of their hypotheses. Because anecdotes, personal experience, and testimonials can suggest hypotheses but are completely inadequate for testing them, they are not admitted as sources of evidence. Rather, designing sound experiments often requires considerable ingenuity, and implementing a necessary design can be time consuming and expensive. Well-controlled experiments that rule out alternative explanations are considered the best way to separate truth from fiction. However, in the absence of such empirical evidence, scientists regard a hypothesis only as a theory, never as fact. Pseudoscientists, in contrast, do not follow even the most basic principles of research design, are unconcerned about rival explanations for the claims they make, and are unwilling to invest the necessary time and energy to perform valid experiments. Instead, they place great faith in anecdotes and testimonials, encouraging people to rely on their personal experience to evaluate the truth of claims to knowledge. As will be shown in later chapters, reliance on personal experience for testing claims can be downright dangerous.

4. Evasion of Risky Tests

A good scientific experiment is set up in such a way that it is extremely unlikely to yield positive results *unless* the hypothesis is indeed true. Thus, an experiment should provide a "risky" test, one that a false hypothesis will not pass. For example, explaining the past is a weak test of a theory, whereas predicting the future is a more risky test. Scientists value evidence in direct proportion to the riskiness of the test. When profitable pseudoscientific beliefs are on the line, their proponents have a strong motive to avoid risky tests. Passing the test would be nice, but may not help business; failed tests, if widely publicized, may hurt business. In the event that a pseudoscientist does present evidence, it is usually of little value because it is based on a very weak test.

5. Retreats to the Supernatural

Science is a method for uncovering principles of the natural world. Even when a mechanism is unknown, observable results are the currency of scientific validity. In contrast, many pseudosciences resort to supernatural explanations when their claims are shown to be false. For example, touch therapy, which is popular in the nursing profession, is premised on a "human energy field" that has never been shown to exist. When research demonstrated that self-proclaimed experts could not even detect this energy field—let alone use it for diagnosis or treatment—practitioners steeped themselves in supernatural claims (e.g., "holistic" or "spiritual" effects that cannot be observed or measured) rather than closing up shop. Supernatural explanations that are unconnected with observable reality do not deliver on promises of experienced, verifiable benefits; instead, they shift the standards of evidence and allow practitioners to further evade reasonable tests.

6. The Mantra of Holism

A major task of science involves making increasingly specific distinctions among events in order to generate increasingly useful theories. For example, scientists identify subatomic particles, chemical elements, physical diseases, mental disorders, and so forth. Pseudoscience, on the other hand, often rebels against such distinctions in the name of "holism." Proponents of holism are almost always extremely vague about just what this term actually means. They use the term to insist that people must "take into account" far more information than is psychologically possible. When a holistically oriented pseudoscientist claims to consider everything in a completely unspecified way, it remains an absolute mystery just what information he or she does utilize, and in what manner, to make important judgments and decisions. "Holism" can be used as a shield against the effortful learning and careful drawing of meaningful distinctions, offering in their place only a rhetoric of empty verbiage.

7. Tolerance of Inconsistencies

Scientists subscribe to a handful of principles of formal logic, chief among them the notion that contradictory statements cannot both be true. Pseudoscientists are noteworthy for their tolerance of logical contradictions within and across "specialties." For example, because the signs of the zodiac are based on the seasons of the year, some astrologers reverse their order in the southern hemisphere; others, however, do not. Orthomolecular medicine involves taking megadoses of dietary supplements to increase potency, whereas homeopathy involves diluting these ingredients to miniscule—often nonexistent—levels to increase potency. It is telling that one seldom, if ever, sees or hears even a casual discussion of these contradictions. Unlike the vigorous debates among scientists that are designed to eliminate contradictions in the search for the truth, pseudoscientists do not question each other. Instead, contradictions are swept aside.

8. Appeals to Authority

Science is based on empirical data. Anyone can read the experimental record and draw conclusions from it. Pseudoscience, however, has little data to offer. In its place, practitioners urge others to believe in their practices based on their say-so. As you will see, history has shown the dangers of subscribing to beliefs based on nothing more than authoritative pronouncements.

9. Promising the Impossible

Science involves respect for the limitations of present knowledge and current technological capabilities. By contrast, pseudoscience is unbounded by reality and actually profits by making grandiose promises. Physical constants (e.g., the speed of light), physical laws (e.g., the conservation of energy), and a knowledge of human fallibility (e.g., mental shortcuts) are readily ignored by avid pseudoscientists. For example, pseudoscientists have claimed that UFOs traverse the interstellar distances at greater than light speed, that perpetual motion machines exist, and that polygraph (lie detector) tests are "100% accurate" in their assessments of deception.

10. Stagnation

One of the most striking characteristics of any healthy scientific discipline is the rapid rate of change that it undergoes—its demonstrable progress in accumulating knowledge. New research refines the old in successive approximations to the truth, leading to observable practical gains.

> For example, human life expectancy held steady for thousands of years, and nearly doubled in the 20th century. What is the cause of this stunning, unprecedented, humanitarian transition? The germ theory of disease, public health measures, medicines, and medical technology. Longevity is perhaps the best single measure of the physical quality of life. (If you're dead, there's little you can do to be happy.) This is a precious offering from science to humanity—nothing less than the gift of life. (Sagan, 1995, p. 10)

In contrast to science, pseudosciences are remarkably static. In fact, their proponents often hail this static quality as a virtue. Thus, the "ancient wisdom" of a pseudoscience is touted as evidence of its value, rather than as a lack of progress or improvement that sets it apart from legitimate science. For example, the ancient healing arts of Eastern medicine have not achieved anything like the dramatic gains in longevity that science has produced in the West, and the time-honored myth that we use only 10% of our brain has survived for generations despite mountains of contradictory neuroscientific evidence. Initial hunches are seldom entirely correct, and unless you can see demonstrable refinement of beliefs or practices, they may well be pseudoscientific rubbish.

In all these ways, pseudoscience is a pretense, a sham. It projects an air of authority despite an absence of experimental evidence and an unwillingness to do the tough work of carrying out sound research. Proponents of pseudosciences cling tenaciously to their cherished beliefs, avoiding true tests as long as possible, denying the relevance of evidence, and—if all else fails—inventing supernatural explanations to explain away contradictions between their beliefs and reality. Although scientists are by no means immune to these weaknesses, they tend to base their beliefs on observable, repeatable experimental evidence and to modify their beliefs more judiciously as new data are obtained.

THE PLAN OF THIS BOOK

The preceding description is just an overview of some of the general problems with pseudoscience that are explored in greater detail in subsequent chapters. Using examples from a variety of pseudosciences, the four sections of this book describe and apply the principles of sound reasoning. These sections are bound together by a dedication to open-minded and skeptical inquiry. Their ultimate goal is to arm you with tools for clear thinking.

Part One: Deception

Part One introduces several methods by which pseudoscientists attempt to influence us. First, Chapter 2 outlines the role of clever word choices in framing issues and shaping beliefs. For example, the use of terms like *pro-choice* and *pro-life* in the abortion debate goes well beyond attempts to capture viewpoints or perspectives accurately; instead, these terms represent a deliberate attempt to influence beliefs through careful use of language.

Chapter 3 describes the time-honored appeal of magical thinking. As a species, we appear to have a longing for something transcendent, something mystical in our lives. Throughout history, we have tended to attribute phenomena that we could not explain to supernatural forces. This chapter uses well-understood psychological principles of learning to clarify how superstitious beliefs are formed and maintained. It also explores magical beliefs in vitalistic, unverifiable energies, and presents a simple test that challenges their existence.

Chapter 4 reviews the power wielded by authority in guiding our beliefs and behaviors. Although a mindful obedience to legitimate authority greatly simplifies life and is often quite justified, we occasionally commit two types of mistakes: being overly dismissive of qualified authorities, or being overly obedient to questionable authorities. This chapter reviews the characteristics indicative of qualified and questionable authorities, and suggests that attempts by pseudoscientists to legitimize their authority through political—rather than scientific—means undermines the legitimacy of their claims to authority.

Part Two: Self-Deception

Part Two considers the strengths and weaknesses of different types of evidence in the context of our tendencies toward unwitting self-deception. Chapter 5 enumerates a number of ways in which even honest, well-intentioned people can deceive themselves and others. For example, we can be seriously misinformed when we place too much faith in testimonials, anecdotes, or case studies. Although these informational sources can serve as a rich source of hypotheses, they are nonetheless wholly inadequate for testing them. This is partly because the cases we hear about are selectively chosen, and selectively chosen cases are often exceptions to the very principles we need to learn.

Chapter 6 explains the role of a plausible theory in the preliminary evaluation of a claim to knowledge. When people make claims that are incompatible with well-understood scientific principles, these claims must be carefully and critically examined. This chapter explores magnet therapy, homeopathy, and alien abduction stories in depth as examples of pseudoscientific claims that contradict well-understood principles of science.

Chapter 7 reviews the variety of ways in which an association between two events, such as a treatment and an outcome, can be established and interpreted. In our everyday lives, we are often presented with incomplete information and cannot conclusively determine whether associations between events are present at all. Thus, when two events are shown to be related, this does not necessarily mean that either event causes the other. Several criteria must be met to establish a causal relationship between events, and these are reviewed in this chapter.

Chapter 8 presents a concise summary of scientific reasoning that centers around six challenges that any claim to knowledge must meet: falsifiability, logic, comprehensiveness, honesty, replicability, and sufficiency. To the extent that a claim passes these simple tests, it warrants at least tentative belief. In addition to spelling out a basic framework for scientific reasoning, the premises and consequences of several challenges to the philosophy of science are reviewed. Although science—crafted and carried out by fallible humans—is admittedly an imperfect tool for discovering truths about the natural world, it is arguably superior to any alternative method of inquiry.

Part Three: Psychological Tricks

Part Three analyzes a variety of psychological tricks that can create and sustain unwarranted pseudoscientific beliefs. Chapter 9 deals with the consequences of selective media coverage on our beliefs. Popular media outlets tend to report unusual or sensational stories, and do so in a vivid style that increases their memorability. Later, the ease of recalling this vivid information can distort our judgments of the threat of a potential hazard, the prevalence of a belief, or the validity of a conclusion.

Chapter 10 shows how easily confidence accumulates for whatever beliefs we choose to hold. We tend to seek and recognize only information that agrees with our views, subjecting disagreeable ideas to a more stringent burden of proof. Similarly, we place too much faith in "explanations" of past events rather than requiring theories to accurately predict the future. Ironically, proponents of the beliefs that have received the least support from research tend to display the most overconfidence.

Chapter 11 reviews the tendency of pseudoscientists to concoct conspiracy theories. Believing in grand conspiracies can add a sense of meaning and purpose to people's lives or defend against rational inquiry. Once the surface plausibility of most large-scale conspiracy theories is penetrated, however, logical contradictions arise that severely challenge their accuracy.

Chapter 12 considers ways in which we sometimes overestimate the degree of control we have over events in our lives. Belief in personal control can feel quite empowering. However, it can also be mercilessly unleashed against the victims of unpredictable, unavoidable misfortunes, as when women who have been raped are held accountable for their own victimization. It is argued that the illusions of control offered by many pseudosciences are dangerous in several ways.

Part Four: Decision Making and Ethics

Part Four examines the process of decision making and considers ethical issues raised by pseudoscientific practices. Chapter 13 introduces classical decision theory as a powerful tool for evaluating the effectiveness of any assessment or decision-making procedure. For example, even valid diagnostic tests run into insurmountable difficulties when the medical conditions they seek to detect are extremely rare. A simple method is outlined that combines the relative rarity of a condition with the strength of the evidence for or against it, thereby improving decision making. It is argued that, in their attempts to portray their practices as universally useful or perfectly effective, practitioners of pseudoscience often fail to construct or utilize tests in a responsible manner.

Chapter 14 reviews research showing that the statistical (actuarial) approach to decision making is equally or more accurate than the clinical (intuitive) approach. After explaining several reasons for this finding, several common justifications for the clinical approach are raised and debunked, and it is argued that the most ethically defensible decision-making methods are those that have the best observable track record.

Chapter 15 integrates multiple lines of reasoning to consider the ethics of administering or promoting unverified treatments. Proponents frequently claim that their treatments are harmless, and potentially helpful, so there is no risk involved in trying them out. In fact, proponents tend to underestimate the potential for and probability of harm, to overestimate the likely benefits, and to ignore the costs of forgoing verified treatments when unverified treatments are used in their place. Given basic ethical principles, this chapter argues that it is unethical to administer or even promote an unverified treatment.

Finally, Chapter 16 provides some general advice for spotting and overcoming faulty reasoning. The various shortcuts that we use to simplify our thinking are reviewed, and methods to resist faulty reasoning are suggested. The concluding chapter is premised on a respect for your capacity to make informed judgments and to reach personally satisfying decisions. My intention throughout this book is not to suggest *what* you should believe, but *how* you can arrive at truly informed choices that are consistent with your own values. It is my sincere hope that this exploration of the psychology of human reasoning will enable you to make smarter choices in areas of your life that are important to you.

one

DECEPTION

LANGUAGE

Misleading and Evasive Tactics

I once attended a sales presentation for a set of magical cookware. The pots and pans were remarkable in many regards. During the "economics" portion of the sales pitch, our host explained that smart consumers could save money because there would be no shrinkage of food in this miraculous cookware: "When you buy a five-pound roast, you will get five pounds of meat on your table." The natural juices, moisture, and flavor of your food would somehow be perfectly sealed in. Many audience members seemed content to accept this assertion. Later on, the "healthy eating" portion of the sales pitch featured a cooking demonstration. Boneless chicken breasts were sautéed before our eyes, and then an entire cup of fat was drained from the pan. We were told that this would have been *two* cups had beef been cooked. The link between fat, cholesterol, and heart disease was explained at some length, with the obvious conclusion driven home repeatedly: Using this cookware would remove more lethal substances from the food as it cooked than any other cookware. Once again, especially in light of the unsightly fat on display in the plastic cup, many audience members seemed content to accept this assertion.

The problem was that there was a clear contradiction between these claims: One cannot simultaneously seal in all of the natural juices, flavor, and moisture of meat *and* drain off a large quantity of its fat!

WEASEL WORDS AND FRAMING EFFECTS

The stark impossibility that both of these claims were true was cleverly disguised by presenting each claim in a distinct, self-contained portion of the presentation. Perhaps more important than the temporal separation of roughly one-half hour was the demonstrator's abuse of language. Had the term *fat* been used in both contexts, it would have been readily apparent that the same substance cannot be conserved and reduced at the same time. Moreover, in addition to the intentional muddying of a problematic contradiction, the choice of terminology at each point was designed to foster the desired reaction. When attempting to argue that meat juices would be sealed in, it was advantageous to refer to them in a positive way—surely everyone can appreciate enhanced flavor and moisture. When the gears were shifted to the elimination of these same meat juices, they had to be cast in a negative light—and who, these days, has not come to loathe fat and cholesterol? Carl Sagan (1995) coined the term *weasel words* to refer to this use of language in a deliberate attempt to influence thought on superficial grounds.

This may strike you as par for the course in advertising, where we recognize that the intention is to persuade. However, weasel words can also have an impact on more personally meaningful, strongly held beliefs. Consider an experiment in which people were asked about their views toward free speech (Rugg, 1941). One group of participants was asked whether "the United States should allow public speeches against democracy," and a majority of participants (62%) said no. However, another group of participants was asked whether "the United States should forbid public speeches against democracy," and a majority of them (54%) also said no! What is one to make of the finding that antidemocratic speeches should not be allowed, yet not be forbidden?

It is striking that the mere substitution of one word had an impact on the way individuals conceptualized this important issue. Asking whether one should "allow" a type of speech frames the question in terms of the acceptability of the speech's content, whereas asking whether one should "forbid" a type of speech frames the question in terms of limiting personal freedoms. Psychologists refer to such a backlash against a perceived loss of freedom as "psychological reactance." We value our personal autonomy highly and do not tolerate threats to it kindly.

This very same principle is at work in the debate over abortion. When one side declares itself pro-choice, it is attempting to play on our natural inclination toward personal freedom. Similarly, when the other side declares itself pro-life, it is attempting to play on our respect for the sanctity of human life. By using these labels, both sides in this debate deliberately frame the issue in a highly suggestive manner, making the underlying issue appear unobjectionable. Do you know anyone who, in his or her general philosophy, is *anti*-choice? How about *anti*-life?

The crafty use of framing in the abortion debate is premised on the idea that even beliefs with life-or-death consequences can be altered through simple changes in language. But is this the case? A classic experiment by psychologists Amos Tversky and Daniel Kahneman (1981) suggests that framing can influence even the most serious of decisions. Participants were asked to make a tough choice:

> Imagine that the United States is preparing for the outbreak of an unusual Asian disease, which is expected to kill 600 people. Two alternative programs to combat the disease have been proposed. Assume that the exact scientific estimate of the consequences of the programs are as follows:
>
> - If Program A is adopted, 200 people will be saved.
> - If Program B is adopted, there is a one-third probability that 600 people will be saved, and a two-thirds probability that no people will be saved.

Before reading any further, take a moment to consider which program you would choose. Once you have made your decision, reevaluate the same situation by choosing one of the following two new options:

> - If Program C is adopted, 400 people will die.
> - If Program D is adopted, there is a one-third probability that nobody will die, and a two-thirds probability that 600 people will die.

Again, consider your choice before reading any further.

Tversky and Kahneman found a surprising pattern of results: Of their participants, 72% preferred Program A over Program B, whereas 78% preferred Program D over Program C. To see why this pattern of results was so surprising, you need to realize that Programs A and C are formally identical (200 out of 600 people living is the same as 400 out of 600 people dying), as are Programs B and D (1/3 of the time all 600 people will live, 2/3 of the time all 600 people will die). Thus, a substantial proportion of respondents reported logically inconsistent choices. When the problem was phrased in terms of lives *saved,* people were generally risk-averse, opting for the sure savings of 200 lives. When it was phrased in terms lives *lost,* people were risk-seeking, opting to take a chance at saving everyone. It is disquieting to think that such superficial framing of an issue might influence policy decisions with such potentially grave consequences. It is therefore extremely important to understand the framing effect of language.

Kahneman and Tversky's (1979) "prospect theory" provided a concise explanation for the seemingly contradictory choices that framing effects can prompt us to make. To get a feeling for the two principles that are involved, consider these questions:

1. Which feels larger to you, the difference between $0 and $1 million or the difference between $100 million and $101 million?
2. Suppose that you have no money. Which arouses a stronger emotional reaction, gaining $1000 or losing $1000?

Most people report that the difference between $0 and $1 million is psychologically larger than the difference between $100 million and $101 million, and that losing $1000 hurts more than gaining $1000 helps. Each of these

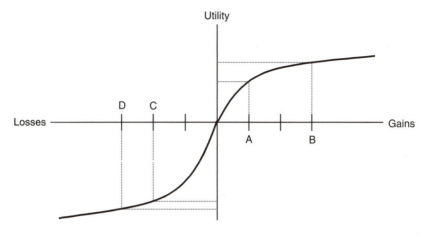

FIGURE 2

The S-shaped curve of prospect theory illustrates the principles that initial gains or losses are valued more heavily than are additional gains or losses and that losses are valued more heavily than corresponding gains.

reactions corresponds to a principle of prospect theory. A simple S-shaped graph (Figure 2) depicts the relationship between actual gains or losses (the objective reality) and their "utility" to us (our psychological perception of value).

Focus on the solid curve in Figure 2; we'll come back to the dotted lines shortly. First, notice that the curve is steepest in the center, flatter toward either end. This shows that we assign greater utility, or importance, to initial gains or losses (e.g., the difference between $0 and the first $1 million) than we do to gains or losses far from our reference point (e.g., the difference between the 100th and 101st million dollars). Second, notice that the curve dips lower for losses than it rises for gains. This shows that losses (e.g., losing $1000) weigh on our thinking more heavily than do equivalent gains (e.g., gaining $1000). These two principles help to explain why we are often risk-averse for gains and risk-seeking for losses. To see this, let's return to the paradox of lives saved versus lives lost.

The four programs, A through D, correspond to the dotted lines in the graph. Let's look first at the choice between programs A and B. Program A provides a sure savings of 200 lives, which has a fairly high utility. Program B offers the possibility of saving all 600 lives, but note that the utility of this outcome is not three times as high as the utility of saving 200 lives; in fact, it's not much greater at all. On the other hand, if program B fails (as it will with a two-thirds probability), no lives are saved, and the utility of this outcome is much lower than that of saving 200 lives. Thus, we perceive little to be gained by taking the risk, and much to be lost, so we opt for program A. We are risk-averse for gains.

Perceptions are reversed, however, when we compare programs C and D. Program C results in a sure loss of 400 lives, which has a strong negative utility. With program D, we do not perceive the risk of losing all 600 lives to be much different from losing 400 lives—their utilities are nearly equal—but there is the possibility of losing no lives, an outcome of much greater utility. Thus, there is little to be lost by taking the risk, and much to be gained, so we opt for program D. We are risk-seeking for losses.

COOPERATION AND CONVERSATIONAL MAXIMS

In addition to the influence of weasel words and framing effects, we are vulnerable to other linguistic tricks. Most ordinary conversation is guided by an implicit goal of cooperation, and pseudoscientists take advantage of our assumption that they are following basic conversational rules when they are not. Grice (1975) described four such rules, or "conversational maxims," that we usually follow to be cooperative:

1. *Quality.* We are truthful, basing our statements on adequate evidence.
2. *Quantity.* We are as informative as necessary, but not overly detailed.
3. *Relation.* We make contributions that are relevant to the topic of discussion.
4. *Manner.* We avoid obscurity and ambiguity by being clear and concise.

Not only do these rules encourage a cooperative conversation, but they are also important cornerstones of good scientific communication. Pseudoscientists, however, routinely violate one or more of these maxims. Let's take a look at what happens when each of these maxims is intentionally breached.

Quality: The Myth of "Health Food"

We will begin with outright dishonesty. Lacking evidence, pseudoscientists will often ignore the maxim of quality by providing false information to the public using linguistic tricks. Perhaps one of the most cunningly deceptive and evasive phrases in modern times is that of a "health food store." For starters, it is worth noting that healthful foods are simply those that contain nutrients: proteins, carbohydrates, fats, vitamins, and minerals. Therefore, most any item in an ordinary grocery store is "health food," and a reasonably well-balanced diet of these items will easily satisfy all of our body's needs. For this reason, one would think that nutritional supplements would be limited to the nutrients listed above. Instead, the chemical ingredients in many supplements sold in health-food stores go well beyond mere nutrients, and their claims involve remarkable curative powers that nutrition alone simply cannot provide. For example:

> In 1989, the FTC [Federal Trade Commission] secured a consent agreement for-
> bidding Miles, Inc., of Elkhart, Indiana, from making unsubstantiated claims for
> its One-A-Day brand multiple vitamins. According to the FTC complaint, Miles's
> ads on radio and television had stated . . . "Defending your lungs against air
> pollution requires vitamins A, E, and C. Daily stress can chip away at your B vita-
> mins. And rigorous physical running can actually knock essential minerals right
> out of your system. That's why One-A-Day vitamins are uniquely formulated to
> help put back what your world takes away." (Barrett & Herbert, 1994, p. 51)

There is no evidence to support any of the claims made in this statement.
The notion that you can knock minerals from your system seems particularly
ludicrous.

Sadly, such claims are now acceptable in the name of "health food," an
industry whose name allows people to pretend that they are not buying and
selling drugs. As will be discussed at greater length in Chapter 4, many people
are unaware that a federal law passed in 1994 allows virtually any drug to be
sold without approval by the Food and Drug Administration (FDA) if it is
called a "dietary or nutritional supplement." Governmental agencies can only
take action on behalf of consumers *after* harmful effects have been observed,
rather than requiring that safety be demonstrated before a product is marketed. Robert Park, writing in a newsletter of the American Physical Society
(June 23, 2000), poses an important question: Is such a "shut the gate after the
cows have escaped" strategy a viable approach to public health? Clearly, buy-
ers must exercise great care when purchasing untested chemicals labeled as
"supplements."

The degree of freedom enjoyed by the health food industry as it hustles
unwary consumers is shocking. For example, legal enforcement actions against
General Nutrition Center (GNC) are so routine that the company appears to
consider such actions simply a part of its operating expenses. General Nutrition Center has been censured by the FDA and the Federal Trade Commission (FTC) roughly once each year over the past 30 years. In a 1994 FTC case,
for example, GNC agreed to pay $2.4 million to settle false advertising charges
involving 41 products. In such cases, the corporate perpetrators of marketing
scams have substituted the dishonest term *health food* for what was once just
plain "quackery."

Quantity: Suggestive and Leading Questions

On the face of it, communicating excessive detail through mildly suggestive
phrasing may seem harmless. However, violating the maxim of quantity by
providing suggestions can tamper with our memories in destructive ways. A
classic experiment on leading questions was performed by Loftus and Palmer
(1974). Participants first watched a videotape of an accident involving a car
and a truck and then answered a series of questions. Those participants who

were asked how fast the car was going when it "contacted" the truck responded with an average of 31.8 miles per hour, whereas those who were asked how fast the car was going when it "smashed into" the truck responded with an average estimate of 40.8 miles per hour. Surely *smashed into* evokes a different frame of mind from the more neutral term *contacted;* it provides additional detail that may or may not be faithful to the actual events. In addition to this influence on estimates of speed, individuals in the "smashed" condition were much more likely to report one week later that the accident had involved broken glass, which it had not. A false memory had been suggested.

Because our memories sometimes blend together, false details may appear plausible if they seem consistent with existing memories. To examine this possibility, Bransford and Franks (1971) presented participants with a list of sentences such as these:

- The ants ate the sweet jelly which was on the table.
- The ants were in the kitchen.
- The ants ate the sweet jelly.
- The ants in the kitchen ate the jelly which was on the table.
- The jelly was on the table.
- The ants in the kitchen ate the jelly.

After a five-minute delay, participants were given a new list of sentences and asked which ones had appeared on the first list. An interesting result emerged. Regardless of whether a sentence had in fact appeared on the first list, participants expressed greater confidence in having seen sentences that contained more details. For example, even though "The ants ate the sweet jelly" did appear on the list, participants were more confident that "The ants in the kitchen ate the sweet jelly which was on the table" had appeared on the list, even though it had not. The use of details led to the false impression that this sentence had been seen before.

In case you suspect that this is a trivial effect, consider more consequential memory distortions that have been achieved through detailed suggestions. Participants in experiments conducted by Elizabeth Loftus and her colleagues have falsely remembered seeing "nonexistent broken glass and tape recorders, a clean-shaven man as having a mustache, straight hair as curly, and even something as large and conspicuous as a barn in a bucolic scene that contained no buildings at all" (Loftus, 1997, p. 177). Perhaps even more dramatic are false memories of observing a drug bust (Nucci, Hoffman, et al., cited in Loftus, 1997); being lost at age five in a shopping mall, department store, or other public place (Loftus & Pickrell, 1995); undergoing an overnight hospitalization for a high fever with a possible ear infection or attending a birthday party with pizza and a clown (Hyman, Husband, & Billings, 1995); attending a wedding reception and accidentally spilling a punch bowl on the parents of the bride or evacuating a grocery store when the overhead sprinkler systems erroneously activated (Hyman & Billings, 1995); getting one's hand caught in a mousetrap and having to go to the hospital to get it removed or going on a hot air balloon ride with classmates (Ceci, Huffman, Smith, & Loftus, 1994); and tripping, falling, and breaking a window with one's hand (Garry, Manning, Loftus, & Sherman, 1996). In each of these experiments, the researchers designed a memory in advance and successfully implanted it in participants through the use of detailed suggestions. Many of these false memories that participants acquired were vivid, detailed, and held with great confidence. The ready distortion of memory through suggestive details should give pause to those who take all eyewitness testimony or "recovered" memories at face value.

Relation: The Irrelevant Language of "Alternative" Health Care

Given the enormous success of science in treating physical and mental diseases and illnesses, it should not be surprising that promoting a questionable, unverified treatment can be challenging. Nonetheless, a number of pseudoscientific practitioners and patients disparage evidence-based health care and applaud "alternative" health care. These individuals employ pseudomedical jargon to evade legal accountability, thereby violating the maxim of relation. The pseudoscientists who promote "alternatives" rely heavily on irrelevancies to gain respectability and carve out a profitable niche in the health marketplace. For example, they describe evidence-based, or scientific, treatments as *traditional, conventional, establishment,* or *Western,* and promote unverified treatments as *alternative, complementary,* or *integrative* practices that involve *rediscoveries*—a *new medicine* in which *East meets West.* Are any of these labels *relevant* to the fact that there is evidence to support some treatments but not others? No. Pseudoscientists distort language primarily for the impressions that they can create: conjuring images of a dated, stagnant scientific enterprise that is resistant to change, accepting of only one cultural perspective, and perhaps more harmful than beneficial. The reality is altogether different.

The existence of an "alternative" treatment implies that it is one of multiple, equally valuable options from which one may select a remedy, thus appealing to the freedom of choice that citizens of a democracy cherish so dearly. But what is the true nature of this choice? A recently published editorial in the *New England Journal of Medicine* discussed the risks associated with untested and unregulated remedies and concluded: "There cannot be two kinds of medicine—conventional and alternative. There is only medicine that has been adequately tested and medicine that has not, medicine that works and medicine that may or may not work" (Angell & Kassirer, 1998, p. 841). Treatments that cannot meet the simple "show me" requirement of research evidence are not alternative health care—they are *alternatives to health care.*

The term *traditional* refers to information that is faithfully passed down through generations by word of mouth, a descriptor that, ironically, accurately characterizes alternative practices that have remained virtually unchanged for hundreds—in some cases, even thousands—of years. For example, there are no "rediscoveries" in the traditional Chinese medicine of herbalism and acupuncture, just stale ideas that have never been subjected to and survived a fair test. By contrast, scientific health care is a relatively recent human achievement, consisting largely of research begun in the 20th century, and is constantly changing in response to newer and better data. This is absolutely *non*traditional: *science* provides the ever-changing, progressive "new medicine."

Terms such as *standard* or *conventional* health care or the *medical establishment* imply the existence of an inflexible, rigid, overly conservative system. However, the legal interpretation of these terms is more precise: This language signifies the existence of supportive research evidence that establishes a practice as a safe and effective treatment.

Referring to scientific health care as Western is misleading in several ways. The term *Western,* when employed in an era that increasingly recognizes and appreciates cultural diversity, seems to suggest that science is hostile toward other points of view. Quite the opposite is true: The standards of scientific reasoning are applied regardless of whether a researcher in the United States or in China submits the data. Alternative practitioners frequently reveal *their* cultural bias by embracing "Eastern" health care and rejecting "Western" health care without considering available evidence. If one truly puts all cultural perspectives on an equal footing, how can any *one* of them be singled out as worthless? That is, why does Western health care merit any less attention than alternative systems? This glaring inconsistency is particularly curious in light of the remarkable gains achieved by scientific research.

The "East meets West" descriptor is bogus not only for the reasons described above, but also for the same reasons that the terms *complementary* and *integrative* health care are flawed disguises. These relatively new terms are concessions to the inadequacy of alternative treatments. They suggest that alternative health care, though not useful on its own, is somehow of value when used in conjunction with scientific health care. This is nonsense. "Complementary" or "integrative" practices merely add an unverified component (the alternative treatment) to one known to be effective (the scientific treatment).

A final type of linguistic abuse enables alternative practitioners to avoid legal accountability for their actions. Simply put, it is illegal to practice medicine without a license, and unsubstantiated health claims constitute crimes. Although many pseudoscientists routinely violate the law by making false claims, some scrupulously avoid the scientific language of diagnosis and treatment and instead use certain legal evasions:

> Instead of promising to cure your disease, some quacks will promise to "detoxify," "purify," or "revitalize" your body; "balance" its chemistry; bring it in harmony with nature; "stimulate" or "strengthen" your immune system; "support" or "rejuvenate" various organs in your body; or stimulate your body's power to heal itself. Of course, they never identify or make valid before-and-after measurements of any of these processes. These disclaimers serve two purposes. First, since it is impossible to measure the processes quacks allege, it may be difficult to prove them wrong. Moreover, if a quack is not a physician, the use of nonmedical terminology may help to avoid prosecution for practicing medicine without a license—although it shouldn't. (Barrett & Herbert, 1994, pp. 27–28)

Such evasive language is nothing but a brazen attempt to skirt the law. What, after all, is the *reason* for not being able to make certain claims or promote unproven products? The health marketplace is—and, to varying degrees, has always been—rife with fraud. One way to protect yourself is to demand evidence for the safety and efficacy of a treatment, and to carefully avoid being misled by irrelevant language.

Manner: The Emptiness of "Holism"

The maxim of manner requires that we be clear and concise in our communication. By intentionally violating this maxim, those who advocate "holism"—as in holistic language instruction, holistic health care, or holistic astrology—achieve considerable obscurity and ambiguity. A holistic perspective discards innumerable, invaluable distinctions. Gilovich (1991, p. 125) quotes Roger Lambert, a character in John Updike's *Roger's Version,* on this point:

> Next to the indeterminacy principle, I have learned in recent years to loathe most the term "holistic," a meaningless signifier empowering the muddle of all the useful distinctions human thought has labored at for two thousand years.

The central fallacy of holism can be demonstrated through a clear analogy. When your car breaks down, do you want a mechanic to assess and repair the specific mechanical failure or to holistically repair the whole car? The choice seems clear enough. On its web site, however, the American Holistic Veterinary Medical Association (AHVMA) presents a common, though grotesque, distortion of this analogy to help promote the full range of "holistic healing" practices for pets. Although they pay lip service to endorsing evidence-based treatments, they perpetuate a continual and only thinly veiled assault on science. After noting that "conventional" treatments "are employed simply to make the symptoms go away," they present the following false analogy that reveals their hostility to science: "Picture a car with a low oil warning light. Extinguishing the light will certainly make the sign go away, but will it solve the problem?" The clear implication is that scientists are so unfathomably inept that they would "extinguish the light" in some way *other* than adding oil! In reality, the "whole car" is not broken—so what, one might ask, would a "holistic" auto mechanic do? The holistic vets are silent on that point. Thus, even the example chosen to disparage science shows that it undoubtedly involves the smartest course of action: to validly detect the *specific* problem (low oil) and *treat it* (add oil). By contrast, holism is empty rhetoric.

Holism is also nonsensical in many circumstances involving well-understood principles of health. For example, if you broke your leg, would you prefer to put your leg in a cast and walk with the aid of crutches while it heals, or have a "holistic healer" *not* deal specifically with your leg, but "treat you as a whole person" by prescribing some mixture of acupuncture, herbs, homeopathy, magnets, nutritional supplements, reflexology, therapeutic touch, and/or other alleged remedies? In other words, should a broken leg be treated directly or considered a broader problem in need of a broader remedy? It seems likely that even the most staunch advocate of holistic medicine, upon breaking his or her leg, would want to put a cast on it and get some crutches.

For many, the logic of making meaningful distinctions becomes murkier when they think about less directly observable events. But why should it? For example, the notion that a modern astrologer must make use of the "whole chart" typifies the futility of holism. Astrology is based on the belief that all natural phenomena are influenced by celestial bodies, and there is partial truth to this: "Every time we wake up with the sun, or plan barbecues on moonlit nights, or go fishing at high tide, we are showing how celestial bodies have real influence in our lives" (Kelly, 1997, p. 1035). But these influences are trivialities, nothing at all like the grand claims of astrology. For centuries, astrologers were consulted for assistance in making important, practical decisions: Should I marry this person? Should I wage war against this nation? Around the 1950s, however, science began to catch up with astrology and test the predictions that astrologers made. It turned out that astrologers were unable to make predictions any better than chance guessing (for reviews, see Dean, Mather, & Kelly, 1996; Kelly, 1997, 1998).

In the face of overwhelming negative evidence, astrologers faced a tough choice: either reject their discredited beliefs or create after-the-fact explanations. In true pseudoscientific form, astrologers embraced a range of evasive tactics, including holism. Modern astrology pays little attention to the evidence against it because, as critic Kelly (1997) puts it, "the horoscope is a whole system in which every part is influenced by every other part" (p. 1044). That is, astrologers objected that scientific investigations tested only one astrological factor at a time, failing to take into account "the whole chart" that professional astrologers supposedly utilize to make their predictions.

In astrology—as in all other empirical matters—the holism defense is fatally flawed. One can rightly ask just what "the whole chart" means, and whether it is psychologically possible to consider it in its entirety:

> Where does the whole chart end? With ten planets [astrologers count the sun and
> our moon, though none of the dozens of other moons in our solar system, as plan-

ets], twelve signs, twelve houses, midpoints, Arabic points, nodes, aspects and whatever other astrological concepts may be used, it is simply impossible to interpret a "whole chart." When astrologers claim that they use the whole chart, they only refer to the fact that they use more factors than just one. Nevertheless, no matter how many factors they use, they always use a restricted number of factors, and therefore only a part of the horoscope. They never use the whole chart. But then the question becomes how many factors would be considered, and which factors? . . . Suppose that I consider as many as 20 factors, then undoubtedly an astrologer will come up who claims that I should use 21 factors. (Van Rooij, 1994, p. 56)

Based on a typical list of factors, Kelly (1997) calculates that there are approximately 10^{28} possible horoscopes. Without providing details for her calculations, one astrologer arrived at the figure of 5.39×10^{68} (Doane, 1956). Either way, both values are *far* in excess of the number of humans that have ever lived. Thus, it is quite likely that nearly every person ever born (excepting, perhaps, identical twins) has had a unique horoscope. This denies any possibility that astrological laws can make predictions. If nobody has ever had your unique horoscope before, how could astrologers know what to expect? The only clues are the individual factors in the chart (which *are* shared with other people) but astrologers cannot use these to formulate rational predictions because then they're not using the whole chart! The "everything influences everything else" nature of holism invariably leads to this crippling paradox.

As will be discussed in greater detail in Chapter 14, all "holistic" practices also suffer from the serious shortcomings of the clinical approach to decision making. Unaided human judgment is simply incapable of dealing effectively with large amounts of complex information. Compounding matters is the resolute refusal of "holistic" practitioners to offer reliable evidence that they use any consistent decision-making strategy at all. Holism is an empty retreat from reality, a method by which pseudoscientists muddy rational thought, avoid clear and concise communication, and follow their own idiosyncratic beliefs to justify doing whatever they please.

CLOSING THOUGHTS: FALSE DICHOTOMIES AND THE SLIPPERY SLOPE

When you suspect that someone may be trying to pull the wool over your eyes through the deceptive use of language, you should dig a little deeper to see what that person is really saying. We have seen that the strategic framing of issues and tactical violations of conversational maxims can be subtle, yet yield powerful effects, but there are other ways that linguistic tricks can be used to influence your thought. For example, to return for a moment to the abortion issue, consider a bumper sticker that I saw while driving one day: The top line read "Smile" in large lettering. I sped up to get a closer look, and eventually read the bottom line: "Your *mom* was pro-life." Now this is vacuous, even for a bumper sticker. The term *pro-life* is an empty catch-phrase, and the full statement is logically flawed. It makes no sense to presume that everyone's mom was pro-life, as plenty of pro-choice women have children! (Are we to believe that all women who are pro-choice will necessarily abort every pregnancy? This obvious foolishness is the only way for the bumper sticker to be truthful.)

Thus, the abortion issue highlights two final linguistic tricks that are often used in the attempt to persuade. First, the entire pro-life versus pro-choice debate can be construed as a *false dichotomy*. Despite repetitions of the simplistic dichotomy put forward by parents, teachers, friends, and the popular media, there *are* other options. For example, one can favor allowing abortions under certain circumstances (e.g., pregnancies that result from rape or that endanger the health of the mother) but not others (e.g., pregnancies resulting from consenting sex without birth control). In a chapter co-written with Anne Druyan, Sagan (1997) argues that what we all object to is killing a *human being*, which forces us to grapple with a perplexing issue: What does it mean to be human? Sagan and Druyan defend the view that certain types of thought processes make us human, and they then provide evidence that we attain the capacity for these uniquely human thought processes at about the beginning of the seventh month of fetal development. Thus, they would argue that abortion up until that point does not take a human life, whereas beyond that point it does.

This is not the place to endorse or critique this, or any other, particular view. My purpose is only to point out that you need not subscribe to a false dichotomy, that you can think more deeply about a number of possibilities before formulating your own beliefs. Why is it, then, that so many people identify themselves as pro-choice or pro-life? One likely culprit is their fear of the *slippery slope:* that any small concession on their part will be taken advantage of by "the other side." This is the old "give 'em an inch and they'll take a mile" fear. For example, pro-life advocates fear that if they concede that there is nothing uniquely human about a fertilized egg, they will be forced to allow abortions at that point. Having conceded this, they fear that their opponents will push the arbitrariness further, that allowable abortions will begin to slide along the slippery slope toward the time of birth. Pro-choice advocates are likewise unwilling to concede that the fetus is a human life just moments before birth for fear that this argument against abortion can be used against them, with the arbitrariness sliding back toward the time of conception.

In this way, the fear of the slippery slope helps to maintain false dichotomies. It is not difficult to see the same process preventing serious debate about a variety of issues of profound significance, such as gun control, environmental protection, or nuclear arms reduction. When rational debate is stifled, misleading and evasive uses of language can be deadly.

INFOTRAC COLLEGE EDITION

To learn more about topics included in this chapter, enter the following search terms:

alternative medicine
false dichotomy
framing effect
health food
prospect theory
slippery slope
suggestion and memory

CHAPTER 3

MAGIC

The Allure of Exotic Rituals, Fantasy, and Mysticism

Who Wants to Be a Millionnaire? As I write, this remains a wildly successful television quiz show. Give Regis Philbin correct answers to assorted trivia questions, and you can win $1 million. Who among us is not drawn in by the allure of such easy money? Of course, the chances of appearing on that show, earning the privilege of being a contestant, and correctly answering 15 questions of increasing difficulty is quite slim. Fortunately, there is another path to $1 million that's open to anybody.

Therapeutic touch is a pseudoscience that has achieved popularity within the nursing profession. Swenson (1999) notes that its proponents claim that therapeutic touch has been taught to more than 48,000 people in 75 countries, is taught at 75 schools and universities, and is practiced at 95 health facilities. What is therapeutic touch? Its practitioners assert that they can diagnose and treat physical disease by sensing and manipulating a "human energy field." They attempt to do this by moving their hands above the patient's body, typically at a distance of about three inches. Thus, one of the many mysteries of therapeutic touch is that no actual touch is involved.

Enter the $1 million challenge. The Philadelphia Association for Critical Thinking (PhACT) and the James Randi Educational Foundation have jointly offered a $1 million award to anyone who can pass a simple test. While blindfolded, by moving your hands about three inches above a person's arms, you must be able to discern, whether the person's arms have been inserted into fiberglass sleeves (the sleeves are used only to prevent heat transfer, which makes arms very easy to detect!). In a series of trials, your rate of correct responses must exceed chance-level random guessing. That's it! If the astounding claims of therapeutic touch practitioners are even remotely true, then any one of them should have an easy time passing the PhACT/Randi test and collecting the $1 million. "This is something they claim to be able to do every day in their practice, so why not come to Philadelphia and show us?" asks Randi. So far, the money remains unclaimed. Why?

BELIEVING IN MAGIC

Throughout all of human history, our thirst for knowledge has been driven by the struggle to survive in an often harsh and unpredictable world. We have worked diligently to learn about the natural world through both formal and informal experimentation. For example, long before scientific methods were formalized, people had developed sophisticated means of tracking and capturing prey, defending themselves against much larger and stronger predators, planting and harvesting crops using the length of the day as an index of the changing seasons, and navigating over great distances by following patterns among the stars. Each of these achievements represents remarkable human ingenuity, a significant step forward in grasping the subtleties of the natural world and utilizing them for practical purposes.

Alongside this march of progress in coming to know reality has been an enduring belief in magic. Magical beliefs provide a sense of control (albeit a false sense) over the potentially threatening aspects of our world that we do not yet understand. When a genuine mastery of our environment eludes us, it is nonetheless comforting to believe that we possess knowledge, and thus power, through magic. Before scientists uncovered the causes of thunder and lightning, for example, these phenomena were often ascribed to angry gods.

The danger of magical thinking lies in the possibility that we will cling so tenaciously to our superstitions that we will be blinded to reality when it becomes clearly understood. A fleeting belief in supernatural forces may be relatively harmless, but if it actively inhibits our quest to know the real world, we suffer. Magical thinking holds no keys to progress and offers only false hope. Moreover, strong belief in one supernatural phenomenon may open the door to belief in others. Once reality has been partially abandoned, it becomes easier to accommodate other magical beliefs.

WISHFUL THINKING

Although it may seem childish, it is surprising just how often we choose to believe in something simply because we wish it were true. Usually, wishful thinking makes the world more interesting or entertaining, and less threatening.

One of the most outspoken pseudoscientists of the past few decades, Andrew Weil, has a true knack for selling wishful thinking. Through a complex mixture of perfect sense and absolute nonsense, his many books and public appearances have generated a large following. The first of his books, *The Natural Mind,* was published in 1972. One of its themes—strongly indicative of the wholesale endorsement of magical thinking that permeates all of Weil's popular writing—is that rational, intellectual thought actually *impedes* the growth of our knowledge. "In order to perceive reality directly, one must sooner or later learn how to abandon the intellect and disengage oneself from the thoughts it produces incessantly" (Weil, 1972, p. 120). He never explains exactly how a disengagement from thoughts and our intellectual processes will allow us to perceive reality. An earlier passage is more overtly mystical and every bit as unclear:

> The conscious experience of unity behind the diversity of phenomena—said by sages and mystics of all centuries to be the most blissful and uplifting of human experiences—may require nothing more than a moment's freedom to stand back from the rush of sensory information and look at it in a different way from usual. (Weil, 1972, p. 96)

The reader is never informed what the "conscious experience of unity behind the diversity of phenomena" actually means, nor how this can be achieved. But what a powerful statement this is. Could it be any more emotionally appealing? Similarly attractive ideas are tossed around in a later discussion of mental telepathy, or the ability to communicate directly from one mind to another:

> Not only do I think each of us can share consciousness, I think all of us are already doing it all the time. We do not have to learn to be telepathic; we just have to notice that we already are by letting telepathic events into our waking consciousness. . . . Telepathy is nothing other than thinking the same thoughts at the same time others are thinking them—something all of us are doing all the time at a level of our conscious experience most of us are not aware of. Become aware of it and you become telepathic automatically. (Weil, 1972, pp. 184–187)

As a scientist, I would be utterly fascinated by the existence of mental telepathy. I would love to learn how it works, and can imagine no end to the exciting new research questions that could be explored. Here are the first dozen or so that occur to me:

- What types of thoughts may be shared: conscious, unconscious, or both? That is, does telepathy require active participation or can others read our minds regardless of our intentions?
- Must the messages be verbal, or can images be included?
- Is there a limit to the complexity of a message that can be shared?
- Over what distances may messages be transmitted?
- How do we target a particular mind to which we will send or from which we will receive a message? There are, after all, roughly six billion people on the planet, and this seems as though it could be awfully confusing!
- How do we signal or recognize the beginning or end of a message? That is, how does our sending or receiving apparatus assure a proper connection?

- How do we distinguish an incoming telepathic message from a hallucination?
- Where in the brain is a telepathic message processed?
- Can we process normal sensory input at the same time as telepathic messages?
- Are we limited to processing one message at a time, or can we simultaneously send and/or receive multiple messages?
- How much individual variation is there in the ability to send or receive messages?
- Can we train ourselves to become better senders or receivers?
- Do primates or other animals possess any telepathic powers as well?

My skepticism in light of Weil's inviting claim should therefore not be taken as a lack of interest. Nor should it be construed as a threat to my scientific worldview. Though I cannot conceive of answers to these questions based on currently understood scientific principles, I am quite open to new discoveries and new evidence. I'm a psychologist, after all, so genuine proof of mental telepathy would utterly fascinate me! At present, however, the evidence is not at all persuasive. To believe in an extraordinary, fantastic phenomenon—such as mental telepathy—based on nothing more than unsubstantiated assertions would be an act of sheer wishful thinking.

BELIEF IN A VITALISTIC ENERGY

But wishful thinking sells, and it can be contagious. For example, many pseudosciences are premised on vaguely specified and poorly understood forms of energy. As noted earlier, practitioners of therapeutic touch claim that they can detect an energy field through the palms of their hands when held about three inches from the patient. This energy is allegedly used both to diagnose and to treat disease. Practitioners of acupuncture believe in a mysterious energy known as "qi" or "chi" (pronounced "chee") that flows along a series of "meridians" on the body. Specific locations along these meridians are said to be "acupuncture points" at which the insertion of a needle will help to "unblock" or "realign" the energy flow in a beneficial way. The relatively new pseudoscience of "thought field therapy" is likewise premised on the blockage or disruption in energy flow along the meridians of the body, but it involves rhythmic tapping at acupressure points to add energy or modify its flow as needed and thereby cure psychological disorders. Similarly, chiropractors refer to "The Innate" (always capitalized) and homeopaths to "vital energy," both conjuring the existence of energy fields. The list of pseudosciences that have created magical forms of energy to suit their purposes is endless.

The fundamental problem with these and other forms of purely hypothetical energy is that they have not been detected by even the most sophisticated physical measurement instruments. There is simply no evidence suggesting the existence of this energy, let alone a human ability to detect it, determine whether it is "imbalanced," or "adjust" it.

Proponents of energy-based pseudosciences attempt to rescue their beliefs by asserting that these energies do not exist in the same physical universe that we experience. They exist in some other realm that is also vaguely specified and unverified. Although this retreat might explain why scientists have not detected these mysterious energies, it is ultimately poses the greatest contradiction. That is, if the energy cannot interact with our physical universe to be detected by our measurement instruments, how can it interact with our bodily organs to cause disease, interact with practitioners to allow them to reach diagnoses, or be manipulated by practitioners as a treatment? Few people seek care for a blockage in the flow of their energy fields. We seek help for problems that we are experiencing, problems that we *can* detect and that we find quite distressing. Ordinarily, these problems can be diagnosed using the type of laboratory equipment that is unable to detect the mysterious energy.

Many people are undeterred by the contradictions inherent in mystical energies that selectively interact with the physical world, and it can be difficult to have a rational debate with someone who chooses to believe in magic: often, the rules of logic are thrown out. Fortunately, it is quite easy to *test* the fantastic energy-based claims made by pseudoscientists to the satisfaction of both proponents and skeptics. To be done well, both sides of a debate must agree to the terms of a test, which then obligates them to accept its results. Such an experiment *has* been carried out to test for the ability of people to detect a "human energy field." Remarkably, one girl's junior high school science project has dealt the greatest blow yet to those who believe in vitalistic energy!

Putting the "Human Energy Field" to the Test

Emily Rosa is the daughter of Linda Rosa, coordinator of the National Council Against Health Fraud's Task Force on Questionable Nursing Practices. Because therapeutic touch has gained such widespread acceptance within American nursing, Linda and Emily frequently discussed it around the house. For a school science project, Emily designed and carried out a simple, elegant test of the most basic assumption of therapeutic touch: that an energy field can be *detected.* Naturally, if this test was failed it would be impossible to maintain that the energy could be utilized for diagnosis or manipulated therapeutically. To test this claim, Emily blindfolded self-identified "expert" therapeutic touch practitioners and asked them, under well-controlled laboratory conditions, to detect the mere presence of another person by identifying which of the person's hands was put forward from trial to trial. The procedure was fully described in advance to participants, each of whom assured Emily that they could perform successfully with great ease. Each then made a series of 10 "left/right" judgments, with the correct answer varied at random from trial to trial. Simply guessing at random would have resulted in 5 correct judgments out of 10. The results revealed that participants averaged just 4.7 correct answers out of 10, a little *worse* than pure guessing! In 1998, at the age of 11, Emily Rosa became the youngest author ever to publish a paper in the *Journal of the American Medical Association* (Rosa, Rosa, Sarner, & Barrett, 1998).

The failure of "experts" at this task, the *easiest* task imaginable for those versed in therapeutic touch, speaks strongly against the existence of an energy field. Clearly, someone who cannot distinguish the presence or absence of another human being would be utterly incapable of diagnosing or treating disease on the basis of a hypothetical energy field surrounding that person. Emily's results, shocking as they were to proponents of energy-based pseudosciences, were perfectly consistent with the conclusions of scientists. A recent book edited by Scheiber and Selby (2000) contains a collection of logical analyses and empirical tests of therapeutic touch, none of which support any of the bold claims made by its proponents. More broadly, a scientific panel at the University of Colorado Health Sciences Center reported in the May/June 1997 National Council Against Health Fraud newsletter: "There is virtually no acceptable scientific evidence concerning the existence or nature of these energy fields."

Just like the failure of experts in Emily's experiment, the fact that nobody has taken advantage of the $1 million PhACT/Randi challenge is telling. No practitioner of any energy-based treatment modality has ever been able to document the existence of this energy. Moreover, all available logic, theory, and research consistently suggest that belief in magical energy is unwarranted.

THE CREATION OF SUPERSTITIONS AND EXOTIC RITUALS

In addition to the belief in magical energy, a host of superstitious beliefs and practices are popular for similar reasons. The way many superstitious beliefs and exotic rituals develop is fairly well understood by behavioral learning theorists, who were the first psychologists to employ the term *superstition* (Skinner, 1948). To understand how superstitious learning takes place, let's start by considering a few of the fundamental principles of learning theory.

When a behavior is followed by reinforcement, the chance of that behavior occurring again in the future increases. For example, suppose your child receives good grades one semester and you want to reinforce his or her studious behavior. Reinforcement may either be "positive," in that something pleasant is given to the child (e.g., a payment for the good grades), or "negative," in that something unpleasant is removed (e.g., a release from household chores). With careful attention to the nature and timing of reinforcements, behaviors can be shaped into more desirable patterns. Animal trainers use the principles of learning and behavior to teach elephants to march in an orderly fashion, to teach bears to ride bicycles, to teach dolphins to leap from the water and kick a dangling ball with their tail, and to teach a wide array of other tricks (Breland & Breland, 1961, 1966). The behavioral approach to psychotherapy successfully treats psychological disorders in this way (Lazarus, 1971; Skinner, 1953). Because our survival has depended on the ability to learn from our environment, it should come as no surprise that these principles of learning are powerful. Though we have some innate or instinctive behavioral tendencies, our success as a species can be attributed in no small part to the adaptability to change that our learning mechanisms make possible.

But what do we learn when no attention is paid to the *schedule*, or pattern, of reinforcement? What if reinforcement is provided at random, as so often happens in everyday life? Observations have suggested that eccentric and idiosyncratic behavior patterns often develop without having been intentionally reinforced (Skinner, 1948). Skinner noted that although the specific behaviors differed from one experimental subject to the next, the behaviors shared a notable persistence despite a lack of scheduled reinforcement. For example, a pigeon placed in a chamber with several gadgets that it was free to manipulate would be given a food pellet at purely random intervals regardless of its behavior. Despite the lack of any planned association between the pigeon's behavior and the reinforcement (receiving a food pellet), the pigeon often happened to operate on some aspect of its environment immediately prior to receiving the food. This accidental reinforcement caused the pigeon to engage in more of the behavior, thereby increasing the chance that the next randomly administered food pellet would again accidentally reinforce the same behavior. Over time, virtually any ordinary behavior performed by a pigeon could become linked in this way with positive reinforcement. Behaviorists referred to this type of accidental learning as "superstitious behavior," and it bears an uncanny similarity to many of our own beliefs and behaviors.

Our superstitions do indeed appear to be developed similarly to those of laboratory animals. For example, it is easy to imagine the accidental reinforcement of "rain dances." A group of individuals suffering through a drought happens to perform some sort of dance and, by chance, it begins to rain. From that point onward, whenever another drought is experienced, the group dances in an attempt to summon more rain. Perhaps they will have to dance for a few days before it rains again, perhaps they will have to perform a more elaborate dance, but with perseverance it will rain again—after all, every drought comes to an end eventually. In a similar way, the perception that various amulets, talismans, or other "good luck charms" bring good fortune may be readily confirmed. All one needs to do is actively search for evidence of good fortune and disregard both misfortunes and the chances of experiencing the same good fortune had the charm not been used.

All of this is reminiscent of the belief that chicken soup has some special effectiveness against the common cold. In fact, there is an old saying that you can cure the common cold in a week with chicken soup, or you can just wait seven days. Often we are duped by superstitious learning. Whatever action is taken gets credited with success whether it brought about the desired outcome or not, and a superstitious belief is born.

SUPERSTITIONS AS REPRESENTATIVE THINKING

Superstitions can be very compelling because they are often based on cause and effect pairings that are superficially plausible and therefore easy to believe. Many superstitions merely reflect the notion that "like goes with like" (Potter, 1983), which psychologists refer to as "representative" thinking (Kahneman & Tversky, 1972). Here's a question to illustrate the power of representative thinking:

> Linda is 31 years old, single, outspoken, and very bright. She majored in philosophy. As a student, she was deeply concerned with issues of discrimination and social justice, and also participated in antinuclear demonstrations. Please select the most likely alternative:
>
> • Linda is a bank teller
> • Linda is a bank teller and is active in the feminist movement.

If you chose the second option, then you are not alone. Nearly 90% of the participants in a study by Kahneman and Tversky (1972) believed that Linda was more likely to be a bank teller and active in the feminist movement than just a bank teller. However, the second choice is logically *less* likely to be true than the first, for the simple reason that there are some bank tellers who are not active in the feminist movement. Feminist bank tellers are a subset of all bank tellers, so the first option has to be more likely to be true. Why do so many of us make this mistake? Because the second choice *seems* more consistent with all we know about Linda. The fact, though, is that a more general statement is always more likely to be true than a statement that includes the same information plus additional details.

The lesson to be learned is that we can easily be misled by things that appear to fit together nicely but may in fact have no real connection. For example, one of the two fundamental principles of homeopathy is the "law of similars" that was "discovered" by Samuel Hahnemann in the late 1700s. He proposed that the same substance that would produce disease in a healthy person would cure someone afflicted with that disease. A more dangerous example of representative thinking would be hard to imagine, for administering the cause of a disease to someone who already has it certainly will not help matters! (Fortunately for patients, Hahnemann also believed in the "law of infinitesimals" and therefore diluted his medicines; homeopathy is discussed further in Chapter 6).

MAINTENANCE OF SUPERSTITIONS

If a superstitious behavior is based on accidental learning or representative thinking, you might wonder why it endures. Are we not smart enough to root out and eliminate our more foolish beliefs? The answer is that another principle of learning makes superstitious beliefs particularly hardy. When a behavior is followed by reinforcement every time it occurs, the behavior will stop fairly rapidly if the reinforcement ceases. For example, if you pay your child every time he or she gets good grades, a clear connection will be learned. If for any reason you stop paying your child, and studying is maintained only by continuous reinforcement, the studying will rapidly disappear (or extinguish) in the absence of payment.

How can you provide reinforcements in order to shape a desirable behavior but avoid the problem of rapid extinction? The key is to not provide reinforcement every time the behavior occurs, to use what psychologists call an intermittent schedule of reinforcement. For example, you might reinforce every other good report card (a fixed schedule), or you might haphazardly reward a good report card every once in a while (a variable schedule). Although both of these intermittent schedules result in somewhat slower learning than does continuous reinforcement, they also result in behavior that extinguishes much more slowly. The reason is this: If you establish that your child will only sometimes be paid for good grades, he or she will not take the absence of payment to mean that the deal is off. The child will continue to study because he or she will presume that there is still some chance of being paid next time. After all, not all good report cards were reinforced. In particular, if the schedule of reinforcement was variable, your child would have to experience a whole series of good report cards without receiving payment before his or her studying behavior might begin to extinguish.

It is therefore important not only to consider whether learning has been shaped though intentional or accidental reinforcement (with the latter sometimes the cause of superstitions) but on what schedule the reinforcement was administered. Consider someone who tries a homeopathic remedy for the flu and happens to recover almost immediately. Even though the purported flu remedy may have had nothing whatsoever to do with the recovery, it will likely be credited a success. A superstitious belief has been created through accidental reinforcement. Now the chances are greater that this person will use the same homeopathic remedy the next time the flu sets in. Because the treatment itself has no physiological effect, it will only happen to coincide with recovery from the flu on occasion, by chance. Thus, across repeated flu episodes, the accidental reinforcement will follow an intermittent, variable schedule, solidifying the use of the homeopathic remedy. Belief in its efficacy will become highly resistant to extinction. Among other reasons discussed in Chapter 5, testimonials are virtually worthless as evidence because it is impossible to tell whether superstitious learning has occurred in any individual case. Only well-controlled scientific experimentation can rule out this possibility.

ABUSES OF SCIENCE IN FAVOR OF MYSTICISM

Science is routinely abused by those who prefer mysticism, fantasy, and exotic rituals. In particular, several counterintuitive aspects of scientific theories are used to argue that reality itself is extremely complex, that anything is possible. The first generalization is quite true: Reality is enormously complex. Robert Park (1997) calls relativity, quantum mechanics, and chaos theory the "three weirds" of science. Each reveals subtleties of nature heretofore unimagined. However, this does not justify the second generalization, that anything is possible. This freewheeling "anything goes" attitude reflects a gross misconception that does violence to the spirit of scientific inquiry.

Science can be viewed as a series of successive approximations to the truth, with each new insight bringing us a little closer. The goal of good science is in fact to eliminate incorrect hypotheses so that the hypotheses that survive are more likely to be correct. This is not to argue that scientists are never surprised, and indeed some of the most impressive scientific discoveries—such as penicillin or X-rays—have been made accidentally. However, even as each new discovery opens up additional lines of research, it also provides a more complete understanding of reality. The notion that "anything is possible" denies those aspects of reality that we currently understand. Pseudoscientists would like us to set aside the pieces of the grand puzzle that are already in place so that the rationales for their mysterious and untested beliefs no longer conflict with the best available research evidence.

A closely related abuse of science perpetrated by pseudoscientists is the claim that they are misunderstood geniuses with brilliant ideas that are not accepted because they are ahead of their time. Throughout history, many people who were unable to convince a reasonable audience resorted to delusions of persecution (see Gardner, 1952). The fashionable comparisons these days—"they laughed at Galileo," "they laughed at Newton"—suffer from a serious logical flaw satirized perfectly by Carl Sagan: "They laughed at Bozo the Clown, too." The simple truth is that, among promoters of revolutionary or "fringe" theories, the geniuses with brilliant ideas have always been overwhelmingly outnumbered by those who were simply wrong. Many pseudoscientists actually use their self-proclaimed persecuted status as a selling point, wearing it as a badge of honor, apparently holding the naïve belief (or, more insulting, expecting *us* to hold the belief) that the theories of Galileo and Newton were later accepted *because* their discoverers were persecuted.

It is interesting to note that, historically, scientists have been the most readily converted to radical new ideas supported by evidence. *Scientists* did not laugh at Galileo or Newton. Even Einstein's ideas on special and general relativity, which revealed the incompleteness of long-held and deeply-respected theories in physics, were accepted rapidly within the scientific community. The theories of Galileo and Newton were eventually acknowledged (as will be Einstein's contributions) among wider circles based on persuasive scientific evidence, not on sociological, religious, or political grounds.

The Magic of Modern Technology

It is ironic that mysticism appeals to so many people in this age of incredible scientific and technological achievement. Perhaps the very success of science is in fact the problem. To most people, modern technology is indistinguishable from magic. How many among us can explain how electricity is generated, how computers manipulate or exchange information, how a microwave oven cooks food, or even something so simple as how a remote control or cellular telephone operates? None of these technologies is on the "cutting edge," yet they are beyond all but the vaguest comprehension of most people. We have become heavily dependent on devices that, for all practical purposes, work by magic. Once we begin to lose touch with how things work, we may be more susceptible to accepting other claims based on enigmatic principles. Without a basic level of scientific literacy, we cannot tell which magic is real, which magic is only fantasy. But if we cannot tell the difference ourselves, we ought to at least recognize the need to defer to qualified scientists when it comes to matters of science.

Learning the style of thinking and understanding the knowledge base of science is challenging. Science requires sophisticated methodological solutions to complex problems as well as careful attention to ethical, legal, and practical issues. It calls for creative thought to consider all possible theories as well as tough-minded skepticism to help sort the fruitful theories from those that are bogus. It encourages you to keep your mind open, but, as the old saying goes, "not so open that your brains fall out." How much easier life would be if we could simply dismiss the need for science and come to know our world by following the path of least resistance. If only our wishes did come true.

Mysticism, fantasy, and exotic rituals often represent a recklessly simple-minded approach to knowledge. When you hear someone use terms like *relativity, quantum mechanics, chaos,* or the similar-sounding *complexity,* you may well ask yourself whether the speaker has any true understanding of these theories. Each requires extensive scientific and mathematical training to even glimpse its deep meaning, and perhaps a decade or more of dedicated study to fully comprehend it. Might someone be casually tossing around a shorthand version of a theory with which he is unfamiliar because it serves the purpose of muddying important distinctions, legitimizing mysticism, or glossing over the stark contradiction between his own theory and a well-understood corner of reality? When people compare themselves to Galileo, Newton, or other "persecuted geniuses," might they in all truth bear a greater similarity to Bozo the Clown?

INFOTRAC COLLEGE EDITION

To learn more about topics included in this chapter, enter the following search terms:

mysticism
superstition/superstitious
therapeutic touch
thought field
wishful thinking

AUTHORITY

Appeals to Blind Obedience

Between five and six million Jews were killed in the concentration camps of Nazi Germany. In the aftermath of World War II, psychologists tried desperately to understand what caused the atrocities of the Holocaust. Specifically, research investigated how the Nazi philosophy could have been accepted by so many Germans. One idea was that a personality characteristic known as "authoritarianism" made some people particularly likely to follow orders. This hypothesis met with only limited success when tested in research. In the 1960s, Stanley Milgram turned the entire question on its head. Rather than ask how the Nazis could be so different from us, he asked instead how each of us is a little like a Nazi.

MILGRAM'S OBEDIENCE RESEARCH

Imagine that it is the 1960s, you live in New Haven, Connecticut, and a newspaper ad is soliciting volunteers for an experiment on "the effects of punishment on learning" being conducted in the Psychology Department of Yale University. The pay that is offered is modest but fair: $4.50. You respond to the ad and are scheduled to participate in the experiment. When you arrive, you find that another person is there to take part as well. When you are greeted by the experimenter, he thanks you both for coming and explains that to test the effects of punishment on learning, one of you, the "teacher," will administer electric shocks to the other, the "learner," when mistakes are made. Straws are drawn, and you are relieved to learn that you will be the teacher. As you watch, the experimenter escorts the learner to another room, straps him into a chair, and attaches an electrode. To give you a sense for what the shocks are like, you are given a 45-volt shock. Before you and the experimenter return to the other room, the learner mentions that he has a heart condition and asks whether the shocks will pose any threat. By way of reassurance, the experimenter states that although the shocks will be painful, they will cause "no permanent tissue damage."

The experimenter then escorts you to the room from which you will control the learning task. You are seated before a large device, a shock generator that is connected to the learner in the adjacent room. The shock generator has a series of 30 switches. The first switch delivers a 15-volt shock, the next a 30-volt shock, the next 45 volts, and so on up to the last switch, which delivers a 450-volt shock. In addition to voltages, verbal descriptions of the shocks' intensities appear below groups of switches. The lowest group is labeled "Slight Shock," and a group further up the scale is labeled "Moderate Shock." The labels progress up through "Danger: Severe Shock" and end with the last switches being labeled only "XXX."

After you have had a moment to look over the device, the experimenter explains your role as teacher. First, you will read a lengthy list of word-pairs to the learner through an intercom system. His job is to remember which words go together. Then, you will read one word from the list along with a set of four other words from which the learner will make a selection. If his selection is a correct match, then you move on to the next word. Otherwise, you will inform the learner that his selection is incorrect, read the correct answer, and deliver a shock. The most disturbing aspect of this procedure is that each time you administer a shock, it must be 15 volts more intense than the last. For the first mistake, the learner will receive a 15-volt shock, for the second mistake a 30-volt shock, and so forth. The experiment will continue until the learner responds to the entire list without making any errors.

You begin the experiment, and the learner remembers several of the word pairs but occasionally makes a mistake. You dutifully administer brief electric shocks whenever the learner makes a mistake. As the voltage of these shocks begins to climb, the learner grunts, cries out, and eventually screams in pain. The learner repeatedly demands to be released, expressing concern about his heart condition and complaining about the intense pain. Uncertain what to do, you turn to the experimenter, who simply tells you to "please go on." If you protest further, you are told that "the experiment requires that you continue." In increasingly agonized shouts, the learner insists that he be let out, that the experiment must stop. Still, the experiment continues. At 300 and 315 volts, the learner shouts his refusal to respond any longer. Once the 330 volt level is reached, there is no sound whatsoever coming from the other room. Not only does the learner cease responding to the questions, but he no longer cries out in pain—a worrisome sign indeed. Nonetheless, the experimenter says that "you have no choice, you must go on," and that a failure to respond should be treated as a mistake. Although by now you have begun sweating, laughing nervously, and occasionally pausing to plead with the steadfast experimenter, you continue in your role as the teacher. The shocks continue all the way to the "Danger: Severe Shock" level and beyond, finally reaching the highest level, 450 volts, labeled as "XXX." After you have administered the most intense shock that the device will produce, the experimenter instructs you to continue delivering a 450-volt shock for each mistake. Once you have done this several times, the experimenter finally informs you that the experiment is over. Your nightmare has come to an end.

At this point, you may be thinking that you would never have gone so far, that you are not the type of person who would willingly cause harm to another human being no matter what an experimenter ordered you to do. If you believe that this scenario depicts the actions of a sadistic teacher, dramatically unlike most normal individuals, then you are not alone. Prior to conducting the experiment, Milgram polled 40 psychiatrists. Provided with a detailed description of the experimental procedure, they believed that just 1 in 1,000 people—the true sadists—would continue in the teacher role all the way to the highest shock level. However, this is far from what happened. In the version of the experiment described above (see Milgram, 1974), 65% of the teachers fully obeyed the experimenter and delivered shocks all the way up through the maximum intensity! Moreover, even among the 35% who disobeyed the experimenter, relatively few of them did so before 300 volts had already been administered and the learner stopped responding. These results, to use an unavoidably bad pun, were shocking.

Before proceeding, it is important to address the ethics of this research. First, it is crucial to understand that no shocks were actually delivered. The experiment's purpose was not to study the effect of punishment on learning, but rather to study obedience to authority. The initial drawing was rigged so that the one true participant was always the teacher, whereas the learner was a confederate of the experimenter whose reactions were staged. His complaints and protests were carefully executed, standardized so that each participant experienced precisely the same situation. Once the experiment was terminated, the teacher was reunited with the learner and shown that he had not been harmed in any way. As you might imagine, this usually came as a tremendous relief to the participant. Then, the experimenter led an extensive discussion about the true nature of the study and the reasons deception had been necessary. Finally, Milgram contacted all the participants after the experiment was over to ensure that they were not experiencing residual distress. A panel of expert psychiatrists attested to the mental health of the 40 participants who had been most strongly affected by the temporary stress of the experiment. Most of the participants (84%) reported being glad to have been a part of the experiment; only 1% reported regret over having participated. Many people reported that they learned something that, although disturbing, provided invaluable insight into human nature and changed their lives—they became less likely to mindlessly obey authority figures and more likely to speak up for themselves. Several individuals even volunteered to participate in any other experiments that Milgram was conducting.

UNDERSTANDING MILGRAM'S RESULTS

When you first learn about this experiment, undoubtedly one of the most famous in all of psychology, a common reaction is that you, personally, would surely not continue to obey to the very end. However, subsequent research has failed to reveal any differences between those who obey and those who disobey. Neither age, sex, occupation, nor personality, for example, successfully predicts who will be more or less obedient. Therefore, if you believe that you would have disobeyed before administering a 300-volt shock, you may well be wrong. In fact, there is no known reason to suspect that you would behave any differently from Milgram's participants, 65% of whom fully obeyed orders. If you think otherwise, you are probably underestimating the power of the situation.

Many factors, some more subtle than others, contribute to the high level of full obedience (administering shocks all the way to the 450-volt level) that Milgram observed. To understand these factors, the obedience rates of a whole series of experiments with slightly different procedures were compared. Although full obedience never dropped completely to zero, the pattern of results did reveal many contributing factors. One important factor was the perceived legitimacy of the authority. The original experiment was performed at a reputable institution (Yale University), but when it was repeated in a rented warehouse by a team identifying themselves as the "Research Associates of Bridgeport," the rate of obedience dropped to 48%. A second factor was the proximity of the authority figure to the participant. When the experimenter provided orders over the telephone, obedience dropped to 21%. A third factor was the teacher's emotional distance from the learner. When the learner was seated in the same room as the teacher, obedience dropped to 40%. When the teacher was required to physically hold the learner's hand on a shock plate to administer punishment, obedience dropped further still, down to 30%.

There are other situational factors that research showed to be important determinants of obedience. One subtle aspect of the situation that was never manipulated in a follow-up experiment was the gradual escalation of voltages. There was such a slight difference between each shock level that it may have made disobedience seem arbitrary at any given point in time. That is, the situation did not change sufficiently from one shock level to the next to justify (to oneself or to the experimenter) a refusal to continue. For example, after having administered 150 volts, would it not be somewhat hypocritical to refuse to administer 165? If 165 is cruel, then so was 150. Had the voltage levels been more widely separated, it is plausible that obedience would have dropped. The only available evidence on this point comes from the observation that those who did disobey tended to do so at a similar point: around 330 volts, when the learner stopped responding. The possibility that the learner had suffered some horrible fate as a result of the shocks profoundly altered the situation in a way that mere 15-volt increments could not. This may be another example of the deleterious effects of a slippery slope.

WHEN SHOULD WE OBEY?

More than anything, Milgram's results reveal the remarkable obedience to authority that lurks within each of us. In a way, this should not surprise us so much. After all, it would be virtually impossible to get through life without obeying authorities. We cannot verify everything that we are told because we cannot spend the time to do so and we simply do not possess the expertise to fully understand the evidence on which all assertions are made. We must accept the authority of experts or else remain woefully uninformed. The trick is to distinguish between legitimate authority, based on true expertise and a genuine concern for our well-being, and illegitimate authority, based only on the appearance of expertise and less noble intentions.

Unfortunately, it is often difficult to make this distinction. For example, doctors possess considerable expertise based on formal training and experience, yet they are not infallible. Do others challenge their mistakes? When a doctor makes an obvious mistake on a prescription, for example, does the nurse administering the medicine question it? Sadly, the answer is typically "no." Consider first the strange case of a "rectal earache" reported by Cohen and Davis (1981). Robert Cialdini, an expert on the psychology of persuasion, describes it in this way:

> A physician ordered ear drops to be administered to the right ear of a patient suffering pain and infection there. But instead of writing out completely the location "right ear" on the prescription, the doctor abbreviated it so that the instructions read "place in R ear." Upon receiving the prescription, the duty nurse promptly put the desired number of ear drops into the patient's anus. Obviously, rectal treatment of an earache made no sense. Yet neither the patient nor the nurse questioned it. (Cialdini, 1993, pp. 219–220)

Is this story symptomatic of a larger problem? It appears so. In a systematic study involving a more serious treatment error (Hofling, Brotzman, Dairymple, Graves, & Pierce, 1966), nurses were ordered to administer medication to a patient. However, there were four good reasons they should have challenged the order:

1. The order was made over the telephone, which violated hospital policy.
2. The individual giving the order claimed to be a doctor without any verification.
3. The drug was listed as experimental, not yet approved for administration to patients.

4. The order called for a clear overdose, fully double the maximum that was allowed.

The experiment was carried out with nurses on 22 different surgical, medical, pediatric, and psychiatric wards. A secret observer was placed outside the intended patient's room. In 95% of all instances, the nurse arrived fully prepared to administer the medicine! (The observer intervened at this point and explained that this was an experiment.) This is chilling obedience, underscoring the need for individuals to more carefully consider the legitimacy of authoritative pronouncements.

UNTRUSTWORTHY AUTHORITIES

Pseudoscience often involves appeals to questionable authorities and self-proclaimed experts whose judgments are not based on well-controlled scientific research. In many ways, the proponents of pseudoscience seek to blur the distinction between legitimate and illegitimate authority. A few commonly heard arguments will be reviewed as examples of the fallacies committed to legitimize authority. This listing is by no means exhaustive, but it should provide you with some tools to help you think about other arguments and evaluate their merits on your own.

The "Ancient Wisdom" Fallacy

An appeal to "ancient wisdom" is often substituted for actual evidence. Proponents suggest that any belief that has been held for a long period of time must be valid. This type of argument has dangerous consequences, however. If beliefs are granted truth owing merely to their age, this would provide justification for sexism, racism, anti-Semitism, and a host of other repellent notions that have been widely held throughout human history. Social progress involves the continual questioning of ancient wisdom, and there is no reason that any belief system should be exempted from such challenge.

Modern-day advocates of traditional Chinese medicine, such as acupuncture or herbs, rely heavily on appeals to ancient wisdom. Unfortunately, the effectiveness of a treatment cannot safely be assumed based on its age. In fact, there is little or no support for the assertion that these ancient practices have "stood the test of time," because they have seldom even been subjected to— let alone passed—meaningful tests. It is easy to claim success for a treatment when, as in China, no accurate medical record-keeping has existed until recently. After all, how can you tell whether treatments have done more good than harm when health outcomes are not tallied in any way?

The Popularity Fallacy

Another ploy is to overestimate the extent to which others subscribe to a given belief. The suggestion that many people agree lends at least a superficial aura of legitimacy to authoritative claims, referred to by Robert Cialdini (1993) as "social proof." In 1993, David Eisenberg and his colleagues published the results of a survey that has become one of the most frequently cited—yet poorly understood—reports in the alternative health literature. The researchers asked people what types of health care they had used during the previous year, focusing on what were considered "unconventional" treatments: those not widely taught at U.S. medical schools or widely available in U.S. hospitals. The authors concluded that 34% of Americans use unconventional treatments, which has been often been rounded to the more quotable figure of "1 in 3."

Although this figure is well known to many people owing to its popularity with the media, there are serious problems with it. When the authors discuss unconventional treatments, they list homeopathy, acupuncture, and herbal remedies as exemplars, implying that these alternative practices are fairly popular. However, a closer look at their data shows something quite different. Very few people in the study sought homeopathic treatments (about 1%), acupuncture (less than 1%, *down* from earlier surveys), or herbs (about 3%). Moreover, even these few users of unconventional treatments relied primarily on over-the-counter homeopathic and herbal products; only 1.33% consulted a practitioner. Thus, the examples that are frequently linked with the "1 in 3" statistic are in fact noteworthy for their rarity, their *lack* of popularity.

On the other hand, the researchers counted many widely taught and widely available practices as unconventional anyway (e.g., commercial weight loss programs, relaxation training, and biofeedback). For example, weight loss programs are based on the principles of diet and exercise taught in *every* medical curriculum. When people repeat the claim that "1 in 3 Americans use alternative medicine," you should recognize the deceptive disconnect between the message and the data. This is a bogus appeal to authority based on (greatly exaggerated) popularity.

The Fallacy of Self-Proclaimed Expertise

A colleague of mine once attended a conference presentation on "perceptual learning modalities," the notion that students vary in their ability to learn by reading, listening, or watching. The "expert" on this theory explained that students' learning styles can be assessed and that teaching must be adapted to match these styles. This is certainly plausible, and if it is true it may have tremendous practical importance. If it is false, however, it may have destructive consequences. Many instructors constantly struggle to improve their teaching style; suggesting that those who have managed to develop effective techniques should change them without reason would be most unwise.

My colleague decided to inquire about the methods by which students' learning styles were classified. What is the evidence for the validity of the questionnaires being recommended? How do we know that these learning styles even exist? Such requests for documentation are quite standard in any scientific discipline. In this case, however, they were received with indignation, rather than a reference to relevant research.

Undeterred, my colleague posed another important question: What is the evidence that altering teaching to match these learning styles will enhance learning? The theory predicts that students' learning styles should *interact* with teaching styles such that appropriate matches result in superior learning relative to mismatches. There are many studies on the effectiveness of different teaching styles, but in these studies teachers usually use just one style apiece for all the students that they teach. The critical question here is whether teachers should adopt different styles for different students. For example, when given instruction in a visual way, visual learners should learn better than auditory learners, whereas the auditory learners should learn better when taught in their preferred modality. When asked about the existence of research data bearing on this question, however, the expert became flustered and evasive. She handed my colleague a list of references and quickly moved on; clearly, the challenge for evidence was incompatible with her intended message. Among the references listed—many of which were conference presentations, few of which were experiments published in peer-reviewed scientific journals—not one appeared to have tested the most fundamental claim being made: the interaction effect. When asked one last time, the presenter confirmed my colleague's suspicion that nobody, in fact, has ever directly examined whether learning is enhanced through a match between teaching and learning styles. Thus, despite the pressure to adjust one's teaching to match hypothetical learning styles, there is currently no scientific evidence to support this practice. Rather, educators are asked to modify their beliefs and teaching behaviors based on nothing more than speculation.

The problem of self-proclaimed expertise is pervasive and troubling. How much easier our lives would be if we could simply check an individual's credentials (education, professional affiliations, etc.) to gauge his or her expertise. Unfortunately, expert status does not guarantee veracity. A provocative paper by David Faust and Jay Ziskin (1988), grounded in research on human fallibility, argued that psychologists and psychiatrists are often unable to meet the legal definition of expertise. In particular, a considerable body of research suggests that one of the most "obvious" markers of expertise—clinical experience—is unrelated to the accuracy of one's statements (for reviews see Garb, 1989, 1999). Although it is surely disquieting to recognize that we should place no more faith in the authoritative pronouncement of a psychologist with decades of clinical experience than one with a freshly-minted Ph.D., this is surely knowledge worth knowing. Expertise derives not from opinion, not even from the consensual agreement of an entire profession, but from a demonstrated ability to contribute valid judgments and reach truthful conclusions.

POLITICAL LOBBYING AS A WARNING FLAG

One final type of questionable appeal to authority involves certain types of political action. What better way to achieve a veneer of respectability and authority than through governmental recognition? There is nothing wrong with lobbying, so long as its justification is ultimately rational and ethically defensible. There is a world of difference in lobbying for policy change from an evidence-based to an ideologically driven position, although this distinction is not always clear-cut. Whereas some important social issues are intrinsically ideological, others lend themselves well to scientific investigation. In these latter cases, it is quite disturbing when a well-organized political lobby serves as a substitute for—rather than a vehicle to disseminate—scientific research.

An argument can be made that when health practices enter the political arena, this is usually a warning sign of pseudoscience. Effective treatments need little political support; solid evidence and successful health care largely speak for themselves. Did Jonas Salk need to lobby a governmental agency to support the polio vaccine? Of course not! Awards and recognition are showered on those who present real cures. Thus, intensive lobbying efforts signal that advocates are bypassing the normal channels that shape health care policy via research evidence, attempting instead to pass a questionable practice through a legislative body. This strategy is gravely problematic. Legislatures are accountable not to patients, but to voters, and our elected officials are motivated to keep people happy, not necessarily healthy. Moreover, legislators often do not possess the technical expertise necessary to fully understand and fairly evaluate health claims. They are thus highly susceptible to misinformation in this area. Two health-related political battles of the 1990s demonstrate the dangers of this illegitimate route to authority.

The National Center for Complementary and Alternative Medicine

As a result of a massive political campaign, the Office of Alternative Medicine (OAM) was created as a branch of the National Institutes of Health (NIH) in 1992. In 1998, this office was renamed the National Center for Complementary and Alternative Medicine (NCCAM). The alleged purpose of this office was to investigate alternative approaches to health care by funding research into their effectiveness. A direct quote from the "Frequently Asked Questions" section of NCCAM's web site states this clearly:

> People sometimes ask whether the NCCAM uses the same standard of science as conventional medicine. Complementary and alternative medicine needs to be investigated using the same scientific methods used in conventional medicine. The NCCAM encourages valid information about complementary and alternative medicine, applying at least as rigorous, and, in some cases, even more rigorous research methods than the current standard in conventional medicine. This is because the research often involves novel concepts and claims, and uses complex systems of practice that need systematic, explicit, and comprehensive knowledge and skills to investigate.

The respect for scientific research methods evident in this passage is praiseworthy, as is the intention to apply them to all investigations of health. However, the track record of the OAM/NCCAM contradicts its avowed mission. A *New England Journal of Medicine* editorial reviewed this record and summarized it as follows:

> So far, the results have been disappointing. For example, of the 30 research grants the office awarded in 1993, 28 have resulted in "final reports" (abstracts) that are listed in the office's on-line data base. But a Medline search almost six years after the grants were awarded revealed that only 9 of the 28 resulted in published papers. Five were in 2 journals not included among the 3,500 titles in the Countway Library of Medicine's collection. Of the other four studies, none was a controlled clinical trial that would allow any conclusions to be drawn about the efficacy of an alternative treatment. (Angell & Kassirer, 1998, p. 839)

To call this merely "disappointing" is quite an understatement. Even though additional publications of research funded by NCCAM may be "in the pipeline" (under review, being revised, etc.), by any standards of research productivity this is especially poor performance. More important, however, is the deplorable *quality* of the research. For five out of nine of the studies to appear in two journals so obscure, with such low standards and poor prestige, that they are not included in a vast medical index is telling. The fact that not a single well-controlled experiment was conducted is remarkable; it directly contradicts the assertion that rigorous research methods are being employed.

In 1993, its first year of operation, the OAM had a $2 million budget. Despite the lack of well-designed studies or practically useful results arising from this organization, its budget has grown at an average annual rate of over 65%. In 2000, the NCCAM was allotted $68.7 million! It is tragic to consider the advances in other, more promising fields of medicine that could have been achieved through a better allotment of limited federal research funds. Looking closely at how little the NCCAM has actually accomplished, one is forced to wonder whether this center serves any purpose other than lending a superficial sense of credibility to a collection of questionable health practices that cannot muster support through scientific research.

The Dietary Supplement Health and Education Act

For decades, United States governmental regulatory agencies have protected consumers by requiring that medicines be proven both safe and effective before they are marketed to the public. These agencies, such as the Food and Drug Administration (FDA) and the Federal Trade Commission (FTC), were created specifically to act on our behalf by preventing profiteering hucksters from marketing worthless or unsafe products. Throughout history, quack remedies have caused a tremendous amount of physical harm—not to mention financial hardship—because they were not tested prior to being sold. The establishment and empowerment of regulatory agencies that ban the sale of unsafe products and levy fines and criminal charges against those who seek to take advantage of consumers in the health marketplace represents an impressive achievement.

Consistent with decades of consumer advocacy and protection, enforcement actions were becoming quite intense in the 1980s as crackdowns on many of the fraudulent products and practices in the "health food" industry gained momentum. In 1984, the U.S. House of Representatives defined a "quack" as "anyone who promotes medical schemes or remedies known to be false, or which are unproven, for a profit." As the threat of enforcement loomed larger, the health food industry was faced with a decision: It could be more careful about offering only products and services supported by research evidence, or it could band together to fight government regulations. Unfortunately, it chose the latter course.

One of the most intense lobbying efforts that America has seen in recent history was led by a group called the Nutritional Health Alliance (NHA). Although the name of this organization suggests a trustworthy authority, it actually reflects weasel words used to disguise the group's true intentions. The NHA supported a complete deregulation of the health food industry by removing the requirement of FDA approval for new drugs sold as "dietary supplements." Such deregulation trades consumer protection for commercial gain. The lobbying campaign was based in large part on two key pieces of misinformation: (1) if retailers did not support the proposed legislation, they would be put out of business, and (2) if consumers did not support it, the FDA would make vitamins unavailable for sale. Both of these claims, though patently false, were highly effective in spurring people to action. The entire campaign was framed as a "freedom of choice" issue. The end result of an extended and intense lobbying effort was the 1994 passage of the Dietary Supplement Health and Education Act (DSHEA).

Under DSHEA, it has become legal for anyone to sell almost any drug to the public, provided they refer to the drug as a "dietary supplement" and do not make specific health claims about its effects. Unproven remedies—which constitute "quackery" by an earlier congressional definition—are now officially tolerated under the guise of dietary supplements. Vague wording and the sheer number of people who routinely violate the provisions of DSHEA have resulted in insufficient enforcement of even these weak standards. In one noteworthy action, the FTC conducted an "internet surf day" on November 10, 1998, to scan for illegal health claims featured in on-line advertisements. This single day's work resulted in 1200 warnings sent to companies that were making illegal health claims about their supplements. The scope of illegal activities is skyrocketing.

More frightening, though, is that government agencies are not allowed to intervene until *after* adverse effects are observed and reported for drugs labeled as supplements. No longer is there a safety check before a product reaches the shelves of the "health food" market. It is now up to you and me to determine which products are safe and effective, a demanding, time-consuming, and hazardous chore that used to be handled for us by qualified experts. The "health food" industry itself has taken a lackadaisical attitude toward quality control:

- In an analysis of ten brands of St. John's Wort (a dietary supplement used to treat depression) commissioned by the *Los Angeles Times* in 1998, seven brands contained much lower potencies than stated on the labels. One of the worst offenders—evidencing only 20% of the labeled potency—was Sundown Herbals, a division of Rexall, the nation's leading distributor of dietary supplements.
- The November/December 1998 newsletter of the National Council for Reliable Health Information summarizes the findings of a study published in *The Pharmacist's Letter:* "The content of herbal products varies a great deal. How the plant is grown, harvested, and stored; the plant parts selected; the extraction process used; and other factors can have an effect. The ingredients of some herbal products can vary from 0 to 10 times the label amount."
- In its March 1999 issue, *Consumer Reports* published an article that was highly critical of the herbal supplement industry. It urged Congress to reconsider the Dietary Supplement Health and Education Act "in light of the free-for-all it created in the marketplace." It also encouraged readers to "view the word 'natural' with skepticism; after all, hemlock and arsenic are natural, too."
- In a *New England Journal of Medicine* article, Ko (1998) reported that 83 of 260 Asian patent medicines that were analyzed contained undeclared pharmaceuticals or heavy metals. About 10% contained lead, 15% contained arsenic, and another 15% contained mercury. The median levels of the arsenic and mercury were well above the safety limits set by U.S. Pharmacopoeia.
- "Steel Bars," marketed as a healthy, nutritional snack, have been found to be seriously mislabeled. For example, although the coconut bars were

claimed to contain 4 grams of fat and 35 milligrams of sodium, laboratory testing revealed 16 grams of fat and 235 milligrams of sodium. In September 1998, the company reached a settlement in a class action lawsuit that included consumer refunds of $750,000, payment of the plaintiffs' attorney fees, donation of 1 million bars to a food bank, and future compliance with labeling laws.

Following the passage of DSHEA, there has been an explosion of new "dietary supplements" available to consumers. They are no longer relegated only to "health food" stores, which would be easy to avoid, but appear alongside tested remedies on the shelves of pharmacies and grocery stores, and are offered through hundreds of mail order outfits and internet sites. This legalized free-for-all underscores the importance of staying informed and using critical thinking skills.

As was made all too clear by the creation and expansion of the National Center for Complementary and Alternative Medicine and the passage of the Dietary Supplement Health and Education Act, political action that is openly hostile to scientific research can erode even the most fundamental tenets of consumer protection. This is a false authority in its most dangerous form. Our modern-day information age has made it easier than ever both to educate and to misinform large numbers of people. Because determining the legitimacy of authorities and identifying whose interests they are serving is often exceptionally difficult, we must cultivate the ability and the motivation to think for ourselves. But don't just take my word for it.

InfoTrac College Edition

To learn more about topics included in this chapter, enter the following search terms:

ancient wisdom
authority and obedience
expertise
national center complementary alternative medicine

SELF-DECEPTION

CHAPTER

5

EXPERIENCE

The Limitations of Testimonials as Evidence

Martha M. Christy published a book in 1994 with a rather immodest title: *Your Own Perfect Medicine: The Incredible Proven Natural Miracle Cure That Medical Science Has Never Revealed!* David G. Williams, writing in the *Alternative Health Newsletter,* had nothing but praise for this book: "If you buy only one health book this year, this is the book you should get. It outlines a therapy that can be used by anyone, anywhere, for practically any complaint known." What do you suppose this "perfect medicine" might be? The book is about *urine therapy!*

So how does one use urine for medicinal purposes? Some "experts," such as Andrew Weil (1998), believe that it may have some value when applied to the skin. Helen Kruger (cited in Gardner, 1999, p. 14) wrote:

> In some parts of the South, a baby's face is washed with urine to protect the skin. Elsewhere, it's used as a gargle for sore throat and for acne, cuts, and wounds . . . the French had a custom of soaking a stocking in urine and wrapping it around the neck to cure a strep throat. . . . People have put urine into the eyes to "cure" cataracts, a habit that gives my eye doctor the shudders. It could cause the cataract to grow denser, he says. And only recently, I heard about a new reducing treatment given by some doctor in Florida. The urine of a pregnant woman is injected into the obese patient to "break down the fat cells."

Christy, in her truly unique book, has a different use in mind. She explains that *drinking* one's own urine will cure cancer, arthritis, tuberculosis, AIDS, and countless other diseases. Not surprisingly, Christy personally attests to the effectiveness of urine therapy based on its role in curing her many health problems. She describes herself as having been a "walking encyclopedia of disease," reporting more health problems than you might think possible for one person ever to have, including pelvic inflammatory disease, ulcerative colitis, ileitis, chronic fatigue syndrome, Hashimoto's disease, mononucleosis, severe chronic kidney infections, chronic cystitis, severe candida, external yeast infections, marked adrenal insufficiency, serious chronic ear and sinus infections, and extreme food allergies. Christy spent over $100,000 of her own money plus years of her life trying a nutrition scheme, a megavitamin therapy, acupuncture, chiropractic, and "every herbal preparation and drug-free natural health therapy" she could find. And then something magical happened.

> Desperately ill and severely depressed, even contemplating suicide, Christy came across a book that recommended drinking one's own urine. She gave it a try. The result was "almost instantaneous relief" from her symptoms. Her hair, which had fallen out, grew back again "thick and lustrous." She gained weight and her energy returned. She says she now swims, hikes, and rides horseback. "Much to my own and my family's amazement, I am back to work and after thirty years of almost nonstop illness, I have a rich, full life again—and all because of an unbelievably simple and effective natural medicine." (Gardner, 1999, p. 15)

These astounding claims, seemingly gross exaggerations or outright fabrications, are typical of the testimonials readily offered by proponents of pseudoscience, whose claims are unbounded by the constraints of scientific evidence.

SELF-DECEPTION

Although there are legal prohibitions against making unsupported health claims, the law does not forbid storytelling. Because pseudosciences are not backed by research evidence, their promoters rely almost exclusively on personal experiences, anecdotes, and testimonials to support the bold claims that are made. These stories can be extremely vivid and compelling, and many people find them not only fascinating but sometimes highly persuasive. In the health sector, there is an obvious profit motive driving some outright fraud and conscious deceit. However, sometimes people motivated only by a desire to help others by sharing their experiences unknowingly communicate misinformation. There are a great many ways in which an individual can be misled about his or her own experiences. This chapter will explore many of the reasons the sincere testimony of even the most honest, well-intentioned person can be wrong.

One of the earliest lessons learned in the history of psychological experimentation is that introspection—looking inward to learn about the nature and causes of our own thoughts or behaviors—is highly unreliable. We are capable of self-deception, whether intentional or not. A complete description of all the forms that self-deception may take—and the factors that prompt it—is beyond the scope of this book. Instead, the present analysis will focus on our tendency to misconstrue the causes and cures of our own health problems, for this is the domain in which misunderstandings can have the most dire consequences. The limitations of personal experience as evidence apply with full force regardless of the nature of the claim being evaluated.

Fundamental to self-assessments of health is the distinction between "illness" and "disease." In an article, "Why Bogus Therapies Seem to Work," from which I will draw heavily in this discussion, Barry Beyerstein (1997) explains this disease/illness distinction:

> Although the terms disease and illness are often used interchangeably . . .
> I shall use disease to refer to a pathological state of the organism due to infection,
> tissue degeneration, trauma, toxic exposure, carcinogenesis, etc. By illness I mean
> the feelings of malaise, pain, disorientation, dysfunctionality, or other complaints
> that might accompany a disease. Our subjective reaction to the raw sensations we
> call symptoms is molded by cultural and psychological factors such as beliefs, sug-
> gestions, expectations, demand characteristics, self-serving biases, and self-
> deception. The experience of illness is also affected (often unconsciously) by a
> host of social and psychological payoffs that accrue to those admitted to the "sick
> role" by society's gatekeepers (i.e., health professionals). For certain individuals,
> the privileged status and benefits of the sick role are sufficient to perpetuate the
> experience of illness after a disease has healed, or even to create feelings of illness
> in the absence of disease. (p. 30)

COMPETING EXPLANATIONS

Bearing in mind the critical distinction between disease and illness, we can now turn to the ways in which an honest person might mistake a worthless treatment for one that works. When someone tries a treatment and then feels less ill, this is often viewed as ironclad evidence that the treatment was effec- tive. It is not. The logic behind the statement "I tried this treatment and felt better, therefore it works" suffers from the problem that there are many com- peting explanations for perceived improvement that cannot be ruled out, *any* of which might be the real cause of this upturn. Below are ten such compet- ing explanations for alleged treatment effects.

The Placebo Effect

One of the most curious of all health-related phenomena is that the simple expectation of recovery sometimes has a positive effect. That is, merely sug- gesting that treatment is being administered can be enough to make one feel better. In scientific parlance, the power of suggestion is called the "placebo effect," and it can be quite strong. As but one example, a recently published review of antidepressant medication trials suggests that roughly 75% of the effectiveness of these drugs can be attributed to the placebo effect (Kirsch & Sapirstein, 1998).

But how can you tell when someone has improved simply through the power of suggestion? And even if you can determine this, how can you tell how much improvement can be attributed to the treatment and how much to sug- gestion? Both of these questions can be answered by comparing the outcomes of consenting patients randomly assigned to one of three experimental conditions. In the example of an antidepressant medication, one group would receive the antidepressant (treatment), a second group would unknowingly receive sugar pills in place of the treatment (placebo), and a third group would be placed on a waiting list and treated once the experiment is finished (control). It is critical that neither the patients themselves nor the research assistant who delivers the medication knows who is in which experimental condition; this "double-blind" procedure equates the power of suggestion by creating comparable expectations in both groups of patients. As the experimenter, you would monitor the depression of all patients using standardized assessment procedures, and—after a prespecified amount of time—compare the results across groups.

If the treatment and placebo groups show comparable outcomes, but both are superior to the control group, then the safest conclusion is that the power of suggestion accounts for the entire treatment effect: The real medication produced no better outcomes than did sugar pills. If the treatment group surpasses both the control group *and* the placebo group, you could safely conclude that the antidepressant has an effect above and beyond mere suggestion. In this case, you could also calculate how much of the difference between treatment and control groups was achieved by the placebo group, thereby estimating the proportion of the effect that is attributable to suggestion.

Although a control and a placebo group are essential when testing the efficacy of a drug, in some cases the side effects of an active ingredient can "unmask" the treatment group and therefore undermine experimental controls on the power of suggestion (Greenberg & Fisher, 1997). If the presence and absence of side effects indicate who is receiving the medication and who is not, the comparison between treatment and placebo groups is tainted. For example, in a review of all the studies of the effectiveness of Prozac that employed a double-blind, placebo-controlled design (Greenberg, Bornstein, Zborowski, Fisher, & Greenberg, 1994), there was a strong correlation between the proportion of participants in each study who reported side effects and the size of the treatment effect in the study. It seems likely that side effects of Prozac reintroduced the power of suggestion by unmasking many members of the treatment group. On the basis of this and other studies of antidepressants, Greenberg and Fisher (1997) argued that, contrary to its manufacturer's claims, not only is Prozac no more effective than earlier antidepressants, there is as yet no convincing evidence that it is more effective than a placebo. Moreover, these authors suggest the intriguing, and highly ironic, possibility that Prozac, marketed as a drug with fewer side effects than its rivals, may derive much of its effectiveness through the production of side effects and promotion of physiological reactions. Of course, this hypothesis can be tested. How? Rather than giving the placebo group an inactive sugar pill, you could give this group an "active placebo" that has no medicinal value but produces bodily sensations similar to those of the treatment being investigated. This would allow you to rule out the competing hypothesis that the treatment effect resulted from poor experimental control because side effects unmasked the treatment group.

Without conducting an appropriately controlled experiment, there is no way to know for sure that the placebo effect is not responsible for any health effect. Therefore, testimonials—based as they are on limited personal experience without benefit of comparison groups or other experimental controls—cannot possibly tease apart real effects from the power of suggestion.

Spontaneous Remission

For poorly understood reasons, diseases—even cancers—sometimes disappear without any treatment at all. To be sure, this is a rare occurrence for some conditions. Beyerstein (1997) notes that one oncologist witnessed 12 cases of spontaneous remission out of about 6000 patients that he had treated. However, for these 12 fortunate individuals, any treatment that had been attempted would no doubt be credited as a fantastic success. Sagan (1995) analyzed the success rate of Lourdes' mystical healing powers in light of this phenomenon of spontaneous remission. Approximately 100 million people have visited Lourdes, France seeking cures from various afflictions. Although the Catholic Church rejects most claims of miracles, it has accepted 65 at Lourdes. This means that the odds of a miraculous cure are less than one in a million, about the same odds as dying on a commercial airline flight to Lourdes! Moreover, the spontaneous remission rate among cancer patients is actually lower at Lourdes than it is among those who stay home. One out of every 10,000 to 100,000 cancers spontaneously remits, so if even just 5% of those who visited Lourdes had cancer, we could reasonably expect 50 to 500 miraculous cancer cures. Of the 65 miracles confirmed by the church, only 3 were of cancer.

The Disease Ran Its Natural Course

Provided that a disease is not chronic or fatal, it may well be self-limiting in that our own recuperative processes will eventually restore full health. As noted earlier, "You can cure the common cold in a week with chicken soup, or you can just wait seven days." Like the misinterpretation of spontaneous remission, however, the coincidental use of any treatment at the time when the disease finally runs its natural course may be falsely credited with success. Moreover, some practices are rigged so that they automatically receive credit, no matter what. For example, Livingston (1998, p. 27) cites the instructions for a magnetic necklace that "cures" headaches, which cleverly create a false sense of effectiveness: "The necklace should be put on as soon as the headache appears and removed as soon as it goes away." If you strictly followed these instructions, the magnetic necklace would always appear to work. Of course, you could just as easily stand on one leg until your headache went away and then credit this strategy with success.

The Cyclical Nature of Many Diseases

Even chronic conditions like arthritis, multiple sclerosis, allergies, depression, and anxiety tend to go through phases, alternating between ups and downs. When is an individual most likely to seek treatment? At the depth of a downturn, when suffering is greatest. Owing to nothing more than normal cyclical variation, then, the treatment will likely coincide with improvement. Through repeated cycles, a treatment has multiple opportunities to be paired, by chance, with improvement. Given the ease of superstitious learning with an intermittent and variable reinforcement schedule (see Chapter 3), an unshakable belief may easily develop in the efficacy of a worthless treatment.

Misdiagnosis

Health practitioners are by no means perfect, and even with the most sophisticated laboratory tests available, some misdiagnoses are inevitable. If an individual misdiagnosed as having a disease seeks treatment and is later correctly diagnosed as healthy, the treatment will be credited a success even though—unbeknownst to doctor or patient—there was no disease in the first place. As illustrated in Chapter 13, pseudoscientific health practitioners often use dubious diagnostic tests that lead to questionable diagnoses.

The "Worried Well"

Partly because of the heavy emphasis that is increasingly placed on preventive health care, many people with no disease nonetheless seek health care. Ordinary aches and pains, along with a range of purely subjective concerns (earlier defined as illness), are elevated to the status of disease. Individuals who experience such symptoms have been termed the "worried well." Testimonials made by these individuals do not speak to true cures, as their complaints were not based on disease to begin with. Using pseudomedical jargon, practitioners of pseudoscience eagerly create legions of worried well patients. Here's what a newspaper ad for "Colon Therapy" (reproduced in Barrett & Herbert, 1994) had to say:

> You clean your teeth, why not clean your INTESTINES?? We offer a health program to clean your intestines, removing the toxic build-up that makes you tired, ill, gassy, depressed, bloated, and craving carbohydrates! Intestinal cleaning can offer relief from constipation, Candida, and parasites. It enhances energy, mental clarity, and RESULTS IN WEIGHT LOSS TOO!

What an original way to try to convince healthy people that they are in need of health care! Having attracted a clientele with normal health and fitness, practitioners are free to prosper through their treatments and then bask in the apparent treatment successes.

Symptomatic Relief

It is a relatively simple mistake to confuse relief from a symptom of illness, such as pain, with the curing of an actual disease. However, the alleviation of symptoms does not necessarily mean that the underlying pathology has been treated. For example, AIDS patients may take medications to relieve some of their suffering without elimination of HIV, the root cause of their disease. Here, again, it is important to remember the distinction between illness and disease. With symptomatic relief one may feel less ill even when the disease persists. Crediting a treatment with success solely on the basis of symptomatic relief may divert patients from much-needed care for an ongoing disease.

Hedged Bets

Many patients who seek pseudoscientific treatments also "hedge their bets" by simultaneously receiving evidence-based health care. The May/June 1998 National Council Against Health Fraud newsletter reports a dramatic case of hedging the health bet:

> Anne Frahm's breast cancer was widely disseminated by the time it was diagnosed. She underwent surgery, chemotherapy, radiation, and hormone therapy. When these failed to send her disease into remission, she underwent an experimental autologous bone marrow transplant. She was then told that there was nothing else that could be done. Five weeks later, her disease was in total remission.
>
> Curiously, Frahm did not credit the biological effects of the bone marrow transplant with her recovery. Rather, she credited having adopted an extreme regimen of enemas (to "detoxify"), two weeks of juicing, eating raw fruits and vegetables, and avoiding sugar, meat, and dairy products.

None of the latter methods of combating cancer has any demonstrated validity, yet they received full credit for the remission of Anne's breast cancer. She believed so strongly in the treatments that had "cured" her that she and her husband started a ministry in Colorado Springs to teach them to others. Where would you place your bet: with the bone marrow transplant or with Anne's HealthQuarters ministry?

Derivative Benefits

Many health practitioners are uplifting and persuasive. They may provide a patient with a sense of purpose, meaning, hope, and any of a variety of other psychological benefits. For example, Andrew Weil—quoted earlier on the subject of mental telepathy—is both a remarkably charismatic speaker and a truly gifted writer. Many people find his unique mixture of sense and nonsense to be highly satisfying, perhaps giving them a "new lease on life." As a result of the purely psychological benefits provided by a practitioner, patients may begin to take better care of themselves. They may eat more well-balanced meals, exercise more, sleep better, or spend more time socializing. Any of these spin-off, or derivative, benefits may have positive effects on health. When the time comes to ascertain the cause of a successful recovery from disease, however, derivative benefits are less visible than the treatment itself and can easily escape one's notice.

Psychological Distortion of Reality

The final way in which health-related testimonials may be misleading involves one of the most heavily researched principles in social psychology. Whenever we hold two or more beliefs that contradict one another, we experience a state of discomfort known to psychologists as cognitive dissonance. Something must be done to reduce this dissonance, and common resolutions include the modification of existing beliefs or the creation of new beliefs (Festinger, 1957). Let's look at some intriguing examples to see how dissonance reduction works.

First, consider the case of the Jewish tailor (a story originally told by Ausubel, 1948, and cited in Plous, 1993, p. 22):

> There was once a Jewish tailor who had the temerity to open his shop on the main street of an anti-Semitic town. To drive him out of town, a gang of youths visited the shop each day, standing in the entrance and shouting, "Jew! Jew!"
>
> After several sleepless nights, the tailor finally devised a plan. The next time that the gang came to threaten him, the tailor announced that anyone who called him a Jew would get a dime. He then handed dimes to each member of the gang.
>
> Delighted with their new incentive, members of the gang returned the next day, shouting "Jew! Jew!", and the tailor, smiling, gave each one a nickel (explaining that he could only afford a nickel that day). The gang left satisfied because, after all, a nickel was a nickel.
>
> Then, on the following day, the tailor gave out only pennies to each gang member, again explaining that he could afford no more money than that. Well, a penny was not much of an incentive, and members of the gang began to protest.
>
> When the tailor replied that they could take it or leave it, they decided to leave it, shouting that the tailor was crazy if he thought that they would call him a Jew for only a penny!

Through a clever psychological trick, the tailor created the tension of cognitive dissonance in the gang members' minds. Once the wise tailor pretended to be pleased with the gang members' behavior and they accepted his offering of the dimes, they came to see shouting "Jew! Jew!" as a job. When the payment was lowered, their jobs no longer seemed to pay well enough to justify the effort, creating cognitive dissonance which was relieved by quitting the job.

We are also confronted with cognitive dissonance arising from decisions that we make. In a classic demonstration of such "postdecision" dissonance reduction, Robert Knox and James Inkster (1968) evaluated the confidence of people betting on horses at a race track. They found that those who had placed bets within the past 30 seconds expressed greater confidence in their wagers than those who were questioned 30 seconds before betting. How can one's perception of the odds of winning on a gamble change within so short a time? The answer lies in the cognitive dissonance created by placing the bet. To have committed money to your belief while remaining uncertain about your chances generates dissonance; it would seem foolish to have bet with poor chances of winning. The solution: Increase your perception of the odds of winning, thereby reducing cognitive dissonance.

The same principle is at work in many individuals' evaluations of treatment. Having committed considerable time, money, effort, and hope to a treatment that you sought voluntarily, would it not reflect poorly on your judgment to declare it a complete failure? You cannot change the fact that resources have been committed, nor that these resources cannot be recovered. The solution: Modify your belief in the efficacy of the treatment. Surely there is *some* measure of success that can be claimed for the treatment, even if only at the symptom level. With some slight distortion, the treatment can be elevated to a reasonably successful venture. In this way, the motivation to reduce cognitive dissonance allows the patient (and, indirectly, the practitioner) to snatch a success from the jaws of failure.

The Bottom Line

None of the ten factors described above requires conscious fraud or dishonesty, yet each significantly undermines the value of testimonials as evidence. When faced with so many competing explanations for perceived recuperation, there is simply no way to know which one is correct. Therefore, the most reasonable reaction to any anecdote, case study, or testimonial is that although it may be interesting as a story and suggestive of a lead to pursue in future research, it is of *no value* in determining whether a general principle is true or false.

For these reasons, assembling a collection of testimonials is of little or no help. None of the problems identified above can be overcome by a large number of testimonials; these competing explanations plague every case. The *only* trustworthy solution is the experimental method of science, which can systematically isolate a genuine treatment effect from all of these potentially confounding factors.

PROBABILISTIC GENERAL PRINCIPLES

In addition to the significant problem of competing explanations, learning from testimonials can be downright dangerous because single cases can be found in support of most any belief, no matter how thoroughly mistaken. For example, a fascinating report in the *New England Journal of Medicine* (Kern, 1991) documented the normal blood cholesterol level of an 88-year-old man who had been eating 25 eggs a day for at least 15 years! Though frequently vilified in the popular press, moderate egg consumption (averaging up to an egg a day) does not affect one's risk of cardiovascular disease (Hu et al., 1999) and may in fact be more healthy than a diet in which other foods are substituted for eggs (Vaupel & Graham, 1980). Nonetheless, no responsible nutritionist would recommend eating 25 eggs a day just because one man was able to do so in good health. This patient came to the attention of medical specialists interested in cholesterol metabolism precisely because of his atypicality. Keep in mind that one individual's experience—whether your own or anyone else's—is just that: a single case that may be highly unusual.

Knowledge is based on *general principles* that can be applied with a certain degree of accuracy to new cases, events, patients, and so forth. If there is absolutely no commonality across cases, knowledge cannot accumulate. It is also critical to remember that any general principle of human thought or behavior is *probabilistic* in nature. General principles reveal a noteworthy relationship between events, a tendency for events to be related to one another to some extent. There are therefore exceptions to *any* probabilistic trend, including all of those in the health sciences that relate symptoms, diseases, prognoses, and treatments. A single counterexample does not disprove a probabilistic rule.

For example, consider the question of whether purely quantitative measures of academic performance, such as high school grades and standardized test scores, predict who will succeed in college. If anyone foolishly stated that these measures perfectly predict college success, then just one counterexample would be sufficient to prove this statement wrong. We can probably all think of someone we know who had good grades or test scores in high school but did poorly in college, or someone who did poorly in high school but excelled in college. Does this imply that grades and test scores do not *tend* to predict success in college? Not at all. Consider a graph of the SAT scores of high school seniors and their first-year college GPAs (see Figure 3).

As can easily be seen in the graph, there is a general association between these two variables, but also some counterexamples. A handful of points toward the upper-left region of the graph represents students with below-average SATs who made the Dean's List in college, and another handful of

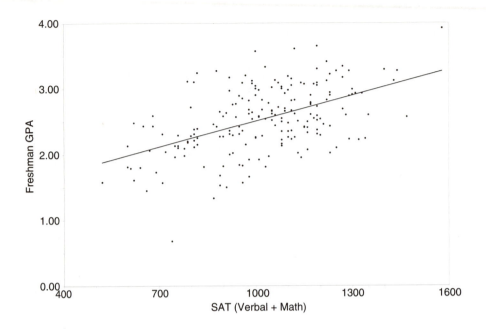

FIGURE **3**

The relationship between students' SAT scores and college GPAs. The line shows that, despite considerable variability, a probabilistic general principle relates higher test scores to higher college grades.

points toward the lower-right region of the graph represents students with above-average SATs who were placed on academic probation in college. These isolated examples do not eliminate the overall trend in the data, however. The bulk of the points represents students whose college performance was predictable, within a certain known margin of error, from their SAT scores. Thus, research reveals a probabilistic general principle: High school students with higher scores on college entrance exams tend to achieve higher grades in college. If you overgeneralize from a couple of high school acquaintances who were counterexamples to this principle, you may wrongfully conclude that college entrance exams are useless as admissions criteria.

This example demonstrates the danger of learning through testimonials: They may well be the counterexamples to probabilistic principles. However, it is quite likely that we will be selectively exposed to many such counterexamples in our everyday lives. Which personal story is more likely to catch people's attention, the student with an SAT score of 1300 who does well in college or the student with an SAT score of 1300 who does poorly? Counterexamples are often more "newsworthy" (see Chapter 9), whereas cases that fit expected patterns go without notice.

Whenever we overgeneralize from testimonials, particularly those that are the very counterexamples of the probabilistic general principles we need to learn in order to understand reality, we may formulate erroneous beliefs. Perhaps the most important, though counterintuitive, rule is that our own experience is only the equivalent of one testimonial. Thus, we should be especially wary of any belief system that encourages us to overweight our unique experience. Our knowledge can begin to accumulate only after we recognize the inconclusiveness of our own experiences and the need to gather evidence through more systematic observations.

INFOTRAC COLLEGE EDITION

To learn more about topics included in this chapter, enter the following search terms:

cognitive dissonance
placebo
spontaneous remission
urine therapy
worried well

PLAUSIBILITY

All Beliefs Are Not Created Equal

As Zeke awoke one morning, something terrifying happened. He was completely paralyzed, yet he had the bizarre sensation of floating weightlessly through the air. Soon he sensed a strange presence in the room around him, and then it became clear that there were in fact alien beings present. These tiny gray creatures with disproportionately large heads and eyes abducted Zeke in their saucer-shaped craft. There, the aliens performed invasive medical experiments, probing Zeke's body and stealing some semen. When finished with their grisly procedures, the aliens warned Zeke of the urgent need to clean up the Earth's environment and combat the worldwide AIDS epidemic. Then, the aliens returned Zeke to his bedroom. The medical experimentation had left no visible scars on his body, and his wife—who was sleeping peacefully beside him—never noticed that he had left. This was an emotionally powerful event. But what exactly happened?

Although there is no Zeke, this account—varying only modestly in its details—has been offered by large numbers of alleged alien abductees (Sagan, 1995). Many people retell their stories with compelling emotional content and seem to sincerely believe them. John Mack, a Harvard University psychiatrist, takes all alien abduction stories at face value, citing their apparent agreement with one another as corroboration of their validity. But what is the evidence? And is this evidence sufficient to justify such fantastic beliefs? Scientists have a saying that "extraordinary claims require extraordinary evidence." The alien abduction scenario contains so many extraordinary elements that it would be prudent to demand strong proof of its veracity.

We have seen how purveyors of pseudosciences use a range of tricks to lend credence to their beliefs and practices, including deceptive language, magical or wishful thinking, and appeals to authority. One of the hallmarks of a successful pseudoscience is surface plausibility, a cover story that many people find appealing. Beneath the surface, however, lurk contradictions and violations of well-understood, evidence-based conceptualizations of reality. It is important, then, to scrutinize the cover story and evaluate the true plausibility of a claim to knowledge. Because some beliefs are simply more likely to be true than others, plausibility provides one useful preliminary gauge of the validity of a claim.

To illustrate the dangers of accepting cover stories at face value, three branches of pseudoscience will be explored. An in-depth evaluation of their plausibility reveals how stunningly out-of-step with reality—and thus how unlikely to be true—they actually are. Before returning to the alien abduction paradigm outlined above, we will investigate two health pseudosciences that lack plausible theories: magnet therapy and homeopathy.

MAGNET THERAPY: CLAIMS VERSUS REALITY

Miguel Sabadell (1998) has compiled a list of some strange claims that have been made about magnets and magnetic fields:

- Cells live on magnetic energy, and most of this energy is provided by water.
- The magnetic field modifies water structure, changing some of its physical properties.
- Spring water is magnetized. But if you bottle it, after five days it loses its power.
- Magnetic water loses its curative properties in contact with metals.
- Eighty percent of common diseases have their origin in Magnetic Field Deficiency Syndrome.
- Drink magnetic water. It's so easy. . . . By this method you can get cured of abscess, acne, allergy, anemia, arthritis, asthma, bronchitis, cellulitis, sciatica, diabetes, diarrhea, dyspepsia, stringent, frigidity, impotency, flu, herpes, headaches, zoster, and a lot more!
- In the body, the magnetic field increases the dilution of oxygen in plasma, transporting more oxygen together with the hemoglobin mechanism.
- Apply the therapeutic magnets in the zone of the disease. North is for pain; south is to recover lost energy and vitality.

Magnets and magnetism have been widely misunderstood throughout history. Franz Anton Mesmer (1734–1815), father of "animal magnetism," began treating severe mental illnesses with strong magnets. He later determined that he could "magnetize" just about anything—such as paper, wood, water, and so on—and that the same positive results were achieved regardless of the source of the magnetism. Eventually, Mesmer concluded that *he* possessed the real power, that his alleged cures could be attributed to the flow of a "universal fluid" between him and his patients. "Mesmerism," as the practice came to be called, gained a strong following in Paris. It was not without controversy, however.

> In 1784 King Louis XVI established a Royal Commission to evaluate the claims of animal magnetism, a commission that included Antoine Lavoisier and Benjamin Franklin among its members. They conducted a series of experiments and concluded that all the observed effects could be attributed to the power of suggestion [the placebo effect], and that "the practice of magnetization is the art of increasing the imagination by degrees." Thomas Jefferson, arriving in Paris soon after the Commission report, noted in his journal: "Animal magnetism is dead, ridiculed." (Livingston, 1998, p. 26)

Sadly, the demonstration that Mesmerism was merely one instance of the placebo effect—having no more value than sugar pills or other ineffective treatments—did not put an end to its practice. Indeed, a variety of pseudo-sciences were born of this belief. For example, sympathetic practitioners developed the notion of healing through hand gestures into what is now called therapeutic touch. Mary Baker Eddy, who believed that she had been cured by a magnetizer, later decided that prayer was a more effective means to the same end and founded Christian Science.

Based as they are on the placebo effect, none these practices has been able to demonstrate any effectiveness beyond the power of suggestion. In Chapter 15, it is argued that administering or promoting any unverified treatment is unethical. Discussions in Chapter 3 revealed the experimental emptiness of claims for therapeutic touch, whereas Chapter 12 examines the religion-motivated medical neglect of children that is fostered by Christian Science. Rather than delve further into these questionable offshoots of Mesmer's animal magnetism, we will confine ourselves here to an exploration of the remarkable healing powers attributed to a related phenomenon that has become a multimillion dollar industry: magnet therapy.

A vast array of products containing permanent magnets are available to consumers, including necklaces, bracelets, earrings, seat cushions, pillows, mattress pads, and belts. Magnetic wraps have been created to fit most any part of the body: hands, wrists, elbows, knees, ankles, and feet. Magnetic insoles are particularly popular; recently, Florsheim Shoes decided to cash in on the fad by building magnets into some of their shoes. Magnets are offered not only for the treatment of disease or relief from pain, but also to boost athletic performance: Magnets are popular with golfers and are used on thoroughbred race horses. The rationale for the efficacy of allegedly therapeutic magnets will be explored in light of the known effects of magnets on water and the human body as well as the strength of the magnets that are commonly offered for sale.

Magnets and Water

Many of the claims gathered by Sabadell and reviewed earlier in this chapter revolve around a supposed influence of magnets on water and of magnetized water on our bodies. But can water *be* magnetized? James Livingston, an expert on the properties of magnets, summarizes the relevant science:

Water is diamagnetic, i.e., weakly repelled by magnetic fields. In response to an applied magnetic field, the electrons in water molecules make slight adjustments in their motions, producing a net magnetic field in the opposing direction about 100,000 times smaller than the applied field. With the removal of the field, the electrons return to their original orbits, and the water molecules once again become nonmagnetic. (We perhaps should note that some promoters of magnet therapy also promote "magnetized water." You can't magnetize water. Although water responds weakly to an applied field, the response disappears as soon as the field is removed.) (Livingston, 1998, p. 30)

There is partial truth, then, to some of the claims that opened this chapter. Magnetic fields *do* change the structure of water, although the effect is slight, repellent (not attractive), and fleeting (it ceases the instant the magnetic field is removed). This is a far cry from the spring water that supposedly remains magnetized for five days after it is bottled. It thus becomes obvious that the only way one can "drink magnetized water" is to drink water while in a magnetic field.

Magnets and the Human Body

What, then, of the alleged healing power of magnets as they interact with our bodies? The suggestion for how a magnetic field might be useful in curing disease is that it increases the flow of blood (which contains iron) to a targeted area, thereby bringing extra nutrients and carrying away the waste products of our metabolism. This theory, too, is directly contradicted by known facts. Blood, like other bodily tissue and fluids, is composed primarily of water. Thus, the fact that water is slightly repelled by a magnetic field is especially relevant. Why? Because the primary constituent of the human body—including not only our blood but, as in most forms of life, all of our tissues and fluids—is water. We are therefore weakly repelled by magnetic fields. In principle, a strong enough magnet could be used to levitate a person, as has been done with water drops, flowers, grasshoppers, and frogs! The small amounts of iron in our blood's hemoglobin do not exist in sufficiently dense quantities to offset the repulsive effect of the much larger amount of water. Therefore, to the extent that magnets have *any* influence on our blood—and this influence is minimal—they will drive blood *away* from the targeted areas!

The Strength of "Therapeutic" Magnets

Finally, it is worth noting that the magnetic fields of therapeutic magnets commonly available for sale are in fact so weak that one need not even worry about driving blood away from vulnerable areas. The strength of a magnetic field depends on several factors, including the magnet's size and whether the individual "north" and "south" poles making up the magnet are aligned (as in a "unipolar" magnet) or not (as in a "multipolar" magnet). Naturally, a larger magnet will generate a stronger magnetic field, all else being equal, but the influence of north-south pole alignment is also important. The north and south poles of old-fashioned horseshoe-shaped magnets, for example, are aligned, producing the relatively strong field characteristic of a unipolar magnet. Newer refrigerator-style magnets, on the other hand, contain north and south poles arranged in an alternating, circular, or triangular pattern, which produces the relatively weak field of a multipolar magnet. This much is obvious in that many refrigerator magnets will support only thin, lightweight pieces of paper.

Most so-called therapeutic magnets are multipolar, meaning that their magnetic fields will penetrate only a few millimeters, barely reaching beneath the skin. Thus, one need not worry that blood is being driven away from the magnet-bound area. Though disappointing to believers in magnet therapy, this should be enormously reassuring to the rest of us, suggesting that we need not fear the indiscriminant destruction of our credit/check/ATM cards, audio- or videotapes, floppy disks, hard drives, or other magnetic devices due to magnets worn by ourselves or others. The very weakness of therapeutic magnets protects us from the potential havoc that people could let loose on our possessions in their own misguided attempts at healing.

HOMEOPATHY: EMPTY PROMISES

Whereas magnet therapy involves devices that do interact with our bodies (albeit in a negligible and useless manner), homeopathy involves an even weaker connection to reality. Homeopathy, founded by the German physician Samuel Hahnemann (1755–1843), is premised on two "laws," each of which is contradicted by considerable scientific evidence.

The Law of Similars

Imagine that you arrive at the emergency room for the treatment of a poisonous snake bite. Which would you rather receive: the antidote to the poison or a little bit more of the poison itself? This is not a rhetorical question, for a true believer in homeopathy would opt for more poison!

The first principle of homeopathy is that the same substance that *causes* a disease in healthy people will *cure* those who are already afflicted with it. This is known as the "law of similars." Hahnemann spent much of his working career testing substances, noting the symptoms that they produce, and prescribing them for people with these same symptoms. This practice truly stands reality on its head, because administering more of the same pathogen or toxin is certainly not the way to cure a disease.

The law of similars may sport some superficial resemblance to immunization, though the effects of the two are entirely different. Immunization works through the injection of a small quantity of a pathogen *into a healthy person* so that his or her immune system can defeat it. In the process, the body builds up its own natural resistance to later infections. Homeopathy, on the other hand, is said to work through the addition of a small quantity of a pathogen or toxin *into an unhealthy person* already suffering from its effects. If this were actually done, the immune system would have to struggle even harder to fight the disease. No plausible theory—let alone evidence—is offered in support of this practice, only rhetoric.

The Law of Infinitesimals

Fortunately, diseases are *not* usually worsened through homeopathy. This is because of the second principle "discovered" by Hahnemann, which protects the patient from the dangers of the first principle by diluting pathogens or toxins to their vanishing point. Contrary to known principles of chemistry, Hahnemann advocated a method by which a substance is repeatedly diluted in order to *increase* its potency. This is known as the "law of infinitesimals," and it, too, thoroughly contradicts reality. Chemists have shown that substances actually demonstrate a "dose-response curve" so that increasingly high doses of a substance cause increasingly strong effects. The steepness of the curve varies from drug to drug. Homeopaths offer no plausible explanation for why any of their drugs should prove an exception to—in fact, a complete *reversal* of—this established rule.

The folly of this law of infinitesimals is even greater than its contradiction of the dose-response characteristics of medicine. For many homeopathic remedies, the active ingredient has not only been severely diluted but is altogether *gone*. It can easily be shown that the degree of dilution ("30X") advocated by Hahnemann—and still widely employed today—will create a solution in which not a single molecule of the original substance remains! As chemists say, the "dilution limit" of the solution has been passed. The "X" refers to dilution by a factor of 10; if one drop of a substance is used, it is then diluted to one-tenth of a drop. The "30" indicates that the process of dilution is carried out 30 successive times. That is, the one-tenth of a drop will then become one-one hundredth, one-one thousandth, and so on, with the original substance ultimately diluted by a factor of 10^{30}.

Avogadro's number, you may recall, represents the number of molecules of a substance present in one mole, and it is roughly 6.02×10^{23}. What this means is that you would have fewer molecules in an entire mole of a substance than are necessary to survive the dilution factor of 10^{30}. Because it is impossible to have fractions of a molecule, you eventually reach a point where dilution has likely removed even the last one.

Park (1997) has calculated that you would need to take approximately *two billion* homeopathic pills diluted at 30X to expect to get a single molecule of the supposed medication! As if this was not bad enough, still more extreme dilutions are sometimes used. On the labels of some homeopathic remedies you will see "200C." The "C" refers to dilution by a factor of 100, and the 200 means this is repeated 200 times! The dilution factor is therefore 10^{400}. To see how preposterous this is, consider the fact that there are only approximately 10^{100} molecules in the entire universe! Thus, if you began with all the matter that exists, you would reach its dilution limit long before you had carried out the whole 200C process.

Hahnemann's theory of homeopathy was published in 1810, one year before Avogadro's number became known. Thus, he may not have realized that his preferred dilution exceeded the dilution limit. We do know this today, however. Although homeopathy has survived virtually unchanged since Hahnemann's time, some manufacturers of homeopathic products do appear to recognize that exceeding the dilution limit is exceedingly foolish. Two ways of handling this break with reality have been developed, although each introduces more problems than it solves.

Evasive Maneuver #1: Lowering the Dilution Factor

Many homeopathic drugs sold today are diluted by more modest amounts than their predecessors, such as 6X. This dilution factor corresponds to one part per million of the original substance. As Park (1997) notes, the pills themselves would be expected to contain many impurities at the parts-per-million level. Thus, although it no longer exceeds the dilution limit, the process is still too extreme to allow a potent level of any medication to survive. Moreover, this action is no longer consistent with homeopathic theory. It is a concession that the law of infinitesimals is false, that potency is not increased through dilution. Rather than monkeying around with differing dilution factors, it would seem far more sensible to simply abandon this fatally flawed pseudoscience.

Evasive Maneuver #2: "Water Memory"

Other proponents of homeopathy have created yet another magical belief in an effort to salvage the first two. They claim that, although not even a single molecule of the original ingredient remains after dilution, the water in which the ingredient was diluted "remembers" what was once dissolved in it. This flight of fancy received tremendous media attention in 1988 when a paper in one of the premier scientific journals, *Nature,* reported no drop-off in potency with increasing dilution of a substance (Davenas et al., 1988). It was speculated that the "water memory" hypothesis had been experimentally supported.

Unfortunately, the serious flaws of this paper have not received as much media attention as its purported findings.

A major flaw is that its results have failed to replicate. None of the teams of researchers who carefully repeated the procedure could achieve similar results. As will be discussed in Chapter 8, replication is one of the cornerstones of science, and the failure of conscientious experimenters to successfully obtain comparable results using the same methods suggests that the original work contained either a fluke result or a mistake, conscious or otherwise. Second, the 1988 results were not consistent with the law of infinitesimals, which predicts an *increase* in potency with increased dilution, not a flat amount that fails to drop off. To date, nobody has ever demonstrated a single reversal of the standard dose-response curve. Third, consider what our world would be like if water *did* have "memory." Think how terrifying it would be to take a sip of water that remembered all of the substances that have passed through it! Sewage is the first thing that comes to my mind, though I will not offend the reader with a graphic list of revolting and toxic substances that our water regularly passes through before it is cleaned and treated for consumption. The only way around this problem is to grant water a *selective* memory that remembers only substances that we regard as helpful. It is apparent that this line of reasoning makes matters far worse before they get better, straining plausibility beyond the breaking point.

In light of its many extremely dubious aspects, Barrett and Herbert (1994) describe homeopathy as "the ultimate fake," and Park (1997) calls it the "no-medicine medicine." In 1999, the *Medical Letter on Drugs and Therapeutics*—the most highly respected source of drug information for physicians—concisely summarized the current status of homeopathy:

> The chemical content of homeopathic products is often undefined, and some are so diluted that they are unlikely to contain any of the original material. These products have not been proven effective for any condition. There is no good reason to use them.

ALIEN ABDUCTIONS: A MODERN-DAY MISUNDERSTANDING

The story of Zeke's alien abduction that opened this chapter is also questionable on many grounds. Although similar accounts are offered in earnest by many people, are they true?

The Contamination Effect

Scientists refer to the consistency or repeatability of a phenomenon as its "reliability." However, reliability is a necessary—but not *sufficient*—condition to establish truth, or validity. For example, your bathroom scale must give consistent (reliable) readings if you step on and off of it several times in order for its readings to be considered valid. But, the scale may reliably give a read-out that is in fact wrong (invalid). The fact that reliability does not necessarily imply validity has a direct bearing on whether the apparent agreement across many people's stories should count as evidence of their truth.

For the sake of argument, let's overlook the inconsistencies among accounts of alleged alien abductees and grant that their stories are generally "reliable"—that is, that they agree well enough with one another in their central details. The question then becomes one of determining *why* they are reliable. There are at least two possibilities. First, it could be that aliens are indeed abducting large numbers of people, and that the accounts are as accurate as can be expected of any fallible humans. This, of course, is what abductees would have us believe. Second, it could be that there are no actual abductions, but that there is a culturally shared stereotype, or script, for how an alien abduction proceeds. The available evidence provides considerable support for the latter possibility.

Take a moment to try something for yourself. Close your eyes, and visualize a UFO. Get a very clear picture in your mind's eye, and continue reading only after you have a describable image. What do you see? Virtually all the students with whom I have tried this simple demonstration report that they see something roughly disc-shaped, like a "flying saucer." But why should they? None of my students have told me that they, personally, have ever seen such a craft, much less been abducted by aliens. So where does this shared image come from?

In 1947, civilian pilot Kenneth Arnold reported seeing a group of cigar-shaped objects in the night sky that moved like saucers thrown across water. When this account was *misquoted* by a reporter as a "flying saucer," a cultural image was born. Once the flying saucer entered the popular imagination, many observers reported seeing them, and the image persists to this day (Sheaffer, 1997). Thus, culturally shared images are possible in the absence of any validity.

And what of the curious fact that the alien abduction phenomenon is largely restricted to North America? Do aliens preferentially abduct Americans, or does our popular entertainment media—captivated by alien beings—provide the grist for a seductive alien abduction myth? The prototypical alien of today—with a disproportionately large, bald head and big, elongated eyes—was created for the 1975 film *The UFO Incident*, based on Betty and Barney Hill's abduction story. Since that time, countless other movies, television programs, books, magazines, and internet sites have popularized nearly identical versions of the stereotypical alien. Moreover, these sources describe abductions using a highly similar sequence of events. Is there anyone who does not "know" how abductions take place? We are indoctrinated into a media-driven culture from a young age and quickly come to know the shared expectations for even purely fictitious events.

Dull Fantasies and Contradictions

A number of beliefs concerning the alien abduction paradigm either imply contradictions or betray a serious lack of imagination. Four questions that challenge these beliefs will now be addressed.

First, why do aliens look so much like *us*? Take a look around at the stunning diversity of life here on our own planet. We are one life form among millions. The chance of an independently evolved being from another planet even remotely resembling us is astonishingly minute. This uninspired homocentrism might be called the "*Star Trek* fallacy":

> There must be dozens of alien species on the various *Star Trek* TV series and movies. Almost all we spend any time with are minor variants of humans. This is driven by economic necessity, costing only an actor and a latex mask, but it flies in the face of the stochastic nature of the evolutionary process. If there are aliens, almost all of them I think will look devastatingly less human than Klingons and Romulans (and be at wildly different levels of technology). *Star Trek* doesn't come to grips with evolution. (Sagan, 1995, p. 375)

Second, can aliens pass undetected through walls? If not, how else could they evade the security systems installed in many homes? Do they know in advance who has such a system and avoid those homes? Similarly, why have they never been filmed on security cameras? Can they selectively make themselves invisible? If so, why do they allow us to see them at all?

Third, aliens can supposedly levitate or otherwise magically transport human bodies and travel vast interstellar distances using life-support systems to survive outside of their home environment. This requires technology far more sophisticated than any we have yet developed. If this is so, why are aliens so remarkably inept at biology? Why do they need to abduct us, one at a time, for "medical experimentation?" Why can't they simply take a quick sample of human tissue and clone people? *We* can nearly do this.

Fourth, why is the advice that alien visitors offer to their abductees so prosaic, so much a product of *our* trials and tribulations, the current problems of modern life on Earth? Unless Zeke has lived in a cave for the past decade or more, he is aware of environmental concerns and the AIDS epidemic. If aliens want to convince us of their superior intelligence or wisdom, why not tell us something that is verifiably correct but goes beyond our present knowledge? Abductees have frequently invited Carl Sagan, an outspoken nonbeliever in abduction accounts, to "ask anything" of the aliens with whom they were in contact. So, Sagan provided them with questions to ask the aliens, and he sometimes received answers. When he asked for anything concrete, such as a short proof of Fermat's Last Theorem (a deceptively simple mathematical proposition whose proof has long eluded scholars), he never heard back. However, when he asked

> something like "Should we be good?" I almost always get an answer. Anything vague, especially involving conventional moral judgments, these aliens are extremely happy to respond to. But on anything specific, where there is a chance to find out if they actually know anything beyond what most humans know, there is only silence. Something can be deduced from this differential ability to answer questions. (Sagan, 1995, p. 100)

If aliens sincerely wish to alert us to realistic dangers, why didn't they tell us about environmental degradation or the AIDS problem in advance, when this information would have been so much more helpful? Why don't they tell us now about threats that scientists have not yet discovered?

Sleep Paralysis

Perhaps the most damning piece of evidence bearing on the plausibility of the alien abduction paradigm is its uncanny similarity to an often-overlooked but genuine phenomenon called "sleep paralysis." Sleep paralysis occurs at the borderline between sleeping and waking states. Individuals feel wide awake yet cannot move—an experience that can be extremely distressing—and often report a pressure on their chest combined with a sensation of weightlessness, as though they are floating. Auditory and/or visual hallucinations—such as bright lights, people, aliens, demons, ghosts, and so forth—are commonly reported, as is the sense of a strange presence in the room. There is often a strong sexual component to the experience. All of this has the full force of our most emotionally compelling dreams.

There are clearly many striking similarities between the typical episode of sleep paralysis and the standard alien abduction story (Blackmore, 1998). Alien abductions are said to take place just as people are falling asleep or waking up, or on long drives, when there is a danger of falling into a trancelike state. Abductees are floated into flying saucers with bright lights, where alien beings physically restrain them, perform experiments on them, and have sex with them. All of this is both spellbinding and distressing, demanding an explanation or meaning. Someone who has never heard of sleep paralysis but has learned much about alien abductions from popular culture may be quite likely to misinterpret the experience.

Indeed, the alien abduction (mis)interpretation of sleep paralysis appears to be merely the latest in a long line of culturally shared delusions about this experience. For example, in ancient times there were stories that followed this same script, occurring either at the point of drifting off to sleep or just awakening, that were interpreted in terms of devils or demons. In medieval times, female demons called "succubi" mated with men to steal their semen and then transformed into male demons known as "incubi" to impregnate women. The offspring of these unholy encounters were believed to be witches. These stories read like the alien abduction accounts of our time, like episodes of sleep paralysis. The obvious connections are persuasive, and to deny them raises thorny questions. Where were all these aliens throughout recorded history? Alien abduction accounts date back just over 50 years, from around the time of the bogus "flying saucer" report. Where are all of the devils, demons, succubi, and incubi now? It is an uncanny coincidence that, throughout human history, mystical creatures have tended to disappear when cultural preoccupations changed, and fanciful new creatures have emerged just in time to meet the new expectations.

Today we look back on medieval allegations of witchcraft as the imaginative products of human fantasy. It seems monstrous that the outlandish claims made by citizens of the corrupt political and religious institutions which flourished in an overly credulous society were taken at face value. Doesn't the nature of the modern-day incarnation of this supernatural tale—the alien abduction story—teach us about our own fantasies, fears, and longings? Have alien beings recently traveled vast interstellar distances to abduct us and carry out medical and breeding experiments without leaving a shred of physical evidence, or are abductees misinterpreting a relatively well-understood sleep-related phenomenon just as humans have for millennia, putting flesh on the bones of a frightening experience using culturally shared expectations?

The reports of self-proclaimed alien abductees may reveal nothing about alien beings, but they speak volumes about the psychology of human beings. In much the same way, the purchase of a therapeutic magnet or a homeopathic product reveals something about human nature. We are prone to flights of fancy, with a capacity for belief in the face of implausible theories. Digging beneath the surface of a claim may serve to unearth logical contradictions or negative evidence.

INFOTRAC COLLEGE EDITION

To learn more about topics included in this chapter, enter the following search terms:

alien abduction
extraterrestrial
flying saucer
homeopathy
sleep paralysis
UFO

ASSOCIATION

Establishing and Interpreting Correlations

In *The Three Faces of Eve* (Thigpen & Cleckley, 1957), a popular book that was also adapted as a movie, three personalities fought for control of a single body: Eve White, Eve Black, and Jane. Eve White and Eve Black held dramatically opposing views and engaged in radically different behaviors. Jane, who emerged last in therapy, was more of a compromise between the extremes. In the "Family Tree" and "Cast of Characters and Dates of 'Birth'" sections that open the book *Sybil* (Schreiber, 1973), we are introduced to a staggering array of personalities. The original Sybil Dorsett allegedly split into a writer and painter, two carpenters (both male), two intensely religious personas, a teenager, two young children, a baby, and seven other personalities described only in terms of their predominant emotions, for a total of 16! These personalities are said to have been "born" one or two at a time from the years 1923 to 1965, and readers are provided with distinct *physical* descriptions of these characters. For example, Mary Lucinda Saunders Dorsett is "plump and has long dark-brown hair parted on the side"; Vanessa Gail Dorsett is "a tall redhead with a willowy figure, light brown eyes, and an expressive oval face"; and Sid Dorsett "has fair skin, dark hair, and blue eyes."

An individual diagnosed with multiple personality disorder, or MPD, behaves as though two or more distinct personalities—by some accounts, even hundreds or *thousands* of personalities—take turns guiding his or her thoughts and actions. (Although the most recent revision of the *Diagnostic and Statistical Manual of Mental Disorders*, American Psychiatric Association, 1994, now refers to multiple personality disorder as "dissociative identity disorder," the more familiar name of MPD will be used here.) As in the cases of Eve and Sybil, these "alter" personalities are frequently reported to differ from one another in ways that are astonishing (e.g., Eve White acts and dresses conservatively, Eve Black acts and dresses flamboyantly) or even patently unbelievable (e.g., one of Sybil's personalities is a woman with light brown eyes, another is a blue-eyed man). But what *creates* such imaginative beliefs and behaviors? MPD is often proposed to result from childhood trauma, such as physical or sexual abuse (e.g., Putnam, 1989). The trauma theory of MPD maintains that a traumatic experience is too stressful for a child to successfully cope with, so he or she "dissociates," or splits consciousness, into an "alter" personality who will absorb the trauma and retain the threatening memory of the event. Before considering other possible origins of multiple identity enactments, let's see how the trauma theory must be evaluated.

To establish that there is indeed a link between reports of childhood trauma and diagnoses of MPD, four pieces of information must be collected through systematic investigation: the number of individuals reporting childhood trauma that (1) are diagnosed with MPD and (2) are not diagnosed with MPD as well as the number of individuals who *do not* report childhood trauma that (3) are diagnosed with MPD and (4) are not diagnosed with MPD. These four pieces of information can be arranged into a 2 × 2 table for ease of comparison:

Diagnosed with MPD

		Yes	No
Reported History of Childhood Trauma	Yes	Cell 1	Cell 2
	No	Cell 3	Cell 4

All four of these pieces of information are absolutely essential because without any one of them, the necessary comparisons cannot be made. To establish that childhood trauma and MPD are related, the *rate* of MPD among individuals with traumatic histories must be different from the *rate* of MPD among those all without traumatic histories. To put these rates into simple ratio form:

- Rate 1 $= \dfrac{\text{Cell 1}}{\text{Cell 1 + Cell 2}} =$ diagnosed MPD among all those who report childhood trauma

- Rate 2 $= \dfrac{\text{Cell 3}}{\text{Cell 3 + Cell 4}} =$ diagnosed MPD among all those who do not report childhood trauma

If these two rates are equal, this would suggest the absence of an association: MPD is just as likely to develop in the presence or absence of childhood trauma. If the rates are unequal, however, there would be evidence of an association between childhood trauma and MPD:

- If Rate 1 > Rate 2, there is a *positive association* (e.g., reports of childhood trauma are associated with an increased rate of MPD diagnoses).
- If Rate 1 < Rate 2, there is a *negative association* (e.g., reports of childhood trauma are associated with a decreased rate of MPD diagnoses).

If even one of the four cell values is missing, the necessary rates cannot be computed and no legitimate conclusion can be reached. Although this simple ratio test is very easy once you get the hang of it, many people fail to recognize the need for this test and for consideration of all four pieces of information. These individuals commonly make one of the two kinds of mistakes that are described below.

Presuming an Association Through Mere Examples

The first mistake involves presuming that a relationship exists based on nothing more substantial than a handful of examples. If somebody notices a few people with traumatic histories who have been diagnosed with MPD and then concludes that there is a positive relationship between these variables, he or she is overweighing the "yes-yes" cell in the table shown on p. 81 (Cell 1; Nisbett & Ross, 1980). Suppose, for example, that a clinician familiar with the cases of Eve and Sybil documents the case histories of individuals who report childhood trauma and are diagnosed with MPD, but fails to notice or document people who did not fit this expected pattern. Of 20 hypothetical patients, perhaps five fit the expected pattern (reported trauma and diagnosed MPD) but five patients also fall into each of the other three combinations (no reported trauma but diagnosed MPD, reported trauma but not diagnosed MPD, no reported trauma and not diagnosed MPD). To determine whether there is an association between reported trauma and diagnosed MPD, the two relevant rates would be these:

$$\text{Rate } 1 = \frac{5}{5+5} = .50; \ \text{Rate } 2 = \frac{5}{5+5} = .50$$

Because these rates are equal, the ratio test reveals that there no association whatsoever between reported childhood trauma and diagnosed MPD in this case. Thus, although it can be tempting to conclude that an association exists after seeing several examples of cases from Cell 1, this is insufficient evidence.

In fact, not only might there be *no* association between the variables, but mere examples provide such incomplete information that it is even possible to have an association in the *opposite* direction from what is initially presumed. Suppose again that a clinician has described five patients who report childhood trauma and are diagnosed with MPD, but failed to document 10 people who fall into each of the other three cells. The two relevant rates would be as follows:

$$\text{Rate } 1 = \frac{5}{5+10} = .33; \ \text{Rate } 2 = \frac{10}{10+10} = .50$$

This time, because Rate 1 < Rate 2, the ratio test reveals a *negative* association, the opposite of what was presumed. That is, although the small handful of patients whose case histories were documented contained both reports of trauma and diagnoses of MPD, it turns out that those who report childhood trauma are actually *less* likely to be diagnosed MPD than those who do not.

The danger in drawing conclusions about relationships from mere examples should be obvious. A small number of examples may be highly unrepresentative of most people's experiences, which may lead to over- or underemphasizing information in ways that reinforce the expectations of the observer. Salient examples abound in our personal experience, in testimonials, in the lives of fictional characters, and in media reports. Many who have read or watched *The Three Faces of Eve* or *Sybil* have fallen into the trap of concluding a relationship based on these mere examples. This is indeed an enticing trap *unless* you remember that there are always four pieces of data required to determine whether a relationship exists. Mere examples fail to provide you with three-quarters of the information that you need, which is precisely why scientists strive to collect data in a more systematic way and use objective statistical comparisons to inform their conclusions.

Presuming an Association Through a Lone Rate

The ratio test outlined earlier involves the comparison of two rates. Often, however, people presume a relationship based on only one of these rates. For example, someone may intensively study a sample of individuals who are all diagnosed with MPD and find that a high percentage of them report trauma in their childhood histories. Thus, one rate is shown to be high, and a positive association is pronounced. However, this is insufficient evidence to establish an association, for the simple reason that we have no information about the other rate. This unknown rate might be just as high as the known rate (which would mean there is no association), or possibly even higher (which would mean there is a negative association), drastically changing the apparent relationship between reported trauma and diagnosed MPD.

In fact, life history interviews conducted with groups of individuals with almost *any* psychological disorder tend to reveal high rates of reported childhood trauma. Moreover, even among a population of 100 adults carefully screened to remove individuals with any sign of mental disorder, Renaud and Estess (1961) still found that childhood trauma was very common. Simply searching for trauma will reveal at least traces of it in the life of many people, so the experience of trauma fails to explain why a given person develops a psychological disorder. It is therefore essential that anybody who believes childhood trauma to be associated with a particular psychological disorder must use a consistent definition of trauma and show that the *rate* of the disorder is higher among those with than those without this trauma. This evidence has not yet been provided for many of the presumed relationships between childhood trauma and psychopathology, including the unsubstantiated link between trauma and MPD (Lilienfeld et al., 1999; Spanos, 1996).

INTERPRETING A CORRELATION

Now that we have seen how a true correlation must be established, we can move on to the proper interpretation of correlations. As we come to know reality, our goal is almost always to know what events *cause* other events to occur. An association between events is surely worth knowing, but it is not as theoretically or practically useful to us as a causal relationship. For example, suppose for now that a positive correlation between reports of childhood trauma and diagnoses of MPD has been established. If this relationship is *causal*, it suggests that preventing trauma will in turn reduce the incidence of MPD. However, if it turns out that this relationship is *not causal*, that something other than trauma is causing individuals diagnosed with MPD to act as they do, then attempts to prevent MPD by reducing trauma will fail and attention devoted to a traumatic memory in the treatment of MPD will be a waste of time, expense, and effort, because the true cause of MPD is not being addressed. We will return to this possibility shortly.

Because causal interpretations are extremely powerful and intuitively appealing, it can be enormously tempting to reach causal conclusions even in the face of insufficient information. In fact, we routinely make this leap based on flimsy evidence. Recall from Chapter 5 the allure of believing that "I tried a treatment and felt better; therefore, it cured me." A lengthy list of alternative causal interpretations (e.g., the placebo effect, derivative benefits, symptomatic relief rather than a true cure, etc.) is routinely overlooked. To steer clear of trouble, there is a simple phrase that you should always remember: "Correlation does not imply causation." It is *not* necessarily the case that childhood trauma causes the symptoms of MPD. There are many other potential causal explanations for any single observed correlation.

Causal Relationships Between Correlated Events

In general, there are three types of causal relationships that may hold between two correlated events (X and Y):

1. X may cause Y. For example, childhood trauma that is reported in therapy (X) may be the cause of diagnosed MPD (Y).
2. Y may cause X. Perhaps it is the diagnosis of MPD that brings about a report of childhood trauma. Recall the horrific tale of MPD treatment gone wrong that opened Chapter 1. Bennett Braun believed that virtually everybody diagnosed with MPD was sexually abused as a child.

Therefore, as soon as Patricia Burgus received the questionable diagnosis of MPD, her therapists *assumed* that she had been abused and began to pressure her to recover memories consistent with their beliefs. Thus, it may be the case that a diagnosis of MPD could cause therapists to search for and elicit false memories of abuse, producing a positive correlation between reported trauma and diagnosed MPD.

3. Z may cause X and Y. Here, Z represents any outside factor that you can think of, and there are almost infinite possibilities for any correlational relationship. For example, perhaps trauma does not cause MPD and MPD does not cause therapists to elicit memories of trauma. Instead, some other variable may cause therapists both to diagnose patients with MPD *and* to elicit memories of abuse. What could such a variable be? How about hypnotizability, or fantasy-proneness, or suggestibility? These are all variables that a therapist could assess in an informal way and use to determine whether the patient is likely to accept a diagnosis of MPD and willingly undergo memory retrieval procedures. Indeed, there is evidence that supports this possibility. Hyman and Billings (1995) found that people who scored highly on the Creative Imagination Scale (a measure of hypnotizability) or the Dissociative Experiences Scale (a measure of disintegration of awareness, thought, and memory) were most susceptible to the creation of false memories.

Thus, for any correlation there are many distinct causal interpretations that cannot be ruled out using only the correlation itself. Additional information is needed to choose correctly from among these possibilities.

Three Conditions for Causality

To show that one event *causes* another to occur, several conditions must be met:

1. X and Y must be correlated.
2. X must precede Y in time.
3. All other factors (Z) must be ruled out.

The first condition is satisfied by virtue of having a correlation in need of interpretation, but the other two conditions can be tricky.

The second condition is often referred to as the "directionality problem" because determining the direction in which the causal influence goes can be difficult. In the trauma theory of MPD, the cause (trauma) must occur before its effect (MPD) is observed. Because MPD is frequently diagnosed in the *absence* of any evidence of trauma (Piper, 1997), some therapists feel compelled to solve the directionality problem by eliciting recovered memories of the abuse. These "memories" are then taken as evidence that trauma did in fact precede the onset of MPD symptoms.

As another example, consider the well-established correlation between self-esteem and academic achievement (Sykes, 1995). Many educators have been quick to assume that self-esteem causes achievement, which suggests that boosting children's self-esteem will likely yield educational payoffs. However, might it be that causality operates in the other direction? Perhaps those who do well in school tend to feel good about themselves. This is at least as plausible as the first interpretation, and it predicts that time spent trying to boost self-esteem will yield no educational gains. Instead, it suggests that education be pursued for its own sake, with increased self-esteem likely to follow as one derivative benefit. Or, perhaps there is some truth to *both* of these explanations, and a situation of "reciprocal causality" exists in which self-esteem influences achievement, which in turn influences self-esteem, and so on. Based on the correlation alone, there is simply no way to determine which of these explanations is correct. We need additional information to help us solve the directionality problem.

The third condition is often referred to as the "third-variable problem" because determining whether an outside factor, or "third variable," causes both X and Y can be extremely challenging. Typically, this is an even more serious problem than directionality because the number of possible outside factors may be very large. As described above, there are several factors (e.g., hypnotizability, fantasy-proneness, suggestibility) that may prompt therapists both to diagnose a patient with MPD and to begin memory recovery procedures. These factors have not been ruled out as causal explanations. Likewise, perhaps neither self-esteem nor academic achievement causes the other; rather, one's upbringing and home environment cause both. Or maybe it's not the home environment, but peer influences, inherited components of personality and intelligence, or any of a number of other potential factors that cause both self-esteem and achievement.

Interpreting a correlation as a causal relationship can be risky. How can you definitively establish the direction of causality? How can you ever hope to rule out every possible third variable? Even if *you* think you have ruled out all other plausible explanations, couldn't somebody else always think of something you forgot?

Examining Patterns Across Multiple Correlations

Although it is difficult to argue for a causal relationship when all you have is a correlation between events, the situation is not always as bleak as it may seem. Even though correlations, by themselves, are weak evidence for a causal relationship, a *pattern* of correlations may combine to produce a potent argument for causality. Hill (1965) proposed the following criteria for determining whether associations are likely to be causal in nature:

1. *Consistency.* Do results replicate across multiple tests and multiple studies, ruling out "flukes"?
2. *Strength of association.* Is the association clinically meaningful, ruling out trivialities?
3. *Dose-response relationship.* Are higher levels of the presumed cause paired with higher levels of the presumed effect, ruling out coincidental associations with other factors?
4. *Plausibility.* Can the relationship be meaningfully explained by sound theorizing? As discussed in Chapter 6, explanations that conflict with known principles of reality are unlikely to be true.
5. *Coherence.* Is the explanation consistent with other known facts? This helps to build a body of information that is collectively stronger than any single correlation.

To see how these criteria can be employed to construct a causal argument from purely correlational data, consider the question of whether smoking causes lung cancer. For ethical reasons, we cannot carry out the conceptually simple experiment that would directly answer this question: Randomly assign some people to smoke, some not to smoke, and observe everyone's health over time. Instead, we are faced with purely correlational results that severely constrain causal explanations. We are particularly limited by the third-variable problem. Because some people choose to smoke whereas others do not, any differences in health across these self-selected groups might well be attributed to existing differences that have nothing to do with smoking, such as personality, socioeconomic status, or attitudes toward healthy eating and exercise.

Few would deny the massive amount of evidence showing that more smokers contract lung cancer than nonsmokers. But can a causal relationship be inferred? Let us consider Hill's criteria for establishing the causality of a relationship. There is certainly *consistent* evidence for the association between smoking and lung cancer, as the data from many large studies all show the same trend. The *strength of association* is fairly high; for example, tables of life expectancy reveal that smokers can expect to live substantially shorter lives than nonsmokers. There is, in fact, a *dose-response relationship*, in that the more an individual smokes, the greater are his or her chances of contracting lung cancer. The argument is quite *plausible*, in that there are known carcinogens in cigarettes and that cigarette smoke is inhaled into the lungs. Abelson (1995) articulates the plausible theory and explains the powerful *coherence* of the total argument by summarizing several lines of evidence:

> The postulated mechanism for the causal link, in simplified, nontechnical form, is that tobacco smoke contains substances that are toxic to human tissue when deposited by contact. The more contact, the more toxicity. Now, what are some empirical implications of such a mechanism?

1. The longer a person has smoked cigarettes, the greater the risk of cancer.
2. The more cigarettes a person smokes over a given time period, the greater the risk of cancer.
3. People who stop smoking have lower cancer rates than do those who keep smoking.
4. Smokers' cancers tend to occur in the lungs, and to be of a particular type.
5. Smokers have elevated rates of other respiratory diseases.
6. People who smoke cigars or pipes, the smoke usually not being inhaled, have abnormally high rates of lip cancer.
7. Smokers of filter-tipped cigarettes have somewhat lower cancer rates than do other cigarette smokers. . . .

All of these implications have moderate to strong empirical support in U.S. Surgeon General (1964) and a succession of later reports. All of them were established correlationally (by comparing cancer rates in different population subgroups). Yet the case is extremely persuasive because it is so coherent, with so many consequences implied by the toxic smoke mechanism supported by strong evidence. (pp. 183–184)

This example demonstrates that although each of the correlational building blocks is weak, the overall argument in this case is a much more solid structure. The effectiveness of a coherent argument derives from the inability of any single competing explanation to account for all of the evidence. This draws on an important principle of scientific reasoning known as "Occam's Razor," which maintains that—all else being equal—the simplest explanation is preferred. Following the principle of Occam's Razor, the link between smoking and lung cancer can reasonably be interpreted as causal, because it is far and away the simplest explanation that is consistent with all of the data.

BEWARE THE MEDIA

In striving to properly establish and interpret correlations, your biggest obstacle may be the popular media (television, radio, newspapers, magazines, the internet, and so forth). Why? As will be discussed further in Chapter 9, what "works" in the popular media are stories of *individuals*. The more vivid, concrete, personal, and emotionally compelling an individual's experiences, the more media coverage they will receive. The captivation of the audience's attention is of paramount importance to media professionals, while informativeness often takes a distant back seat. Thus, you can expect to be bombarded with testimonials, case studies, and anecdotes that will be dramatic but also largely uninformative. Media outlets incessantly urge audiences to form beliefs based on mere examples or lone rates.

For example, there's an old trick that surfaces from time to time involving longevity statistics. Suppose you are told that orchestra conductors have such fulfilling careers that they have a longer-than-average life expectancy. Indeed,

Atlas (1978) noted that the life expectancy of orchestra conductors was 73.4 years. Because most orchestra conductors were male, this figure was compared to that of males in the general population, who in 1978 were expected to live for 68.5 years. Thus, a correlation between fulfilling careers, health, and ultimately longevity was suggested. But this is a bogus comparison. Think about who is included among a sample of orchestra conductors: healthy adults. The average life expectancy for males, on the other hand, includes all individuals who died as infants, children, and adolescents, strongly biasing the statistic downward. When Abelson (1995) presented a more appropriate comparison, contrasting the life expectancy of orchestra conductors (73.4) with men who have survived to the age of 32 (72.0), the difference all but vanished. Certainly, 1.4 years is not a substantial enough difference to shape a career choice! In fact, an even more appropriate comparison might have reduced the gap even further. For example, whites, who tend to live longer than other ethnic groups, are disproportionately represented among orchestra conductors. This trick of comparing a group of adults to a group also including deceased infants and children can be used to suggest that almost *any* occupation is a smart choice for longer living.

Even if you are fortunate enough to receive more than a mere example or a lone rate through media reports, be cautious about inferring a causal relationship from correlational evidence. As noted earlier, the simplest principle is also the most important: *Correlation does not imply causation.* Keep in mind that we are each subjected to misinterpretations of correlational evidence on a daily basis. Much of the time, this is a naïve mistake, as when news reporters simply do not know (or care much about) the difference between a mere association and a causal relationship.

For example, we frequently hear reports on the purported health benefits of adopting a vegetarian diet. Typically, the evidence in support of this advice consists in showing that a group of vegetarians are more healthy than a group of nonvegetarians: perhaps they lived longer, their cardiovascular functioning was superior, and so on. But what about the third-variable problem? Vegetarians are a self-selected group that differs from nonvegetarians in many other ways. Most notably, many vegetarians are generally very health conscious, and are therefore likely to take good care of themselves in many ways that are unrelated to meat eating (e.g., they are probably unlikely to overeat or smoke, and are likely to exercise). Clearly, a correlation between vegetarianism and health measures tells us close to nothing.

To determine what type of diet is best, an experiment is required. Participants would be assigned to conditions in which the diet was comparable in all regards save for including or excluding meat. Assignment to conditions would be random, so that participants' lifestyles, attitudes, and behaviors would not differ in a systematic way across conditions. This way, the only factor that does differ across the two groups is vegetarianism, and third variables such as total caloric intake or exercise could be ruled out. Researchers would need to monitor participants' diets to ensure that they followed the dietary instructions. They would also assess participants' health at the conclusion of the experiment using "blind" evaluators—physicians who do not know which participants were in which condition—in order to prevent such knowledge from biasing the evaluations. The results arising from such a study would be quite informative. However, in the absence of evidence from appropriately designed experiments such as this, we can draw no conclusions from comparisons of widely differing, self-selected groups.

Some professionals attempt to pawn off correlations as causation often and intentionally in deliberate efforts to mislead the public. Advertisers, political strategists, and proponents of practices, products, or beliefs with only correlational support will often overinterpret the data. For example, a pharmaceutical manufacturer may tell you that its medicine relieves headaches faster than a competitor's product. But does the manufacturer tell you, outside of the fine print, that it compared its "extra strength" formula with its competitor's "regular strength" product? Does the manufacturer give you any reason that you cannot simply take a higher dose of its competitor's product to gain even faster relief? It is all too easy to become ensnared in a correlational web spun by professionals attempting to obtain your money, your vote, your belief, or any other valuable commodity that can be extracted.

What is your best defense? Rely upon experimental, not correlational, data whenever possible. Experiments, if conducted properly, are not subject to the directionality and third-variable problems of correlational studies. If practical or ethical impediments prohibit an experimental test, then insist upon a coherent pattern of correlations. A constellation of correlations that coherently points to the same conclusion is a workable guide for your tentative belief. Anything less opens you up for swindling.

Do Horoscopes Predict Anything?

Let's conclude this chapter with a quick look at one final media example: horoscopes. Many newspapers print "sun-sign" astrological horoscopes, and one might wonder whether the advice or predictions contained in these horoscopes is of any value. Horoscopes presume a correlation between sun-signs and human affairs that is causal in nature. Are there celestial influences on our lives? Here's a very simple test that you can conduct to find out.

Get a group of people together (the more the better) and read them the horoscopes from the previous day, but in a random order and without indicating which birth sign corresponds to which description. Ask each person to consider these carefully, thinking about the extent to which each description corresponds to the events of the previous day. Then, have them choose the one that they believe must be their horoscope. If horoscopes validly predict real-world events, people should be able to correctly identify their horoscope with a substantial success rate—say, at least 75%. If the horoscopes are thoroughly invalid, the rate of correct identifications should be equal to chance-level guessing—about 1 in 12, or roughly 8%. It would be wise to repeat the same test the following day, particularly if you try this with a small group, in which a few people may get lucky by simply guessing. Valid horoscopes should afford repeatable success.

I have tried this test in many classes, and none has ever achieved a success rate in excess of chance. Thus, the "for entertainment only" notices that many newspapers print along with their horoscopes appear to be justified. Until all worthless information carries such disclaimers, you'll have to think for yourself.

INFOTRAC COLLEGE EDITION

To learn more about topics included in this chapter, enter the following search terms:

horoscopes
multiple personality disorder/dissociative identity disorder
smoking and cancer

SCIENCE

Evaluating Claims to Knowledge

There once was a horse who could solve mathematical problems. In the early 20th century, a German teacher presented her horse, Clever Hans, to the public. The horse's trainer (or a member of the audience) would ask Hans what $5 + 3$ is, and Hans would tap his hoof 8 times. If asked what 4×7 is, Hans would tap his hoof 28 times. Clever Hans quickly became quite famous as word of his abilities spread through amazed eyewitnesses. Can you imagine the stir caused by a horse with an uncanny ability to solve math problems?

It turns out that Hans was gifted, but not in exactly the way that most people thought. The eyewitnesses were not mistaken: Hans could tap out the answer to any math problem put to him. However, it was a mistake to infer that he arrived at the correct answers by performing calculations. It was not until Oskar Pfungst, a psychologist, tested Clever Hans's abilities under controlled conditions that the truth of the matter was revealed. Pfungst learned that Hans would only answer correctly if two critical conditions were met: The individual posing the problem must know the correct answer, and Hans must have an unobstructed view of this individual. When testing was arranged such that either of these conditions was not satisfied, Hans could no longer solve any problems. Remarkably, Hans had somehow mastered the subtle skill of reading nonverbal cues.

Hans was able to tell by the tone of someone's voice that a question was being asked of him, at which time he would begin tapping his hoof. He would then carefully watch the individual who had asked the question. When the correct answer was reached, this person would unknowingly and involuntarily tilt his or her head ever so slightly. This was Hans's signal to stop tapping his hoof, leaving observers to conclude that he had correctly performed mathematical calculations! Pfungst's application of scientific reasoning helped to eliminate an incorrect hypothesis—that Hans was doing math—while corroborating another, equally impressive hypothesis: that Hans was an astute reader of human nonverbal behavior.

SCIENTIFIC REASONING

Perhaps because of the way science is typically taught to children, many people come to see science as simply a collection of facts. However, science is far more than the discoveries with which it is equated. It is a method, a process, a way of thinking that offers powerful tools for coming to know reality. Science cuts through wishful thinking by setting up observations under well-controlled conditions to determine what causal factors produce what effects. Science is unique among ways of knowing in that it contains a built-in, error-checking mechanism to root out faulty ideas. The case of Clever Hans and his extraordinary abilities shows precisely how scientific reasoning helps us move beyond premature conclusions to understand reality. By systematically manipulating the situation under which Hans was tested, Pfungst ruled out the hypothesis that Hans could add and multiply. In the end, the only tenable hypothesis was that Hans was reading nonverbal cues to produce his solutions.

The scientific enterprise seeks to continually refine and improve our understanding of reality through a series of successive approximations to the truth. When one interesting or impressive theory is disproved, it is often replaced by something equally or even more fascinating. Of course, how fascinating we find scientific theories to be has no bearing on their validity, which depends entirely on their consistency with reality. The power of science derives from its ability to enhance our knowledge. It simultaneously reduces the threat of an unknown and mysterious world and paves the way for technological innovation. These rewards await anyone willing to engage in an open-minded skepticism, giving all ideas a fair chance but maintaining high standards for what constitutes persuasive evidence.

But what are the tools of scientific reasoning? James Lett (1990) offered a good overview of these tools when he outlined a series of six tests that a claim must pass in order to warrant belief. Each test reflects one essential component of scientific thinking that can protect us against foolish beliefs. The easy way to remember the six tests is by remembering the consonants of the word "FiLCHeRS:" *Falsifiability, Logic, Comprehensiveness, Honesty, Replicability,* and *Sufficiency.*

Falsifiability

For a claim to have even the potential of being scientifically meaningful, it must in principle pose a hypothesis that could be disproved. That is, if indeed the claim is false, there must be some way to demonstrate its falsity. This is called the "falsifiability" of the claim, and it is essential because, without it, the claim is completely insulated from reality. Claims that are so completely shielded from unfavorable evidence that they cannot possibly be falsified are actually devoid of meaning. To demonstrate how vacuous such an unfalsifiable claim is, Sagan (1995) suggests what would happen if he claimed that a fire-breathing dragon lives in his garage. Naturally, you would want to verify this claim. When you ask to see it, you're told it is invisible. Perhaps you could use paint to make the dragon visible? No, it's incorporeal, so there is nothing to which the paint can adhere. What about putting flour on the floor to see its footprints? That won't work because it floats in the air. How about measuring the heat of its flaming breath? No such luck, it's heatless. You continue to pose reasonable tests that are met with increasingly unreasonable answers. Eventually you begin to wonder just what it means to speak of a dragon that is invisible, immaterial, hovering in the air, and breathing a heatlessfire. How is this different from no dragon at all?

This example illustrates the problem posed by an unfalsifiable claim: Because it cannot be tested, the most substantial evidence that is provided is somebody's word. This is simply unacceptable currency in scientific reasoning. The approach taken by scientists is to say "show me," and people who cannot or will not supply evidence are pseudoscientists, even if they take on superfluous trappings of science. Whereas pseudoscientists shield their beliefs from testing by framing unfalsifiable hypotheses, science progresses by eliminating mistaken ideas one by one through careful experimentation. This requires not that hypotheses be false—nobody would waste time investigating beliefs known to be untrue—but that there must be some way to test the hypotheses, that they are falsifiable.

Logic

Naturally, any claim to knowledge must be logically sound. The soundness of a logical argument is based on satisfying two criteria. First, the premises on which the argument is based must all be true. Second, the proposed conclusion must validly follow from the premises. If either of these criteria is not met, the argument is defective.

For example, consider the argument used to contend that crop circles—huge geometric patterns pressed into farmer's fields—constitute evidence of extraterrestrial visitations:

1. Crop circles are extremely complex and numerous.
2. Human beings are incapable of such complexity on so grand a scale.
∴ Crop circles are made by extraterrestrials.

The first premise is certainly true, for elaborate crop circles have been observed all around the world for decades. The second premise, however, is not true. Two Englishmen, Doug Bower and Dave Chorley, confessed to having made crop circles for 15 years to fool gullible people (Schnabel, 1994). Not only did they claim to have done this, but they eagerly showed reporters exactly how simple it is to make crop circles using nothing more than two-by-fours and some rope. Imagine how proud they must have felt to hear that their creations were considered too complex to possibly be of human origin! But suppose the second premise *was* true. Would the suggested conclusion logically follow from the premises? Not necessarily. Natural forces can play tricks on us—they are capable, for example, of fashioning intricate patterns like the pyramids on Mars—and it is conceivable that unusual winds or other natural phenomena could have caused strange patterns in wheat fields. Thus, this argument is shaky on several grounds. So much for the claim that "crop circles are evidence of extraterrestrial visitation."

Comprehensiveness

A claim to knowledge must account for *all* the pertinent data, not just select bits and pieces. One claim that fails this test is still widely known and is commonly referred to as the Blackout of '65. Most people who were alive at the time believe that this was an occasion when an unusually large number of babies were conceived. There was a widespread human-interest story maintaining that a spike in the New York City birth rate occurred on Monday and Tuesday of the week falling nine months after the blackout, which suggests what people do when the lights go out! These data were correct, but only a small part of the relevant evidence was considered. It turns out that a similar spike in births actually occurred *every* Monday and Tuesday, and still does to this day. The cause of this anomaly: Doctors prefer not to work on weekends. Therefore, induced labor and Caesarian section births tend to be scheduled for the beginning of the week. Although it is admittedly more interesting than the mundane reality of doctors' scheduling habits, the story of large numbers of babies being born nine months after a great blackout is simply not true. Whenever a claim cannot explain all the relevant evidence, this is a failure of the comprehensiveness test.

Honesty

It should go without saying that claims to knowledge must be evaluated honestly and without self-deception. However, this is often easier said than done. Judgment can sometimes become cloudy, particularly when a cherished belief is on the line. For example, a study by two psychologists found that children who spent more time in day care received lower grades, worse behavioral ratings by parents and teachers, and lower standardized test scores in the third grade than children who spent less time in day care (Vandell & Corasantini, 1991). This study was at least as methodologically rigorous as comparable studies on related topics, yet it met with fierce objections from peer reviewers at the top journal in their field, *Developmental Psychology*. Given that these reviewers probably work long hours and may be members of dual-career couples, it seems likely that some or all of their own children spent considerable time in day care. Might this have produced some distaste for the results of the study? It is impossible to know for certain, but it is conceivable that the nature of the findings made a fair, honest evaluation of the study difficult to procure. In light of the many ways that we can deceive ourselves, passing the test of honesty is more challenging than it may appear.

Replicability

A claim to knowledge should be based on consistent results observed in multiple experiments, preferably conducted in multiple laboratories. A fluke might occur in a single experiment, but it is highly unlikely that the same problem would plague repeated experiments in the same way. Therefore, consistent results across repeated tests are far more trustworthy than are inconsistent results, or flukes.

Perhaps the clearest failures to successfully replicate have come from research on extrasensory perception (ESP). ESP researchers typically conduct a huge number of tests, and they analyze their data in myriad ways. By nothing more than chance alone, every so often a surprising pattern emerges that gives the appearance of outstanding performance. The key is to replicate this finding in order to guarantee that it is not a statistical anomaly, a mere fluke. Despite more than a century of concerted effort spent on ESP investigations, researchers have failed to demonstrate even a single replicable phenomenon. Several terms in the ESP literature reveal just what a failure this effort has been so far (Gilovich, 1991):

- *Psi missing*. This term is used when someone performs *worse* than would be expected by chance alone. Believers in ESP argue that this poor performance is evidence for the paranormal because it deviates from chance. But is this really the type of evidence that supports the magical beliefs associated with supernatural mental abilities: very *bad* predictions?
- *Experimenter effect*. This effect occurs when individuals are able to perform feats of ESP *except* in the presence of a skeptical observer. Believers in ESP take this to mean that "negative energy" of some sort inhibits mental phenomena. Perhaps what it really indicates is that the experimental conditions allow for cheating—either conscious or unconscious—when no skeptic is present to keep everyone honest.
- *Decline effect*. This effect occurs when someone who initially performs well begins to do worse and winds up at purely chance-level performance. Believers in ESP fail to recognize this effect as an obvious *failure to replicate*. Flukes such as this "beginner's luck" quickly disappear.

Sufficiency

Finally, a claim to knowledge must be backed by enough evidence to warrant belief. There are three related points to consider when evaluating the sufficiency of available evidence:

1. *The burden of proof is on the claimant.* This principle is similar to the operation of our criminal justice system: Someone making a claim to knowledge is in the position of a prosecutor, whose responsibility it is to muster sufficient evidence for that claim. We need not accept the responsibility for *disproving* the claim, for if insufficient evidence is provided, this alone suggests that the belief is unwarranted.

2. *Extraordinary claims require extraordinary evidence.* This fairly commonsensical principle was described in Chapter 6: The more fantastic the claim, the more persuasive the evidence must be to muster belief in that claim.

3. *Evidence based on authority is inadequate.* Do other types of evidence exist besides somebody's say-so? No matter *how* reputable this individual may be, history teaches us that anyone can be wrong. No less a respected scientist than Albert Einstein, for example, seems to have been wrong about an important scientific theory of his time: Einstein rejected the uncertainty principle of quantum mechanics, arguing that "God does not play dice." Physical experiments, however, have verified the predictions of the uncertainty principle with great precision.

The evidence in support of a claim must be satisfactory in all three of these ways to pass the sufficiency test. One final phrase is important to keep in mind: "Absence of evidence does not constitute evidence of absence." For example, those who believe that UFO sightings are good evidence of alien visitation argue that if you cannot prove them wrong, they must be right. Remember, though, that your inability to provide an explanation for each alleged UFO sighting does not mean that there *is* no natural explanation. Indeed, there is a long list of well-understood phenomena and man-made machines that can be and have been misperceived as extraterrestrial spacecraft by human observers, including these (Sagan, 1995):

- Conscious fraud or hoaxes, such as objects suspended on strings against a dark night sky or faked photographs or videos
- Conventional or unconventional aircraft, perhaps spotted during military testing flights and therefore unconfirmed for security reasons
- High-altitude balloons, such as the ones misinterpreted as a crashed saucer at Roswell, New Mexico, in 1947
- Planets seen under unusual atmospheric conditions
- Luminescent insects
- Optical mirages

- Lenticular clouds
- Ball lightning
- Meteors and green fireballs
- Satellites, nosecones, or rocket boosters reentering the atmosphere, two or three of which are destroyed on reentry into the earth's atmosphere each day, many visible to the naked eye

You need not determine which of these, or other, explanations is the cause of a UFO sighting. Rather, as noted earlier, it is the claimant's responsibility to provide sufficient proof that what he or she saw could not be explained by any of these sources. Especially in light of the many things that might be seen and misunderstand in the sky, those who proclaim alien visitation via UFOs bear the burden of proof and must provide extraordinary evidence for such an extraordinary claim.

If a claim passes all six FiLCHeRS tests, you can tentatively place some measure of confidence in the belief. To the extent that one or more tests are inconclusive or failed, you would be wise to exercise caution. Those who routinely demand the highest standards of evidence will tend to form the most accurate beliefs and thereby keep from making foolish decisions.

ANTI-SCIENTIFIC BELIEFS: POSTMODERNISM AND OTHER FALLACIOUS IDEAS

You might think that the benefits of scientific reasoning are intuitively obvious, persuasive on their own merits as well as the observable, verifiable knowledge and astounding technological innovation that they generate. However, there are individuals who directly attack the methods of science or, knowingly or otherwise, hold beliefs that are quite hostile toward science.

Postmodernism

In 1996, Alan Sokal wrote a virtually impenetrable paper entitled: "Transgressing the Boundaries: Toward a Transformative Hermeneutics of Quantum Gravity." In it, he applied the tools of postmodern literary criticism to complex issues in physics, highlighting the subjective nature of the world in a critical assault on science. Peer reviewers responded favorably at one of the premiere postmodernist journals, *Social Text*, where the paper was accepted for publication. Some time after the article appeared, Sokal revealed something shocking: It was a hoax! In detail, he showed how he had intentionally misused scientific and mathematical concepts, structured illogical and nonsensical arguments, and reached completely unjustified conclusions.

How, Sokal asked, could the "expert" reviewers and editors of one of the top postmodern journals be so easily fooled? Could it be that they were personally satisfied with his conclusions and emotionally gratified by his gratuitous citations to the work of postmodern "scholars?" In a subsequent book elaborating upon this hoax, *Fashionable Nonsense: Postmodern Intellectuals' Abuse of Science,* Sokal and Bricmont (1998) reviewed the disturbing consequences of a reckless, "anything goes" attitude toward scholarship in which science, mathematics, and anything else smacking of objectivity or a verifiable external reality is ritually scorned and abused.

In some corners of the academic world, there remain individuals who endorse the extreme forms of certain closely related styles of thinking—such as postmodernism and "cultural relativism"—in which it is believed that science is merely "one way of knowing" no more valid than any other. Although a thorough refutation of this belief is beyond the scope of this book, it is worthwhile to discuss several of the most serious weaknesses of postmodernism (see Norris, 1993, for an extended critique; Sokal & Bricmont, 1998, for a review of the abuse of science and math; or Englebretsen, 1997, for a brief discussion of the degradation in standards of scholarship that characterize postmodern academic disciplines).

Postmodern thinking originated in the field of literary criticism, where scholars decided that a text (a term that includes any written material, image, etc., intended to convey a message) has no fixed meaning but can be interpreted within different contexts. That is, the intended meaning of the author or creator of a "text" is completely irrelevant; all that matters is one's personal reaction to it. Two of the central tenets of extreme postmodernism are these: (1) There is no such thing as an external reality. Rather, we each construct our own personal reality. (2) Logical contradictions between interpretations pose no problem, because knowledge is valid only to the extent that we choose to believe that it is valid.

Perhaps one of the most convincing arguments for the existence of an external reality can be made by considering the possibility of there being no such thing. It is doubtful that anyone truly believes in an existence so empty as this, for it fails to explain the coherence of the world as we experience it, provides no grounds for making choices, and attaches no consequences to any of our actions. There is a certain order to the information that reaches each of us, and our actions produce somewhat predictable results. This is what helps us to make decisions and plan for the future, and the lack of an external reality would produce an existence utterly devoid of direction.

Genuine belief in the nonexistence of external reality also renders education meaningless. If there is no reality—nothing "out there" to know about— then one cannot "teach" or "learn" anything aside from direct personal experience. Given that the relatively few individuals who claim to endorse this extreme version of postmodernism are employed by academic institutions, this situation is both amusing (because they appear to have chosen a futile direction for their lives' work) and troubling (because they are exposing students to such unfounded ideas).

The tolerance for logical contradictions presents another puzzle. If it is the case that "truth is relative," that what is true for one person might be false for another, how can a society function at all? For example, imagine a criminal justice system in which a defendant could cling to a plea of "not guilty" on the grounds that this was most harmonious with his or her personal reality, while a jury could evaluate the evidence and decide that—in their personal realities—the defendant is "guilty." Clearly, criminal justice cannot tolerate such logical contradictions.

Suppose for just a moment that postmodern thinking was allowed into medicine. Here's the situation: One doctor believes that you have a malignant tumor that must be removed, whereas another doctor believes that your tumor is benign and will cause no harm. Can we accept the truth of both of these beliefs? Of course not; they contradict one another. Your tumor will or will not cause you physical harm, will or will not endanger your life. It makes no sense at all to entertain the possibility that both doctors' beliefs might be "true for them."

In fact, the fuzzy thinking that embraces contradictions breaks down in any real-world scenario. The attempt to relieve the sting of error by elevating all ideas to an equally acceptable status through sheer force of will is a reckless practice with dangerous consequences. Nobody has ever demonstrated a theoretical or practical advantage to looking the other way when two ideas contradict one another. Why, then, should this absurd practice be tolerated at all? The clear message delivered by any real logical contradiction is that at least one of the ideas is wrong.

In contrast to the path-of-least-resistance attitude, feel-good reliance on wishful thinking, and political correctness of extreme postmodernism, one of the central tenets of the exploration of human reasoning undertaken here is that a fundamental goal of clear thinkers is the attempt to come to know reality as it is. This entails seeking out better and better approximations to universal truths by constructing logical arguments based on scientific data. The intrusion of postmodernism into questions that involve measurable, testable aspects of reality—the realm of science—is a grave mistake because this sloppy, unproductive, and reckless approach to knowledge may readily lead us *away* from reality.

Though, as mentioned earlier, it is beyond the scope of this book to deal with the unlikely premises and faulty logic of postmodernism, I invite readers to judge for themselves which style of thinking is more likely to stimulate theoretical or practical advances in our knowledge of the world. Whereas science has an error-checking mechanism, postmodernism does not provide a way to detect or rule out invalid ideas. For example, if you meet a postmodern thinker, ask him or her to construct an argument that trephining—drilling holes in the skull to let out evil spirits—is inadvisable as medical care, that storks do not deliver babies, or even that the earth is not flat. Within the confines of extreme postmodernism, no such arguments are possible, because anything goes. Everyone's ideas are granted "personal validity," so critical evaluations or general conclusions are impossible. Proponents of postmodernism see this as a strength, though for obvious reasons this approach would be absolutely disastrous at the level of social policy.

Whereas pseudoscience can cause harm by masquerading as science without delivering on its promises, postmodernism poses an even deeper threat. As our population grows and we become increasingly dependent on technology in many spheres of our lives, a rejection of scientific reasoning is the surest way to stunt human progress and put us on a path back to the dark ages.

The "What Works Is Different for Everybody" Fallacy

Another antiscientific notion is captured by a popular catch-phrase of many pseudosciences: "What works is different for everybody." That is, different treatments are proposed to work for different people. The unstated implication is that scientists fail to recognize this point and pseudoscientists do. In fact, scientific research provides a mechanism by which individual differences can be studied. For example, if you suspect that a particular treatment works better for women than for men, you can tabulate treatment effects separately for each sex and make a comparison between them. In this way, the scientific method allows researchers to examine any potentially influential factor and provide increasingly detailed information regarding what type of person is most likely to benefit from what type of treatment for what type of problem.

All of this specificity is proclaimed but utterly unsubstantiated by practitioners of pseudoscience. Where is the evidence indicating which treatment to choose for a given person? As noted in Chapter 2, the tendency of pseudoscientists is to escape into the empty rhetoric of "holism." But what does one *do* with an assessment of the "whole person?" Without guidelines for systematic decisions based on reliable individual differences, it's anybody's guess. Individuating information is sorely lacking because it can *only* be obtained through well-controlled scientific experimentation.

The truth is that there is no evidential support for the holistic prescriptions of pseudosciences. But think about what a wonderful cover-up for ignorance the "what works is different for everybody" ruse can be. It allows practitioners to diagnose and treat health conditions in any manner that they like, and any inconsistencies or failures can be chalked up to enigmatic and unspecified individual differences. When your own health is on the line, however, it seems well advised to stick with a practitioner who can justify his or her treatment plans with research evidence and offer you a prognosis based on data, not a combination of anecdotes and wishful thinking.

The "Probability Is Irrelevant to the Unique Individual" Fallacy

Another variant on the alleged need to personalize treatments involves the claim that because scientists study groups of patients, scientific results have no bearing on the individual case. Although the premise is true—scientists do study groups—the conclusion is false: Scientific results are *crucial* for understanding the individual case. In fact, the only way to uncover general principles that afford sound predictions for new individuals is to search through data collected from large groups for patterns, trends, or other regularities. The only way to offer rational advice is to generalize from previous knowledge. If there are no general principles, then nobody—scientist or pseudoscientist—could offer advice that would predict the future better than chance.

The conclusion that the patterns discovered in research are irrelevant to unique individuals is absurd. How else could we learn? Is each new case to be an exception to the rules? (If so, how did the rules emerge in the first place?) Is it necessary to consider additional variables? If so, which ones? More to the point, how can you *know* that other variables are important if they have not been studied? Rather than relying on guesswork, experiments must be conducted to determine whether additional variables are in fact important.

Despite this logic (and the fact that denying it only serves to introduce additional difficulties), many people seem to feel that probability is irrelevant. "It makes no sense," the argument goes, "to apply probabilities to the single case. The patient before me is a unique individual." However, a simple thought experiment may convince you that probabilities are quite relevant to each and every single case.

Imagine that you are going to play Russian roulette once, and you are offered your choice of either of two revolvers to use. The first contains one bullet in its cylinder; the second contains four bullets. You will choose one gun, put it to your head, and pull the trigger once. This is a unique event, a single case that will never be repeated—you will either live or die. *If you truly believe that probability is irrelevant to the single case, you should not care which gun is chosen.* I have yet to meet anyone so cavalier! The *only* rational way to select a gun is to consider the probability of dying and choose a one-sixth chance as less risky than a four-sixths chance. That everybody chooses the gun with just one bullet shows that, deep down, we all clearly recognize that probability is of the utmost importance in making a smart decision about each and every "single case" that comes before us. When scientific research evidence—which is inherently probabilistic—is available to guide decision making, ignoring it would violate the most fundamental principles of medical ethics. Throwing up one's hands and saying that "probability is irrelevant to the unique individual" introduces chaos. Clearly, we all know better when our own life is on the line.

THE REJECTION OF SCIENCE AS A PSEUDOSCIENTIST'S DREAM

Postmodernism and the reasoning fallacies described earlier, in addition to many variations on these themes, constitute attacks on scientific reasoning. Think for a moment about who stands to gain from the rejection of science as the best available tool that we have for evaluating the accuracy of knowledge. Science consists of well-established procedures for sorting cold facts from warm, fuzzy fictions and is therefore potentially dangerous to cherished beliefs. Is it any wonder, then, that so many proponents of pseudoscience summarily reject the methods and results of science? Science poses a threatening obstacle to those who wish to make unsupported claims, who wish to find a profitable niche while believing whatever they choose and behaving in whatever manner they like.

How easy it is to sit back and form beliefs based on nothing more than wishful thinking, unconstrained by any burden of proof or accountability. Robyn Dawes (1994) uses the term *argument from a vacuum* to refer to beliefs that are served up without any evidential support. At their core, all pseudosciences are arguments from a vacuum. In contrast to the freewheeling abandon of such arguments, science constrains and focuses our thinking by imposing the limits of known reality. But some people find it bothersome to be limited in this way. They would like to operate completely free of the bounds of reality, and denying the legitimacy of science allows them to do this. The September/October 1998 National Council Against Health Fraud newsletter, for example, reported a disturbing case of a chiropractor who was deeply troubled by the notion that his published health claims should be required to meet any standards of evidence at all:

> In January 1995, the Federal Trade Commission ordered Todd Koren, DC, president of Koren Publications, Inc., to substantiate numerous claims made in Koren's chiropractic brochures. Included were the claims that chiro[practic] care: is more effective than Ritalin; can increase IQ; confers increased resistance to common childhood diseases (measles, mumps, chicken pox); is more effective for symptoms common in neurological dysfunctions syndrome; provides relief for gynecological problems, and more. Koren's attorneys negotiated a less aggressive set of claims which were also rejected by the FTC in 1997. Koren is crying "foul" because the FTC requires scientific evidence to back up medical claims. . . . Koren is trying to raise $500,000 immediately from other chiros to pay his attorneys $400 an hour to fight for his right to make claims of health benefit without having to meet established standards of veracity. Koren doesn't grasp the fact that the scientific method is not the property of the medical establishment. Chiropractors are free to be as scientific as they wish.

What would you think if you learned that your doctor was actively fighting *against* the need for standards of evidence, instead defending the right to make any health claim at all? This problem goes far beyond Todd Koren, beyond all of chiropractic. It is symptomatic of the freewheeling abandonment of rationality that is commonplace among the pseudosciences.

Your safest defense against unfounded claims is to learn some of the rudiments of scientific reasoning. You cannot always count on others to look out for your best interests and must therefore protect yourself. The criteria of "FiLCHeRS" (falsifiability, logic, comprehensiveness, honesty, replicability, and sufficiency) constitute one valuable set of scientific reasoning skills that you can profitably adopt into your own everyday thinking with a little practice. Only by applying the highest standards of evidence can you form and retain the most accurate beliefs. If you have lax standards, you will be mistaken—and taken advantage of—more often.

 ## InfoTrac College Edition

To learn more about topics included in this chapter, enter the following search terms:

daycare and psychology
extrasensory
falsifiability
postmodernism

PSYCHOLOGICAL TRICKS

RISK

Biased Perceptions and the Media Paradox

Do you think that more people die in the United States each year from falling airplane parts or from shark attacks? From tornadoes or from lightning? From diabetes or from homicide? Who is more likely to recidivate (repeat a crime after conviction for a previous offense), sex offenders or nonsexual criminals? When we evaluate the relative degree of danger associated with different hazards, we can easily overlook two subtle biases in the sample of information that comes to mind. First, the popular media report to us, in vivid detail, a carefully selected assortment of unusual events. Second, vivid and unusual events exert a disproportionate influence on our subsequent judgments through their increased availability in our memory. These two biases operate hand-in-hand to create what I like to call the "media paradox:" The more we rely on the popular media to inform us, the more apt we are to misplace our fears.

In one widely cited study, college students ranked nuclear power as the most dangerous of 30 different activities and technologies. Experts in risk assessment, on the other hand, ranked nuclear power 20th on the same list, less hazardous than riding a bicycle (Slovic, Fischhoff, & Lichtenstein, 1979). Ross (1995) reviewed several serious misperceptions of risk and poses the critical question, "Are we then turning our backs on a raging inferno while we douse the flame of a match?" (p. 53).

VIVIDNESS

Many of us rely on the popular media (television, radio, newspapers, magazines, the internet, and so forth) for daily information to help navigate the hazards in the world around us. These sources, however, do not provide us with a

Source: Chapter 9 adapted from "Risky Business: Vividness, Availability, and the Media Paradox," by John Ruscio, 2000, *Skeptical Inquirer,* 24 (2), pp. 22–26. Copyright © 2000 Committee for the Scientific Investigation of Claims Of the Paranormal (CSICOP). Adapted with permssion.

representative sampling of events. For a variety of reasons—including fierce competition for our patronage within and across the various popular media outlets—potential news items are rigorously screened for their ability to captivate an audience. Stories featuring mundane, commonplace events don't stand a chance of making it onto the six o'clock news. The stories that do make it through this painstaking selection process are then crafted into accounts emphasizing their concrete, personal, and emotional content. Each of these aspects of a story promotes its *vividness,* which increases the likelihood that we will attend to and remember the information (Nisbett & Ross, 1980).

Both anecdotal and empirical evidence demonstrates the impact of vividness. Imagine that you are in the market for a new car, and you turn to *Consumer Reports* for advice (this example is adapted from Nisbett, Borgida, Crandall, & Reed, 1976). Several hundred consumers' experiences, plus the opinions and road tests of automotive experts, are neatly summarized, and it appears that the cost and reliability of a Honda Civic will best meet your transportation needs. Before making a purchase, however, you happen to mention your decision to a colleague, who is shocked. "A Honda! You must be joking! A friend of mine bought one and had nothing but trouble. First the fuel injection system broke, then the brakes, and finally the transmission. He had to sell it for scrap within three years!" The vividness of this warning makes it quite compelling. How many of us can honestly say that we would treat it in a rationally appropriate manner, fairly weighing the favorable evidence from several hundred consumers plus a consensus of automotive experts against the unfavorable evidence from one second hand account?

Of course, I would not expect to convince you of the significance of vividness with a single vivid example. Experimental investigations more definitively illustrate the impact of vivid information. For example, Borgida and Nisbett (1977) asked introductory psychology students to rate their interest in taking each of 10 upper-level psychology courses. To help make these ratings, all students were randomly assigned to one of three informational conditions. Those in a "base rate" condition read a statistical summary of course evaluations from "practically all the students who had enrolled in the course the previous semester." Participants in a "face-to-face" condition were exposed to a small panel of advanced students who shared their views on the 10 courses. The panelists prefaced their remarks by reporting the same average numerical evaluations that were provided in the statistical summary to "base rate" participants. Finally, participants in a control condition were given no information about the courses.

Compared to the control group, students receiving the statistical summary expressed slightly greater interest in the recommended courses. More important, students hearing the panel discussion expressed considerably greater interest in the recommended courses. The face-to-face presentation of information had a more pronounced impact on students' preferences than did the statistical summary of a far larger number of previous students' responses. Moreover, this effect was stronger among students who had recently decided to major in psychology than among students who had declared other majors. Thus, personal relevance appears to magnify the power of vividness.

The popular media capitalize on this power in many ways. Why, in a story on the effects of welfare reform on thousands of families across a state, does nine-tenths of the report consist of an interview with one affected individual? Why is the logic of "going beyond the statistics and onto the streets" to examine an issue persuasive to viewers, listeners, or readers? Producers are aware that a scientific analysis is not as emotionally compelling as one (carefully chosen) individual's personal experiences. Why does a television news reporter stand in front of a courthouse when sharing a landmark verdict reached earlier that day? Why does a weather correspondent endure frigid temperatures, sleet, and harsh wind on camera to inform us that a severe storm is in progress? Even superficial background elements appear to add a sense of realism and concreteness to a story.

AVAILABILITY

Having been exposed to a biased sample of vivid information through popular media outlets, what impact does this have on our subsequent decisions? Psychologists have discovered that our judgments of frequency and probability are heavily influenced by the ease with which we can imagine or recall instances of an event. Consider these two problems from the research literature:

1. From among a group of 10 people, are there more distinct ways to form a two-member or a five-member committee?
2. Supposing that you have randomly sampled an English word from a text, is it more likely that it begins with the letter "k" or that "k" is its third letter?

Tversky and Kahneman (1973) found that participants in their studies systematically and predictably erred on both of these problems. In the first problem, it is perhaps easier to imagine forming smaller committees, which readily differ from one another, than larger ones, which overlap substantially. In fact, there are only 45 ways to form two-member committees but 252 ways to form five-member committees. In the second problem, it is surely easier to bring to mind words that begin with "k" than words with "k" as the third letter, but extensive word-counts indicate that the latter outnumber the former by a ratio of roughly two to one. In fact, you might not have noticed that there have already been 12 words with "k" as the third letter in this chapter, but only one occurrence with "k" as the first letter—and even that could be disqualified on the grounds that it was a proper name at the top of this paragraph, "Kahneman."

What these exercises reveal is that our judgments are indeed biased by the ease with which we imagine or recall information, or its *availability*. In everyday life, what makes one event more available in memory than another? One crucial determinant is vividness. When we search through our memory to reach a judgment of frequency or probability, the most easily retrieved instances are often those that are concrete, personal, and emotional. Students in the course selection experiment, for example, were more likely to remember the views expressed by panelists than the comparatively pallid statistical summaries. Likewise, a news report will leave a more lasting impression by documenting one individual's personal experiences than by providing a scientific argument based on "mere statistics."

Because our judgment is affected by the ease with which instances of an event can be recalled (rather than by careful evaluation of all the logically possible events weighted by their actual frequency of occurrence), the simple presence of one memory and absence of another can short-circuit a fully rational evaluation. We seldom take notice of *nonoccurrences,* such as the *absence* of crime or accidents (Nisbett & Ross, 1980). Still more rare are popular media reports on the absence of events—unless, of course, this absence itself represents a dramatic change from the status quo, as when a large city witnesses a significant drop in homicide rates. Richard Bach (1973) once wrote of a young couple's fear when they embarked on their first trip on an airplane:

> In all that wind and engineblast and earth tilting and going small below us, I watched my Wisconsin lad and his girl, to see them change. Despite their laughter, they had been afraid of the airplane. Their only knowledge of flight came from newspaper headlines, a knowledge of collisions and crashes and fatalities. They had never read a single report of a little airplane taking off, flying through the air and landing again safely. They could only believe that this must be possible, in spite of all the newspapers, and on that belief they staked their three dollars and their lives. (p. 37)

THE MEDIA PARADOX

Bach's passage on a couple's fear of flying highlights the joint operation of vividness and availability on our judgment, which ultimately results in the media paradox. We have likely all heard or read that, per mile traveled, flying is much safer than driving. Despite this fact, media coverage of air travel catastrophes may actually steer us in the wrong direction: onto the more hazardous roadways. Indeed, a classic series of studies on the judged frequency of lethal events underscores the powerful impact of media coverage on our perceptions of risk. College students and members of the League of Women Voters were asked to estimate the frequency with which 41 causes of death occurred each year in the United States (Lichtenstein, Slovic, Fischhoff, Layman, & Combs, 1978). Two systematic biases were uncovered in analyses of these judgments. First, frequencies of the least common causes of death were overestimated, whereas frequencies of the most common causes of death were underestimated. In many cases, the judgments were off by more than a factor of 10. Second, relative to the best-fitting curve that captured the overall relationship between judged and actual frequencies across all 41 causes of death, those that were overestimated tended to be the ones that received more extensive media coverage. For example, motor vehicle accidents and homicide were overestimated relative to the best-fitting curve, whereas smallpox vaccination and diabetes were underestimated.

Following up on this evidence suggesting a connection between risk perception and the media, Combs and Slovic (1979) closely scrutinized the actual reporting of deaths in their regional newspapers (the Eugene, Oregon, *Register Guard* and the New Bedford, Massachusetts, *Standard Times*). During alternate months for one year, they counted the number of articles about, the number of occurrences of, and the number of reported deaths resulting from each of the 41 causes of death. The two newspapers were almost perfectly consistent in their coverage of deaths. This is interesting in that newspapers with vastly different readerships nonetheless still seem to find certain types of deaths more "newsworthy" than others. This was not simply a result of each newspaper reporting deaths in accordance with the actual frequencies of occurrence. For example, homicides were reported three times as often as deaths by disease although diseases killed about 100 times as many people. More important, there was an impressive correspondence between participants' judgments and the frequencies with which newspapers reported deaths. (The high correlation was not due to a common link between both judged and reported frequencies with actual frequencies of death. In fact, when actual frequency was statistically held constant, the correlations were even higher for both papers.)

Tempting as it may be, however, we must be careful not to conclude on the basis of this correlational evidence alone that the media are responsible for distorting our perceptions of risk. It may be just the opposite: Perhaps media professionals are simply responsive to our existing fears and interests, reporting what they perceive to be newsworthy to us. It may be that a "third variable"—such as the relative degree of controllability or the catastrophic nature of different causes of death—causes both our fears and media coverage. A case can be made for each of these explanations of the observed link between media coverage and beliefs, as well as others. The broad array of factors that are involved are no doubt complexly intertwined.

Fortunately, however, we are in a position to evaluate these relationships armed with more than correlational evidence. Evidence from controlled experimentation shows a causal influence of vivid information on our judgments. Thus, despite competing influences, vividness does play a causal role in our judgment process. Moreover, the causal influence of availability on our judgments suggests that it is the mechanism by which vividness has its effect. This knowledge makes it particularly challenging to deny that the media exert some measure of causal influence on our fears. Debating the strength of this effect or whether it operates in a reciprocal fashion is certainly worthwhile, but it does not allow us to escape from the conclusion that any systematic departure from reality in the media is likely to be mirrored in our beliefs.

FALLING AIRPLANE PARTS REVISITED

Aside from a close miss by what was reported to be a falling airplane part early in the movie *The Truman Show,* I cannot recall ever having heard of such an incident, fictitious or real. Students over the years have told me that they recall stories of people having *found* fallen airplane parts, but not of an actual fatality related to them. Shark attacks, on the other hand, are easily imagined and widely reported. Moreover, in the first movie that comes to my mind, Steven Spielberg's shark actually did cause several fatalities. It may come as some surprise, then, to learn that in an average year in the United States 30 times more people are killed by falling airplane parts than by shark attacks ("Death Odds," 1990).

By this point, it has probably become evident how the questions at the beginning of this chapter were constructed. Within each pair of causes of death, one tends to be reported more frequently than the other in the popular media. Plous (1993) cites correct answers to the first three problems as falling airplane parts (not shark attacks), lightning (not tornadoes), and diabetes (not homicide). And despite the highly publicized and detailed media coverage of sex offenders who molest children or commit rapes just days after release from prison, sex offenders are on the whole actually *less* likely to recidivate than are nonsexual criminals (Beck & Shipley, 1989).

Simply put, then, the media paradox operates as follows: Events must be somewhat unusual to be considered newsworthy, but their very appearance in the news leads us to overestimate their frequency of occurrence. We may therefore come to believe that relatively rare events are common, taking precautionary measures against unlikely dangers at the neglect of more significant hazards. At any given time, we are bombarded with warnings about particular hazards that often turn out to be far less significant threats to our well-being than initially advertised. For example, Gilovich (1991) discussed widespread media reports on the chances of contracting HIV through heterosexual sex. He quotes Oprah Winfrey as having said that "research studies now project that one in five heterosexuals could be dead from AIDS at the end of the next three years. That's by 1990. One in five. It is no longer just a gay disease. Believe me." This estimate has obviously turned out to be a gross exaggeration. Although the transmission of HIV through heterosexual sex is a serious public health issue, it is nonetheless important to keep the degree of danger in perspective.

A Radical Conjecture

To respond to Ross's (1995) question, it appears that we may sometimes douse a match while ignoring a raging inferno. I would like to suggest something more radical still. I propose that a mindful review of cautionary advisories may paradoxically alert us to pockets of relative safety. That is, some media reports intended to shield us from danger may, upon careful reflection, actually signal precisely the opposite.

Once, when I lived in a suburb of Boston, a local fast-food franchise was temporarily closed for violations of the health code. To put it gently, the illnesses of several patrons had been traced back to unfortunate encounters with food at the salad bar. The local media quite naturally ran stories about this. When the time came for the restaurant to re-open, at least one local newspaper printed a follow-up story to remind local residents of the danger. I would conjecture that, of all the places one could grab a quick bite to eat, this particular restaurant was now among the *safest*, at least in the short run. The restaurant's management surely must have realized that the occurrence of a second problem so soon after the last would have spelled disaster. The knowledge that everyone—patrons and health inspectors alike—would be keeping a close watch on food quality at this establishment would surely have heightened attentiveness to health issues.

If the example of a fast-food restaurant strikes you as trivial, consider a decision with more profound, long-range consequences. On March 28, 1979, an accident occurred at the Three Mile Island (TMI) nuclear power plant in Middletown, Pennsylvania. As we approached the 20th anniversary of this event, there was considerable publicity in south-central Pennsylvania, publicity which no doubt awakened memories and rekindled old fears. Around this time, a candidate for a faculty position at the college where I work declined a job offer because the candidate's spouse refused to live so close to TMI. However, not only do experts in risk assessment consider nuclear power to be quite safe, but I would contend that of all the nuclear power plants in the world, TMI is likely to be among the very safest. Nobody in this region would tolerate another accident, and the operators of TMI have been forced to take extraordinary precautions for the past two decades. They will surely continue to do so, compelled as they are by their own widely publicized track record.

Media professionals have a penchant for dramatizing case studies of mishap, be they accidental or malicious. When an incident is brought to the public's attention, it is possible to overlook the fact that the alleged perpetrators are themselves sensitized to the issue, and are thus likely to be exercising renewed vigilance. Therefore, not only should we be extremely careful about accepting media warnings at face value, but an even more robust skepticism may point to a sensible course of action 180 degrees at odds with the directions mapped out in a vivid story.

MINDFUL ATTENTION TO MEDIA REPORTS

> A bright and curious person who relies entirely on popular culture to be informed . . . is hundreds or thousands of times more likely to come upon a fable treated uncritically than a sober and balanced assessment. (Sagan, 1995, p. 5)

A healthy dose of skepticism is one obvious way to navigate the infotainment media maze. We can routinely ask ourselves simple questions, such as, "Why did the producers choose to air *this* story?" or "How *common* is the problem or practice being described?" In general, asking yourself as many questions as you can may reveal the weaknesses, gaps, or contradictions in the information.

Gilovich (1991) outlines several other strategies for protecting ourselves from misplaced fears. First, consider the source of the information. How reputable is it? Is the information based on scientific research evidence? Is there any obvious motive to take advantage of you, such as the connection between a story and advertising revenue? Second, distrust projections. History is replete with erroneous predictions. Alarmists often stand to profit from scaring you into making foolish purchases, as some of the shameless fear-mongering surrounding the Y2K computer bug clearly showed. Third, as has been said before, be wary of testimonials and case studies. An endless parade of devout believers in each new pseudoscientific fad will earnestly swear to its wondrous benefits. Keep in mind the many, many ways in which even honest, well-intentioned people can be dead wrong about a worthless or even harmful treatment.

Another example demonstrates some of the principles suggested above. By the early 1980s, a search of the world's psychiatric literature revealed only about 200 documented cases of multiple personality disorder (Bliss, 1980). Just a few years later, Coons (1986) estimated that 6,000 cases had been diagnosed in North America alone. In the early 1990s, Ross (1991) speculated that 5 to 10 percent of all adults suffers from MPD, or approximately 100 million people worldwide! How can we account for such explosive, exponential growth in the prevalence of this disorder? It seems to trace back to the books and movies such as *Sybil* and *The Three Faces of Eve*, both of which served to bring widespread attention to MPD. Despite the fact that these cases were dramatized due to their atypicality and uniqueness, many people "learned" about MPD and its purported causes through these stories. The popularity of these dramatized accounts of unusual cases illustrates both the media's eagerness to publicize vivid testimonials and the skewed perceptions, bizarre beliefs, and questionable practices that can result from uncritical acceptance of dubious claims.

I would like to close this chapter with a story that circulated via e-mail recently:

> A student at Eagle Rock Junior High won first prize at the Greater Idaho Falls Science Fair, April 26. He was attempting to show how conditioned we have become to alarmists practicing junk science and spreading fear of everything in our environment. In his project he urged people to sign a petition demanding strict control or total elimination of the chemical "dihydrogen monoxide." And for plenty of good reasons, since:
>
> 1. It can cause excessive sweating and vomiting
> 2. It is a major component in acid rain
> 3. It can cause severe burns in its gaseous state
> 4. Accidental inhalation can kill you
> 5. It contributes to erosion
> 6. It decreases effectiveness of automobile brakes
> 7. It has been found in tumors of terminal cancer patients
>
> He asked 50 people if they supported a ban of the chemical. Forty-three (43) said yes, six (6) were undecided, and only one (1) knew that the chemical was water. The title of his prize-winning project was, "How Gullible Are We?" He feels the conclusion is obvious.

InfoTrac College Edition

To learn more about topics included in this chapter, enter the following search terms:

availability heuristic
risk perception
vividness

BELIEF

Confirmation Bias, Post-Hockery, and Overconfidence

Suppose that you complete a psychological test that generates a personality profile specifically for you, and it reads like this:

> You have a strong need for other people to like you and for them to admire you. At times you are extroverted, affable, and sociable, while at other times you are introverted, wary, and reserved. You have a great deal of unused energy which you have not turned to your advantage. While you have some personality weaknesses, you are generally able to compensate for them. You prefer a certain amount of change and variety and become dissatisfied when hemmed in by restrictions and limitations. You pride yourself on being an independent thinker and do not accept other opinions without satisfactory proof. You have a tendency to be critical of yourself. Some of your aspirations tend to be pretty unrealistic.

How well does this describe you as a unique individual? You may find it useful to re-read this description, considering ways in which each statement accurately captures some aspect of your personality. So, how accurate is your profile? In research studies using this very description, most people say that it is very accurate (McKelvie, 1990).

But how can this be? Everybody's personality differs, so the very *same* profile cannot describe everyone as a *unique* individual! Forer (1949) wrote this profile to be purposefully generic, applicable to everyone, yet most people will readily accept it as a good description of their own unique personality. Moreover, people judge fake descriptions such as this to be more accurate than the results of valid psychological tests (Dickson & Kelly, 1985; Standing & Keays, 1986). Perhaps even more disturbing, many psychologists (and their clients) come to believe in the diagnostic utility of responses to a series of inkblots (e.g., the Rorschach Inkblot Test). How can tests of dubious validity, and even completely generic character sketches, be so compelling?

Source: Chapter 10 adapted from "Perils of Post-Hockery," by John Ruscio, 1998, *Skeptical Inquirer,* 22 (6), pp. 44–48. Copyright © 1998 Committee for the Scientific Investigation of Claims Of the Paranormal (CSICOP). Adapted with permission.

Individuals may cling tenaciously to their beliefs despite the scientific and logical evidence that refutes them. Unfortunately, it is relatively simple for anyone with an active imagination, access to a steady supply of ambiguous data, and a willing suspension of critical thinking to "discover" and "validate" relationships between variables, even when no such relationships exist (Gergen, Hepburn, & Fisher, 1986). The key is to focus on post hoc ("after the fact") interpretations of alleged phenomena, with only selective consideration of existing evidence. This type of thinking can be called "post-hockery."

DISCOVERY VERSUS VERIFICATION: THE IMPORTANCE OF PREDICTION

Post-hockery takes advantage of several interrelated strengths and shortcomings of human judgment. For example, we often blur the crucial distinction between the generation and testing of hypotheses. In the *context of discovery*, our outstanding pattern-recognition and reasoning abilities are indispensable. We can detect potentially relevant information and formulate sophisticated hypotheses about underlying causal relationships. However, unaided judgment can fail us in the *context of verification*. We do not routinely subject our cherished beliefs to rigorous tests, and we often accept the first proffered explanation as fact. Particularly if this explanation is interesting or entertaining, our confidence may become unshakable.

One of the surest signs of post-hockery is the inability of its practitioners to predict future events. Although successful prediction does not necessarily imply deep understanding, the reverse is true. An individual who truly understands the relationship between events can use this knowledge to make valid predictions, whereas the post hoc reasoner can only "explain" past events. Two examples illustrate the importance of prediction in testing claims to knowledge.

The Bible Code

In 1997, Michael Drosnin published a controversial book entitled *The Bible Code* in which he claimed to have discovered God's hidden messages in the Bible. The messages were hidden in the sense that they did not appear as consecutive letters in the text. But how did Drosnin know that the messages were there? He had a computer program perform endless types and numbers of text searches. For example, he found that if you start on one particular "N" in the text, and then count forward every 4,772 letters, the next three letters would be "A," "Z," and "I." There you have it: "NAZI" is spelled out in hidden code in the Bible! To his credit, Drosnin found more than just this. He also found that if, for example, you make a grid out of every 4,772nd letter in the Bible, you will find not just "NAZI," but—running perpendicular, and sharing the "I"—you find the word "HITLER." Drosnin displayed many such word pairings, including "ROSWELL" and "UFO." This, Drosnin claimed, would be highly unlikely to occur merely by chance, and therefore must be a hidden message from God. As further support, he argued that these hidden "messages" occur *only* in the Bible, not in other texts.

This alleged discovery is an example of post-hockery. As David Thomas (1997, 1998) has elegantly demonstrated, the reported probabilities of finding these messages were computed inappropriately. Drosnin ignored the fact that his computer program searched the Bible in a virtually infinite number of ways. Indeed, if you look in enough places, coincidence guarantees that you are bound to find something. Drosnin computed the probability of getting the particular matches that he found as though these were the only searches that he performed, ignoring the far more numerous searches that failed to find patterns. The problem with this is that *any* event, after it occurs, can be viewed as remarkably improbable. For example, in his "Who's Counting?" column for July 2000, mathematician John Allen Paulos noted that "any particular bridge hand has a probability of one in 600 billion of being dealt. It won't do, however, to look at the 13 cards dealt to one and proclaim them to be a miracle." If you look in a fantastic number of places, and count anything that you stumble upon as evidence supporting your hunches, you are guaranteed to discover "meaning" where none exists.

With regard to Drosnin's second claim, it turns out that the same hidden "messages" of the Bible Code *can* be found with statistically predictable regularity in a wide array of texts, including the transcript of the Scopes "monkey trial!" (This 1925 courtroom battle waged over teaching evolution in public schools does indeed seem an unlikely venue for God's hidden messages.) In fact, by taking into account the frequency with which different letters tend to appear in writing, Thomas has shown that one can anticipate with reasonable accuracy how often words or phrases will be found using Drosnin's search methods in any text, including religious, literary, and secular writing. Thus, the "hidden messages" uncovered by Drosnin in *The Bible Code* are not at all restricted to the Bible; rather, they are coincidental and ubiquitous. For example, I would hypothesize that if you remove section codes and numbers, Drosnin's search program would find God's "hidden messages"—or any other messages that one might select in advance—with predictable frequency in the United States tax code.

A more subtle problem with *The Bible Code* is of special relevance here. Drosnin has claimed that important messages are revealed through the juxtaposition of words such as Hitler and Nazi, Roswell and UFO. Here is a challenge to those who believe: *predict something.* Promoters of the Bible Code tell us that it can reveal the future, so by all means reveal it to us! Unfortunately, Drosnin's procedure can only be run by *first* choosing a word or phrase and *then* searching for it. Thus, it is impossible in principle to predict anything that has not already occurred. The fact that "meaning" can be found only *after* events have transpired reveals a message of predictive failure that is certainly not hidden.

The "Hot Hand" in Basketball

A second example of post-hockery is the widespread belief in the streak shooting of basketball players. You would be hard-pressed to watch an entire televised game without at least once being told that so-and-so has the "hot hand." There are two distinct ways to understand this remark. It might simply indicate that a player has made a series of shots. Nobody would take exception with this descriptive use of the term. Those involved in the game, however, agree that this is *not* the intended meaning.

The term "hot hand" is used and understood in a *predictive* sense: The player with the "hot hand" is engaged in streak shooting that is expected to continue. Ninety-one percent of fans, coaches, and players reported that a player has "a better chance of making a shot after having just made his last two or three shots than he does after having just missed his last two or three shots." Eighty-four percent reported that "it is important to pass the ball to someone who has just made several (two, three, or four) shots in a row" (Gilovich, Vallone, & Tversky, 1985). These statements clearly imply two testable propositions: (1) long streaks of hits (or misses) frequently occur and (2) "success breeds success." To test these hypotheses, Gilovich, Vallone, and Tversky (1985) analyzed the shot-by-shot floor shooting records of an entire season of the Philadelphia 76ers and the free-throw shots of the Boston Celtics, along with additional experimental research on the "hot hand" phenomenon. The results were clear and consistent:

1. *Are there more or longer streaks than would be expected by chance?* No. In analyses counting the number of streaks of various lengths, it was found that the observed number coincided very closely to what is expected purely by chance.
2. *Are players more likely to make shots after having made previous shots than after having missed previous shots?* No. Gilovich et al. (1985) counted the relative frequencies of making shots after having made or missed the previous one, two, or three shots. The shooting percentages after three misses (56%), two misses (53%), one miss (54%), one hit (51%), two hits (50%), and three hits (46%) reveal a trend that directly contradicts the hypothesis. Players were slightly more likely to make a shot after having missed previous shots than after having made previous shots.
3. *Does the outcome of a given shot relate positively to the outcome of the previous shot?* No. Consistent with the trend noted above, there was a small negative correlation across shots (−.04).

4. *Do players have unexpectedly varying "hot" and "cold" games?* No. Analyses found that day-to-day performance variations coincided well with statistically expected fluctuations.

Because changes in defensive strategy may have worked against the "hot hand" hypothesis—due to heavy coverage of those who make shots and lax coverage of those who miss shots—the researchers also looked at situations in which defense was not a factor. For example:

5. *Are players more likely to make a second free-throw after having made the first than after having missed the first?* No. The relative frequencies are virtually identical.

Finally, the researchers examined the role of confidence in performance.

6. *Can players at least sense when they themselves have the "hot hand?"* No. Cornell University varsity and junior-varsity players made shot-by-shot wagers (indicating confidence) as they took shots around an arc equidistant from the basket. As expected, players appeared to hold the "hot hand" belief: Their wagers were higher following hits and lower following misses. However, these wagers were totally unrelated to the outcomes of shots. Thus, players' perceptions of being "hot" or "cold," as measured by their own wagers, predicted nothing.

In addition to this evidence amassed by Gilovich et al. (1985), Adams (1992) conducted a test of the "time dependent" hypothesis: that success follows success more closely in time than it follows failure (a belief that coaches act on by calling time-outs to "break the momentum" of the other team).

7. *Is there a "momentum" effect such that success follows success more closely in time than it follows failure?* No. The time interval between two successive hits did not differ from the time interval from a hit to a miss. It made no difference whether this comparison was made across all 83 players in the study or within individual players.

Thus, unfortunately for its adherents, the "hot hand" label appears to hold no predictive value. The seven lines of evidence presented above show that the "hot hand" marks past success but does not predict future performance, and nobody has presented any evidence to the contrary. This by no means implies that the outcomes of shots are determined by chance. In fact, a wide range of factors contributes to success, such as a player's baseline skill level, the difficulty of the attempted shot, the strength of the defense, and so forth. What the research *does* indicate is simple: If you had a complete list of the factors that determine the outcome of an attempted shot, the success of previous shots would not appear on it. Despite the unshakable belief of players, fans, and coaches, the "hot hand" is an illusion.

How can so many people come to believe so strongly in a shared illusion? We are quite adept at recognizing patterns, so much so that we sometimes falsely impose order on what is truly chaos. It seems to us that there is something noteworthy about a player who has made several successive shots. Fans, coaches, and players alike feel compelled to create a causal explanation for this rather than to accept the mundane statistical fact that streaks occur by chance far more often than we imagine. The selective interpretation of ambiguous events can also buttress this belief. For example, if a "hot" player's shot rolls around the rim but falls outside, this may be perceived as a "near hit," whereas the same shot made by a "cold" player may be perceived as yet another miss. This analysis suggests that observers may be biased toward perceiving streaks not only in the performance of basketball players, but in the performance of athletes in any other sport as well.

Although the "hot hand" seems to make life more interesting, taking this scientifically discredited notion seriously can lead to foolish strategy (e.g., altering the defense to cover players on illusory streaks or wasting time-outs to "break momentum" that does not exist). In any sport, players or coaches who instead form their beliefs, and base their strategy, on factors with evidence of predictive success should be able to improve their game, especially relative to those who subscribe to illusions.

These examples show how easy it can be to "discover" illusory relationships. If the distinction between the contexts of discovery and verification was clear, we would not get into trouble. However, research on human judgment has shown how feebly we subject our beliefs to tests, if indeed we test them at all. Instead, we tend to seek weak, experiential support for our hypotheses in lieu of a more balanced pursuit of persuasive evidence. Moreover, many of our mental shortcuts contribute a false sense of validity to our beliefs.

CONFIRMATION BIAS

Our selective search for information that confirms (rather than refutes) our views shields us from relinquishing our cherished beliefs. Given an ample supply of ambiguous information, we can almost always ferret out some support for our views. For example, consider the question posed at the beginning of this chapter: How can most people believe that a generic character sketch is a custom-tailored description of his or her personality? The trick is to use descriptions so vague that they apply to almost anyone. Forer's (1949) character sketch, which opened this chapter, illustrates the technique marvelously. The description does capture almost everyone's personality well, which is actually its greatest weakness: It is generic, not personalized. We can each find some anecdotal evidence to support the statements if we dig deep enough into our memories. What we overlook is the likelihood that the sketch characterizes any randomly selected person. This likelihood is quite high. In this way, rational thought is overwhelmed by the bias toward confirmation.

The Rorschach Ink Blot Test

Employing a double standard of evidence is another common method by which evidence is biased toward confirming our beliefs. We assign great weight to evidence that favors our beliefs and ignore or discredit threatening evidence. The history of Rorschach test interpretation and the evidence that bears upon its validity exposes the danger of the confirmation bias.

The Rorschach is a "projective test" that is claimed to reveal your personality through your responses to ambiguous stimuli: a set of ink blots. There are many competing views about the appropriate way to administer, score, and interpret the Rorschach, which itself seems highly problematic. This lack of consensus indicates that your personality will be conceptualized quite differently depending on who happens to interpret your responses. If "experts" cannot agree among themselves about the meaning of responses, how can these systems be valid? In fact, there is no evidence that the Rorschach has ever provided valuable clues to personality, especially when considered in terms of *incremental validity* (the contribution of new information beyond cheaper, quicker, well-validated measures) or *clinical utility* (usefulness, by any reasonable definition, to the practicing clinician; Hunsley & Bailey, 1999). The Rorschach has received highly critical reviews for decades in the premier resource on psychological tests, the *Mental Measurements Yearbook*. For example, Arthur Jensen wrote the following in the 1965 edition:

> Many psychologists who have looked into the matter are agreed that the 40 years of massive effort which have been lavished on the Rorschach technique have proved unfruitful, at least so far as the development of a useful psychological test is concerned. . . . The rate of scientific progress in clinical psychology might well be measured by the speed and thoroughness with which it gets over the Rorschach. (p. 509)

How well is clinical psychology doing at "getting over" the Rorschach? Here we are, almost *another* 40 years later, and the Rorschach remains one of the most popular psychologist tests. Do practicing psychologists recognize the weak, experiential support for their reliance on the Rorschach? No. Those who routinely employ the Rorschach justify this practice on the basis of extensive *personal* experience (Dawes 1994). Such personal experience is accepted by these individuals while the experience of others, as well as scientific evidence against the validity of the test, is grossly underweighted. Chapman and Chapman (1982) quote the pseudoscientific attitude of some practicing therapists: " 'I'll trust my own senses before I trust some journal article,' said one clinical psychologist. 'I know that paranoids don't seem to draw big eyes in the research labs,' said another, 'but they sure do in my office' " (p. 240). These clinicians are clearly falling prey to the confirmation bias, seeing what they expect to see and discounting discrepant information.

Gilovich and Savitsky (1996) describe the role of confirmation bias in Rorschach interpretation through representative thinking: "like goes with like." For example, seeing eyes is associated with suspicion or paranoia, seeing a large head is associated with insecurity about one's intelligence, seeing monsters or nonhuman figures is associated with homosexuality, and so forth. These are the sorts of superficial, preconceived notions that can strongly bias clinicians' interpretations (Chapman & Chapman, 1967). Thus, the Rorschach ink blot test is a pseudoscientific method of assessment that draws its apparent success from a confirmation bias.

Graphology: Handwriting Analysis

Many employers, particularly in European nations and in Israel, pay graphologists to interpret handwriting samples when making personnel selection decisions (Schmidt & Hunter, 1998). But is there scientific support for graphology? Not really. As with responses to the Rorschach ink blot test, samples of handwriting provide a rich array of ambiguous information from which professionals can pick and choose as they mold their interpretations. Thus, the potential for confirmation bias is high. The scientific evidence on graphology clearly indicates that professionals' judgments are heavily influenced by the confirmation bias.

First, experts are no better at inferring personality from samples of handwriting than are laypersons. Thus, highly paid consultants are unnecessary for this task (Bar-Hillel & Ben-Shakhar, 1986). Second, whereas the *content* of writing (weakly) reveals some personality traits, the *form* of writing reveals nothing. Graphologists can make moderately accurate personality ratings when they allow people to write freely on topics of their own choosing, but they cannot predict anything at all when people copy a standard passage in their own handwriting. Thus, the form and characteristics of your writing reveal nothing about your personality (Neter & Ben-Shakhar, 1989). Any apparent success of graphologists stems from their educated guesses about your personality based on *what* you write. Seeking confirmation, graphologists note aspects of the form and characteristics of your writing that are consistent with their interpretation and ignore aspects that are inconsistent. Thus, graphologists' confidence in their ability to learn from the form and characteristics of handwriting grows for same reason that clinicians become faithful believers in the magic of the Rorschach: confirmation bias.

Polygraphy: The "Lie Detector" Test

As a final example of confirmation bias, let's examine polygraphy, or the use of so-called lie detector tests. It is incredibly difficult to determine when someone is lying, and there is no infallible method for making this determination.

Polygraphy strikes many people as the most "scientific" procedure available, but there is actually much more human judgment involved in this method—and thus more room for bias—than is widely understood. In the "control question technique" (CQT), the most common implementation of polygraphy, a machine continually records an examinee's physiological processes (such as heart rate or skin conductance) as he or she answers a series of questions. The examiner poses a mixture of two key types of questions: "target" questions, such as, "Did you steal from your employer?" and "control" questions, such as, "What is your date of birth?" If the physiological readout for target questions is elevated above that for control questions, the examiner concludes that the examinee was being dishonest.

There are several shortcomings to polygraphy that sharply limit its validity. For example, "control" questions do not truly control for the fact that even honest examinees may feel nervous or threatened when asked target questions by an examiner, therefore displaying an increase in physiological arousal. A more appropriate comparison would be to use control questions that involve fabricated accusations. If target questions about the act under investigation provoke greater arousal than control questions about acts known not to have occurred, dishonesty may be more reliably indicated. Another problem with polygraphy is that dishonest examinees may learn to suppress their physiological responses through a variety of tricks. Therefore, the physiological rationale for the test is not as sound as it may appear, and its accuracy is imperfect. Research suggests that polygraphy can correctly detect dishonesty with 76% accuracy and honesty with 63% accuracy (Phillips, 1999). In Chapter 13, we will see that in practice, accuracy rates can be much lower when the polygraph is used to screen many people, few of whom are dishonest.

More important for our present purposes, there are also psychological limitations to polygraphy. Ben-Shakhar (1991) has presented a four-factor model focused on the role of confirmation bias in polygraph examinations. First, polygraphs provide a great deal of complex information to the examiner. Typically, about three physiological measures are recorded during at least three test sequences of 10 or more questions. Combining all of this information is a daunting task. Second, results are contaminated with other sources of information. Whoever has hired the examiners will provide information, even incriminating information or suspicions, and they may interview an examinee extensively before beginning the polygraph session. Third, the examiner begins with a hypothesis about the examinee's honesty. This hypothesis is derived from some combination of polygraph results and contaminating information. Fourth, polygraph results are used to test the hypothesis, but this testing is heavily influenced by the confirmation bias. When examining the physiological readout, an examiner will be likely to selectively seek supportive evidence, disregard conflicting evidence, and combine the complex information in such a way that it confirms the initial hypothesis. Thus, polygraph results do not necessarily inform the final decision, but provide seemingly objective data from which supportive scraps can be tied together to justify an initial hunch. An intriguing investigation broadcast on *60 Minutes* in 1986 corroborates this model:

> Three different polygraph firms were independently called to test an alleged theft of a camera and lens from a photography magazine office employing four employees. In fact, nothing was stolen from the office, but the polygraph examiners were told that it could only have been done by one of the four employees. Each polygraph examiner was told that "it might have been ____," with a different employee being fingered in each case (a decidedly weak fingering). In each case, the polygraph examiner identified the "fingered" employee as deceptive, and cleared the other "suspects." Moreover, all polygraph examiners expressed complete confidence in their decisions. This demonstrates not only that polygraph examiners can go wrong, but that their judgment and decision-making processes are infected by a systematic and powerful source of bias, a bias caused by contamination. (Ben-Shakhar, 1991, p. 236)

A debate regarding the utility of polygraph examinations has raged for decades. Whenever a security breach arouses the passions of government officials, they are tempted to call for expanded use of the polygraph as the solution (Brooks, 1985). In the early 1980s, President Reagan urged widespread polygraph testing for government employees. Fortunately, a review of the scientific evidence by Saxe, Dougherty, and Cross (1985) brought a rational voice to the debate, and the executive directive was dropped. More recently, government officials have been troubled by security violations at the Los Alamos National Laboratory. Robert Park wrote the following "What's New" piece in the electronic newsletter of the American Physical Society (June 30, 2000):

> LOS ALAMOS: CONGRESS BELIEVES IN THE POLYGRAPH. Whatever the security problem is, Congress seems convinced that the polygraph will cure it. Tuesday night, the House Armed Services Committee approved the Nuclear Secrets Safety Act, which would require polygraph exams "for individuals who have access to any vault containing Restricted Data." A number of senior scientists at Los Alamos insist they will take early retirement rather than submit to a procedure they regard as pseudoscientific garbage. Meanwhile, the Lab is having trouble trying to recruit new staff.

The *60 Minutes* study shows that seemingly innocuous suggestions can exert a dramatic influence on the conduct and interpretation of a polygraph examination. Those in charge of federal policy seem all too eager to ignore the significant limitations of this technique, subjecting government employees and scientists to interviews in which an examiner's initial suspicions may bear more strongly on the outcome than any scientific data. Although the practical problem of lie detection is of the utmost importance, pseudoscientific methods like CQT polygraphy are plagued by the confirmation bias, and thus are not a wise solution.

ABSENT OR MISLEADING FEEDBACK

Another limitation of human judgment involves our desire for and use of corrective feedback. We need such feedback to evaluate and modify our views. However, because of both cognitive and attentional biases (e.g., confirmation bias) and the nature of environments that we seek out and set up for ourselves, we rarely receive or attend to feedback, and that which we do obtain tends to be uniformly positive. Thus, our views are rarely challenged.

Often we receive little, if any, objective feedback against which to test our beliefs. Imagine the case of a clinician who relies heavily on the Rorschach as an assessment tool to aid in reaching a psychological diagnosis. The test is administered, responses are interpreted, and a diagnosis is reached. For some practitioners, diagnostic mistakes may have no consequence for the course of treatment. For example, if therapy is conducted in a similar fashion for all patients, how can a diagnostic error ever be detected? Belief in the utility of the Rorschach thus becomes invulnerable due to a lack of corrective feedback.

Suppose, instead, that successful treatment hinges on a correct diagnosis. Will a clinician receive corrective feedback even when an incorrect diagnosis is made and an ineffective therapeutic technique used? Given the usual reasons that patients seek counseling and the dynamics of the patient-therapist relationship, it should come as no surprise that patients tend to accept and agree with their therapists' diagnoses and advice. Even incorrectly diagnosed individuals will often believe that they are receiving the best available treatment. The lack of treatment success becomes apparent so slowly and gradually that it may never arouse suspicion. Even if it does, neither the therapist nor the patient is likely to question the validity of the original diagnosis, much less the Rorschach assessment on which it was based. There are so many ready-made alternatives. "Perhaps this is an atypical case." "Perhaps therapy did not begin early enough." "Perhaps the patient is resistant to the therapist (or vice versa)." We can generate countless alternative explanations for disappointing outcomes, none of which will call into question a cherished belief. Thus, clinicians may never learn, experientially, that the Rorschach does *not* assist them in reaching valid diagnoses.

The feedback that we do obtain, as a rule, is systematically misleading. Many types of feedback are exclusively positive in nature or easily distorted to become so. How do we evaluate teaching skill? Standardized rating forms can be dismissed by a teacher as worthless and thrown on the same heap with other standardized tests. Teachers learn from experience. Which of a teacher's former students will keep in touch with him or her? Which students ask for letters of reference? If a student enrolls in another of a teacher's courses, this is clear confirmation of teaching skill (never mind that he or she teaches required courses). The student who does not do so, in the unlikely event that this is noticed, must have had other commitments that created a scheduling conflict.

We selectively expose ourselves to situations and environments containing only favorable information. We tend to associate with people who think the way we do, read books and articles that support our views and discard those that do not, join clubs and organizations to interact with others who share our interests, and so forth. With all of these defensive measures in place, where will corrective feedback come from?

HINDSIGHT BIAS AND OVERCONFIDENCE

Once we have discovered a personally meaningful relationship between events, unearthed confirmatory evidence, and received flattering feedback, 20/20 hindsight monopolizes our vision. We begin to feel that we "knew it all along" (Fischhoff, 1975), replacing speculation with certitude through a process of "creeping determinism" (Fischhoff, 1982). We come to hold undue confidence in our beliefs. Perhaps the best way to demonstrate that almost everyone is overconfident much of the time is for you to test your own confidence.

Russo and Shoemaker (1989) devised a simple test of factual knowledge to evaluate confidence. For each of 10 questions, you construct an interval such that you are 90% confident it will contain the correct answer. For example, consider the question, "How much power does the human brain require for normal operation?" If you are 90% certain that the correct answer is between 30 and 90 watts, this is your confidence interval (which, incidentally, would fail to include the correct value of 15 watts; Saravi, 1999). The key to this test is not whether you know the exact answers—although you may for some questions—but whether you can construct confidence intervals that are actually correct 90% of the time. Here, now, are the 10 questions:

1. What was Martin Luther King, Jr.'s age at death?
2. What is the length of the Nile River, in miles?
3. How many countries belong to OPEC?
4. How many books are there in the Old Testament?
5. What is the diameter of the moon, in miles?
6. What is the weight of an empty Boeing 747, in pounds?
7. In what year was Mozart born?
8. What is the gestation period of an Asian elephant, in days?
9. What is the air distance from London to Tokyo, in miles?
10. What is the deepest known point in the ocean, in feet?

The answers to these questions (as quoted in Plous, 1993) appear at the end of this chapter. If you got all 10 questions correct (within your 90% confidence intervals), you may well be *underconfident,* not to mention a member of a breathtakingly small minority! If you got exactly 9 questions correct, your confidence may be *properly calibrated* to your accuracy level; this, too, is exceedingly rare. If you got fewer than 9 questions correct, you are probably *overconfident,* like the vast majority of us. Although this quiz may seem trivial, it is just one measure of confidence. Overconfidence is in fact a pervasive problem across many types of beliefs, tasks, and situations (Alpert & Raiffa, 1982; Oskamp, 1965; Ruscio, 2000), and it is every bit as common among experts as laypersons (Dawes, 1994; Faust & Ziskin, 1988).

FOILING POST-HOCKERY

The proper balance between wonder and skepticism provides a formidable defense against post-hockery. In the context of discovery, exercise a great deal of wonder. The best-known way to minimize the judgmental shortcomings of post-hockery is to consider multiple hypotheses (Arkes, 1991). Confidence in any particular belief is appropriately reduced by the existence of several others, because stronger evidence must be sought to tease apart competing theories. Moreover, the correct hypothesis is more likely to be included in a larger pool of possibilities.

In the context of verification, exercise a great deal of skepticism. It pays to subject your beliefs to the same rigorous tests that you demand of others. Those with the toughest standards of evidence will acquire and retain the most accurate beliefs. Be open to the possibility that you are observing random fluctuations in a probabilistic distribution of outcomes. In his book *Statistics as Principled Argument,* Robert Abelson (1995) sums this up nicely by urging readers to "give chance a chance." When you find yourself proclaiming something to be meaningful and important, ask yourself whether you would accept someone else's idea on the same evidentiary basis.

Finally, when you can only see meaning by looking backward, post-hockery is strongly indicated. You do not truly understand a phenomenon until you can use it to generate testable predictions. When someone makes a claim to knowledge, ask, by way of evidence, "What can you predict?" Adding this simple habit to your repertoire of critical thinking skills will help to clearly differentiate the context of discovery from that of verification. The ability to spot post-hockery in an argument, your own or someone else's, is well worth a bit of practice.

ANSWERS TO THE CONFIDENCE QUIZ

(1) 39 years. (2) 4187 miles. (3) 13 countries. (4) 39 books. (5) 2160 miles. (6) 390,000 pounds. (7) 1756. (8) 645 days. (9) 5959 miles. (10) 36,198 feet.

⑨ INFOTRAC COLLEGE EDITION

To learn more about topics included in this chapter, enter the following search terms:

Bible Code
graphology
overconfidence
polygraph
Rorschach

SCHEMES

The Seductiveness of Grand Conspiracy Theories

In a collection of fictitious newspaper front pages entitled "Our Dumb Century," the publishers of the satirical paper *The Onion* joke about almost everything that occurred in the 20th century. The headline for their November 22, 1963, paper pokes fun at the many conspiracy theories surrounding the assassination of President Kennedy: "Kennedy Slain by CIA, Mafia, Castro, LBJ, Teamsters, Freemasons; President Shot 129 Times from 43 Different Angles." So many conspiracy theories have been proposed to explain this assassination that it now makes for an easy joke. But just how did so many theories develop? Why are conspiracy theories so popular, long-lived, and compelling? And how can we evaluate whether conspiracy theories are likely to be true?

THE THREE ROLES IN A CONSPIRACY THEORY

The first step to understanding conspiracy theories is to distinguish the cast of characters. There are three primary roles involved in any conspiracy: conspirators, saviors, and dupes.

Conspirators

The conspirators are those individuals who are allegedly perpetrating a conspiracy. This role is seldom, if ever, taken on voluntarily, but is rather imposed by others who propose the existence of the conspiracy. What makes a conspiracy "grand" in nature is its massive sweep across time and the sheer number of people said to be maintaining the conspiracy. If any one of the Kennedy assassination theories is correct, the conspirators have been successfully covering their tracks for nearly 40 years. This spans more than a half dozen presidential administrations and would therefore be a surprising testament to a heretofore unknown ability of our federal government to keep secrets.

Saviors

The saviors are those individuals who believe they have uncovered evidence of a conspiracy and want to publicly expose it. They claim to have found a crack in the façade of a massive cover-up or scandal and would like to reveal it for all to see. This role is taken on voluntarily, often enthusiastically, as saviors assert that they hold the key to saving others from the evil deeds or plans of the conspirators. A consideration of the psychological benefits of taking on the savior role goes a long way in explaining how conspiracy theories are created and why they are maintained.

The position of savior is privileged in two distinct ways. First, he or she possesses secret information. Who among us fails to enjoy having some juicy news to share? Second, the savior's unique information promises to wipe clean the conspirators' lies and deceit, replacing them with the revealed truth. Wouldn't you like to be a messenger of truth, a shatterer of corrupt lies? The savior is prepared to deliver the masses to safety by exposing the dangers inherent in the conspiracy. This, too, confers elevated status. The savior is willing to assist all who do not possess his or her keen powers of observation, access to secret information, and well-reasoned analysis of the situation. Those who fail to recognize the immediate danger of the conspiracy are deemed in need of protection, and the savior is first in line to provide this security.

Think how much meaning and purpose such a role could add to an otherwise hum-drum life, how incredibly energizing it may be to latch onto a noble cause such as fighting against a grand conspiracy. Is it any wonder, then, that some people tend to see conspiracies everywhere they look? Should it be surprising that there are always newcomers to continue the fight against a conspiracy whenever a savior tires of a stale idea or a futile struggle? This may reflect nothing more than the desire for special status or a search for greater direction in life.

Dupes

The dupes are neither those accused of being conspirators themselves nor those convinced by the saviors that a conspiracy exists. The dupes are those whom the saviors see as blind, gullible, and being led down a primrose path by the conspirators; they are clearly in need of enlightenment so that they, too, may come to see the dangers of the conspiracy. The dupes themselves remain skeptical about these supposed dangers, challenging evidence supporting the existence of the alleged conspiracy or simply viewing the entire matter a waste of their time and attention. Usually, the dupes greatly outnumber the saviors, which provides a keen incentive for the saviors to carry on their self-appointed mission of enlightenment.

A Grand Conspiracy Theory: "Area 51"

Pop culture abounds in conspiracy theories, though few of these qualify as *grand* conspiracies, involving large numbers of people over extended periods of time. There are, however, a handful of conspiracy theories that many people appear to find quite persuasive and that have stood the test of time. One deeply entrenched belief that has gained widespread popularity is that an extraterrestrial spacecraft crashed near Roswell, New Mexico, in 1947 and is being studied, along with several alien bodies that were also recovered, in a secret government facility located at "Area 51."

Here, the conspirators are hundreds or thousands of government agents and scientists who have kept a tight lid on this operation for over 50 years. The saviors are those who firmly believe that a massive cover-up is being perpetrated by the United States government. By contrast, the dupes remain unconvinced that there was a "flying saucer" crash at Roswell or that alien technology and bodies are stashed in a secret military installation.

The Role of the Media

Phillip Klass is widely recognized among scientists as one of the most credible experts on the subject of alien visitation. He has spent decades examining government records, many of which have recently been declassified, and has come to the conclusion that the *real* cover-up is being committed by the news media. No, he does not charge that CNN is guarding Area 51! Klass has gathered overwhelming evidence indicating that there never was a crash at Roswell, that there has been no alien visitation, and that the entire Area 51 conspiracy theory is bogus.

The popular news media, however, continue to perpetuate the myth because it makes for such an interesting story. Klass has documented in great detail the highly biased, one-sided media coverage of anything relating to UFOs or aliens. In a number of books (e.g., Klass, 1983, 1997a, 1997b), he has revealed the suppression of skeptical viewpoints—and the open acceptance of wild speculation or unverified opinion—that supports the myth of Area 51. For example, to this day the media give plenty of air time to supposed evidence of alien visitation that has been shown to be fraudulent:

- "Crop circles" or more complex designs stamped into open fields. The human creation of crop circles was covered in Chapter 8.
- Photographs of "MJ-12" documents in which references are made to appendices that describe astonishing alien technology. Are the MJ-12 documents authentic? The undeveloped film mysteriously appeared in

the mailbox of a film producer sympathetic to claims of alien visitation and government conspiracy. By this time, the photographed documents were decades old. Where had they been found? When had they been photographed? No corroborating evidence of the existence of the photographed documents has ever been provided. Typographic and lexicographic analyses suggest that the documents are fraudulent, and it seems especially odd that the photographer did not flip to even a single page of these appendices to capture some of the actual information; we are provided with nothing more than unsubstantiated references. All told, photographs of MJ-12 documents appear short on evidence and relatively easy to fake.

• The "Alien Autopsy" film that was repeatedly aired by Fox television. Again, there are many reasons to doubt the authenticity of this evidence. It is odd that such poor-quality, black-and-white film was used when much higher quality, color film was readily available. Its owners have refused to provide a sample of the film itself for dating purposes, whereas the fragment of leader (pictureless film at the beginning of a reel) that they did provide could have been cut from anything, such as easily obtainable old news footage. Anyone who has viewed this film can attest to its grainy quality; the distance, rather than close-up detail, with which the putative alien was filmed; and the oddly hurried manner in which the autopsy was conducted. All of this is especially peculiar given the monumental importance that would be attached to the discovery of a genuine alien being.

Prior to this reading, had you ever heard of crop circles, the MJ-12 documents, or the "Alien Autopsy" film? In my experience, most people have. Had you ever been offered any critiques? In my experience, most people have not. These are but three examples of thoroughly discredited "evidence" that is routinely presented in an uncritical fashion by the popular news and entertainment media (see Klass, 1983, 1997a, 1997b, 2000, for additional discussion of these and other dubious claims).

Thinking Clearly About Area 51

In the spirit of critical thinking about conspiracy theories, here are two things to consider. First, recall from Chapter 6 that most people imagine UFOs as something akin to a "flying saucer," like the one that supposedly crashed near Roswell. However, as Sheaffer (1997) explained, there never was such a flying saucer. Once this erroneous news report spread, however, other reports and photographs of saucer-shaped UFOs became commonplace. The lesson: People tend to see what they want or expect to see. The fact that the original report actually described a cigar-shaped craft says a lot about the authenticity of later "saucer" sightings.

Second, wouldn't the two parties allegedly perpetrating this conspiracy—the government and scientists—stand to *gain* rather than *lose* by proclaiming the existence of aliens? The government funds a tremendous amount of scientific research, so why should it impede its own progress by keeping such a discovery secret from most scientists? For example, the discovery of aliens would allow biologists to directly study an independently evolved species of life. Moreover, imagine the technological breakthroughs that would result. If the extraterrestrials are capable of building a craft that can traverse vast interstellar distances, they are likely far more advanced than we are. NASA, which continually struggles to justify its budget, could lay claim to incredible funding priorities.

But here is the toughest conflict of all, the biggest thorn in the side of the Area 51 conspiracy theory: Why would any government suppress the existence of aliens? After all, one of the basic functions of any national government is to provide for the defense of its people. Without an external threat, a government may have difficulty holding on to its power (and demanding large tax payments). Governments thrive on rallying the populace through fear, sometimes exaggerating or creating enemies and threats for this purpose. Imagine the need for defense spending if we knew for sure that potentially hostile aliens were capable of reaching our planet. Could anyone in the government dream of a more potent reason to increase taxes or of a more effective way to unite us against a common enemy? Our government would be *thrilled* to announce the existence of aliens!

Unfortunately, despite logical analyses and mountains of evidence amassed by Klass and others, delusions regarding Area 51 are willingly passed along by the popular media and remain widespread in our society. For example, a public celebration of the 50th anniversary of the supposed flying saucer crash was held in Roswell during the summer of 1997, and the film *Independence Day* depicted the Area 51 conspiracy as a known fact, perhaps lending it additional credibility.

PROBLEMS FACING ANY GRAND CONSPIRACY THEORY

Scratching the surface of the beliefs surrounding Area 51 reveals some of the common problems with which any grand conspiracy theory must contend. First, it is difficult to believe that the alleged conspirators really are operating in tandem. Does an overarching alliance actually exist? Is it plausible? For example, one common target of grand conspiracy theories is "the government." William Jarvis wrote a short piece entitled "The Government Is Not a Person" for the March/April 1999 National Council for Reliable Health Information newsletter, and it begins by noting:

Although often caricatured as "Uncle Sam," the government is not a person with attributes of character that can be used to define a personality in terms of morality. The government is a complex network of administrative, legislative, and judicial agencies that are often in conflict with each other.

Given this internal conflict, does it make sense that nobody within the system would speak out to reveal the conspiracy? Is there *no* department of the federal or state governments that would stand to gain anything by exposing the alleged cover-up at Area 51? What about officials telling family and friends this juicy secret—can we believe that no one would share this news, or that all who learned of it would keep it to themselves?

This leads to the second major problem with grand conspiracy theories. The same feature that makes the belief so magical—its massive scale—is often its greatest weakness. It seems to strain plausibility to imagine that hundreds, thousands, even millions of people have had access to information that has managed to remain a well-guarded secret. The sheer size of a grand conspiracy theory makes it unlikely from the start. If there are serious dangers involved in the cover-up of secrets at Area 51, as suggested by the saviors, why has not even a single person worked up the courage to anonymously leak information to the press? Are we really to believe that every one of the individuals who has had access to "classified" information within "the government" has willfully and skillfully suppressed this evidence?

Third, the self-interest of the parties involved must be considered. It must be asked whether the alleged conspirators truly have a good reason to perpetrate such a conspiracy, whether they actually stand to gain from it. Often, a close look shows that there is no good reason for such a conspiracy to exist. This, of course, is a compelling argument that it may not. As mentioned above, the defense industry would likely profit tremendously by disseminating proof of alien visitation. Its silence on this matter speaks volumes.

THE "HIDDEN CURE" CONSPIRACY

Armed with these critical thinking tools, let's examine a grand conspiracy theory in the arena of health, one which Steve Novella calls "The Theory of Hidden Cures." Pseudoscientists endorsing this type of theory argue that such cures operate outside the realm of scientific health care because a "medical establishment" is "suppressing" the pseudoscientists' "hidden cures." For example, some pseudoscientists claim to have discovered cures for AIDS, cancer, or other presently incurable diseases. However, they assert, these cures are being suppressed by greedy scientists and practitioners who conspire to protect their own livelihoods. Does this belief stand up under close scrutiny? I argue that it does not, for at least four primary reasons.

Intense Competition Is Ignored

The first major problem with this theory is that there is simply no unified "medical establishment." Believers typically argue that the American Medical Association, medical schools, hospitals, pharmaceutical companies, insurance companies, physicians, the National Institutes of Health, the National Cancer Institute, and others are in league with one another to maintain the status quo. What conspiracy theorists fail to realize is that these individuals and institutions have few connections with one another, that this network is far too extensive to facilitate a meaningful (let alone successful) conspiracy. As with any grand conspiracy theory, there are simply too many people involved to pull it off.

Not only do these institutions operate largely independently of one another, but they are in fierce competition with one another. There is a continuous struggle within and across scientific institutions for resources such as grant funding, recognition, prestige, laboratory space, and so forth. The surest way for any individual researcher or his or her employer to keep pace with others is through productive research. No scientist or scientific discipline stands to gain *anything* by standing still and maintaining the status quo. All available resources—tangible and intangible—go to those who make demonstrable progress in providing more accurate depictions of reality.

Researchers have a vested interest in seeking out novel ideas and subjecting them to rigorous tests, and the reward structure of scientific health care ensures that promising ideas *will* be explored, regardless of their source. New theories of illness and disease, new diagnostic tools, and new treatments are constantly replacing the old. This is in contrast to the stagnation of many pseudosciences, whose proponents *boast* of the fact that their practices have remained unchanged (i.e., have not improved) for hundreds or thousands of years. Anyone who speaks about the existence of a unified "medical establishment" simply has no idea how science really works.

The Alleged Profit Motive Makes No Sense

Believers like to argue that the medical establishment suppresses "hidden cures" because such cures would cut into establishment practitioners' profits. Even if this seems reasonable at first glance, think for a moment about who would be in a position to benefit from or be harmed by new cures. Whereas health care *providers* spend most of their time in the examining room and may feel a pinch if a cure is discovered for a disease within their area of specialization, *researchers* spend most of their time in the laboratory with plenty of hypotheses waiting to be tested. Thus, researchers—who tend not to be practitioners themselves—are unlikely to be threatened by new discoveries. In fact, if a team of researchers developed a cure for a disease—such as AIDS, for example—prestigious awards would be gleefully showered upon them. There would be no end to the fantastic job offers and funding opportunities they would receive, including virtually limitless professional perks. Researchers therefore have absolutely no reason to suppress medical break- throughs. Indeed, they stand to benefit tremendously from any advance to which they can lay claim.

The issue of self-interest can be approached from another angle. Would practitioners jeopardize their own careers? What about the Hippocratic Oath that physicians take to alleviate suffering to the best of their ability? Or, what about the costly malpractice suits they could be slapped with if they do not use the best available treatment? Suppressing an effective treatment creates an enormous vulnerability to ethical and legal challenges—why take the risk?

Science Is Never Going to Cure All Disease

But what of the notion that practitioners might put themselves out of business if they released the miracle cures that they are supposedly suppressing? Look over the history of medicine to see the folly in this poorly conceived idea. When scourges of the past were eliminated through vaccines, did scientific medicine collapse? Did practicing physicians fall on hard times when smallpox or polio was eliminated? Of course not. With any major advance in fighting disease, specializations simply tend to get shuffled a bit. Although few practi- tioners are so specialized that their entire practice revolves around the treat- ment of one particular disease, even then a knowledgeable professional could competently respecialize if the need arose. This happens from time to time, and it is a natural feature not only of health care but of any progressive scien- tific enterprise. There is such a vast array of pathology out there that to seri- ously entertain the belief that medicine is going to cure all disease is perhaps best characterized as woefully naïve.

Monumental Callousness Is Presumed

The final problem with the "hidden cures" conspiracy theory is that believ- ers attribute immense callousness to the alleged conspirators. It would be downright mean-spirited (and unethical) to suppress a treatment that could alleviate suffering by curing disease. Moreover, those who work within the "medical establishment" themselves have family and friends who fall prey to the serious diseases for which cures are said to exist. Are these professionals so heartless as to withhold treatments even from loved ones? To believe that conspirators are capable of such monumental callousness projects a disturb- ing view of human nature. You can judge for yourself whether this seems plausible.

Why Does the Theory of Hidden Cures Persist?

Until solid evidence is produced to demonstrate otherwise, it seems most reasonable to conclude that there is simply no such thing as a cohesive "medical establishment." This belief has too many logical flaws. Moreover, even if there were such a group of conspirators, they would still lack a plausible motive for suppressing miraculous cures. One of the most fundamental principles of human nature is that, to a large extent, our behavior is intended to help us achieve our goals. Because the discovery and promotion of new treatments is certainly in the self-interest of health researchers, there would have to be an even stronger reason for these researchers to suppress effective cures. No such reason has been convincingly argued.

Why, then, would anyone insist on the outlandish claim that there is a medical establishment that suppresses cures? The answer may lie in the psychological benefits of the savior role described earlier. Perhaps the privilege of knowing "the truth" and achieving special status by offering salvation to others is compelling enough.

The benefits of the savior role might be sufficient to account for this grand conspiracy theory, were it not for one remaining puzzle: Why does the "medical establishment" never include pseudoscientific practitioners? I have heard variations on the "hidden cure" theory many times, but it is always "scientists" and/or "the government" who are accused of suppressing a wondrous treatment known only to a lone, marginalized practitioner of some highly questionable ideas. As discussed in Chapter 3, this arrangement might reasonably cause us to wonder whether the outcast individual is, in truth, more a marginalized charlatan than a marginalized genius.

Perhaps, then, the answer has more to do with the antiscientific attitudes of many advocates of pseudoscience. Portraying scientists as cruel individuals who intentionally withhold beneficial treatments paves the way for a new array of business opportunities for pseudoscientists. By diverting attention away from acceptable standards of evidence and framing the choice of health care as a moral issue, pseudoscientists may convince some people to side with the self-proclaimed underdog. Many people have had some unpleasant experience with a health care professional: perhaps we were kept waiting too long, experienced an embarrassingly or painfully invasive test, were misdiagnosed, or were treated rudely or with condescension. These and other problems do occur, and many are inexcusable. It is understandable, then, that people will often harbor some resentment and seek treatment elsewhere.

However, though these issues may be grounds for getting a second opinion or changing practitioners altogether, they do not justify an abandonment of science. Health care professionals are only human, but the ideals of scientific medicine are the best bet we have for our health care. Pseudoscientists are often adept at playing on festering frustration with doctors, and—combined with the public's ignorance of science and fear of the unknown—prospective patients may readily be alienated from the scientific enterprise and steered toward pseudoscience. Thus, charlatans may find the "theory of hidden cures" to be a profitable weapon of influence as they try to carve a niche for themselves in the health care marketplace.

CHALLENGING CONSPIRACIES

Conspiracy theories may seem appealing, but they are often highly implausible if you take a close look. There are three basic questions that you should ask yourself when presented with a grand conspiracy theory. First, ask whether there are really enough shared interests to pull together the alleged conspirators. Be aware that although surface plausibility may be conferred by giving a name to the alleged conspirators, such as "the government" or "the medical establishment," such terms may reflect a false sense of unity among individuals or institutions. It is often the case, in fact, that competition or conflict is prevalent among the alleged conspirators. In particular, any grand conspiracy involving scientists is highly unlikely, as the entire enterprise is based firmly upon a healthy competition.

A second question to consider is whether the grand scope of the conspiracy theory reflects its implausibility. One can get just so many people to conspire, and for just so long. Think about the moral decrepitude that may be implied by the conspiracy. Consider that even when there does appear to be a convincing motive for a conspiracy, not every person involved is benefiting. Think about the ease with which just one person, one conscientious dissenter among the massive web of conspirators, could anonymously leak conclusive documentation to legal authorities or to the press. Determine for yourself whether it seems likely that such a large number of people are either so uniformly dedicated to maintaining the conspiracy or so weak-willed and morally corrupt as to silence their disagreement.

Finally, if answers to the previous questions suggest that the grand conspiracy is probably fictitious, you might ask why someone would want you to believe in it. Is it purely for entertainment, to make life more interesting? Is someone else enjoying the psychological benefits of the savior role, which compels them to attempt to rescue others? Or perhaps there is a darker motive: Might the individual be a pseudoscientist attempting to gain credibility by claiming the persecution of his or her ideas? Those with rejected ideas may fabricate conspiracies to explain why their practices are denounced by the mainstream practitioners. We have seen the folly of this ploy before. Keep in mind each of these as reasons others may use to try to sell you on the notion of a grand conspiracy theory when neither evidence nor plausibility argues in favor of its existence.

INFOTRAC COLLEGE EDITION

To learn more about topics included in this chapter, enter the following search terms:

Area 51
conspiracy
coverup

ILLUSIONS

The Perception of Control

Why do most major lotteries allow you to choose your own numbers? Isn't any randomly chosen series of numbers equally likely to win the jackpot? While it is true that the odds of winning are identical regardless of the numbers that are chosen, people nonetheless find the freedom of choice valuable. How valuable? Let's look at an intriguing experiment.

In this experiment (Langer, 1975), office workers were invited to buy a $1 lottery ticket for a drawing with unusually good odds: 20 people would be allowed to play, and one lucky winner would receive $25. (The lottery in this experiment is unlike any commercial lottery in that the researcher operated at a loss of $5 per drawing.) One-half the people approached with the opportunity to enter this lottery were assigned tickets at random; the other half of the entrants were allowed to choose their own numbers to play. Because the odds were more than fair, all 20 tickets were easily sold. At this point, the experimenter approached each ticket holder, one at a time, with a special plea: Someone else wanted to enter the lottery, but no more tickets could be sold. How much would the ticket holder charge to sell back his or her ticket? The participants' answers to this question revealed two interesting findings.

First, on average, people charged the experimenter more than they paid ($1), even more than the ticket's objective worth (based on the expected payoff, which is $25 per 20 tickets: $1.25) to buy back the ticket. In fact, participants required an average of about $5 to give up their tickets. Economists refer to this overvaluing of one's personal property as the "endowment effect" (Thaler, 1980). In other words, we often attach greater value to something simply because we own it.

The second finding of the experiment was quite novel. Those who had been assigned tickets at random required roughly $2 to sell them back to the experimenter, only modestly above the $1.25 objective value. In contrast, those who had chosen their own numbers required roughly $8 to sell their tickets! It appeared that freedom of choice increased the perceived value of the lottery tickets by a factor of four. This is stunning, given that these tickets were not objectively more valuable—the odds of winning remained 1/20, and the payoff that one could reasonably expect per ticket remained $1.25. Langer coined the term *illusion of control* to denote this kind of misperception of control over purely chance-determined events.

THE ILLUSION OF CONTROL

Illusions of control develop as we misinterpret randomness in the world around us. Random events are uncertain, and therefore threatening. Even an imaginary reduction in uncertainty enhances perceptions of predictability and understanding. Thus, we tend to impose order on chaos by perceiving a sense of control, even if it is only illusory, over purely chance-determined events. The distinction between situations that primarily involve skill, such as an athletic competition, and those that involve chance alone, such as a lottery, can easily become blurred. What often serves to blur this distinction is that characteristics of a chance situation may resemble those of a skill situation. For example, choice is one feature of a skill situation that, when introduced into a chance situation, produces an illusion of control.

Langer (1975) uncovered several other features that promote the illusion of control. For example, in a card game involving pure luck, participants wagered less against a well-dressed, seemingly competent "dapper" confederate than against a poorly dressed, less competent "schnook" confederate. Even though personal characteristics of the opponent have no effect on a purely chance-determined game, participants perceived more control over the situation when betting against a schnook than a dapper confederate. This pattern of wagers is irrational. So, too, is the fact that participants paid more for lottery tickets with letters on them than for lottery tickets with numbers on them, despite equal odds of winning. In additional experiments, Langer (1975) found that practicing, even when it could not improve chance performance, led to an increased illusion of control, as did personal experience and even the mere passage of time. It appears, therefore, that we are motivated to control our environment, even when we cannot reasonably and objectively expect to "beat the odds."

Chance and skill are often difficult to distinguish. The perception of control in a skill situation is correct, and it confers advantages. However, the mistaken perception of control in a chance situation may yield mixed results. For example, gamblers often throw dice hard if they want high numbers, soft if they want low numbers (Goffman, 1967), and this sort of superstitious behavior that results from a stable, predictable, and controllable view of the world may be harmless. There are chance situations, however, in which an illusion of control can be detrimental. For example, in one of Langer's (1975) lottery experiments, participants operating under an illusion of control declined the opportunity to exchange their tickets for tickets with better chances of winning. We will return shortly to the potential for danger inherent in illusions of control. First, we will explore a related phenomenon that likewise serves to reduce uncertainty.

THE CERTAINTY EFFECT

Because uncertainty is threatening, the preference for certainty over uncertainty is a strong motivator in our decision making. It should therefore come as little surprise that we overvalue the complete elimination of risk (e.g., from 10% to 0%) as compared to the reduction in the probability of harm (e.g., from 15% to 5%). Consider the following situations to test your own preference for certainty:

1. Suppose you are forced to play a standard round of Russian roulette: You will spin the cylinder of a gun that contains one bullet, aim the gun at your head, and pull the trigger once. How much would you pay to remove the bullet from the cylinder?
2. Now imagine that you are going to play Russian roulette, but there are four bullets in the gun's cylinder. How much would you pay to remove *one* of these bullets at random?

If you are like most participants in one (hypothetical) experiment (Tversky & Kahneman, 1981), you would be willing to pay more money to remove the only bullet from a revolver in Russian roulette than to remove one bullet out of four from another revolver. Objectively, removing one bullet from either revolver reduces the chance of death by 1/6. However, this reduction appears to be worth more when the probability changes from one chance in six to *none* than from four chances in six to three.

In fact, insurance companies amass great wealth due to this certainty effect. Insurance is only profitable because many people are willing to pay more for the elimination of risk than to pay the (likely lesser) costs of choosing to live without insurance. Just as when you gamble by playing the lottery and are unlikely to win as much as your ticket cost, when you gamble by purchasing insurance you are unlikely to get back in reimbursement as much as you pay in premiums. Nonetheless, the offer seems attractive because the only other choice—living without insurance—involves taking your chances against a huge loss that you might not be able to afford. Thus, insurance companies are profitable for the same reason as casinos: The odds are stacked in their favor. Moreover, insurance has even broader appeal because of our strong aversion to heavy losses and our preference for certainty.

The certainty effect creates order from chaos by eliminating uncertainty altogether, providing the strongest possible perception of control. However, when we deceive ourselves, when these perceptions of control are mere illusions, we begin to play with fire.

THE DANGERS OF ILLUSIONS OF CONTROL

A sense of certainty or control can be nice in that it reduces the uncertainty in the world and feels empowering. However, the misperception of control can have undesirable consequences, including the inappropriate placement of blame or the development of a helpless outlook.

Belief in the "Just World" and the Blaming of Victims

Our perception of the social world is sometimes simplified through what Melvin Lerner (1980) refers to as a fundamental delusion, the belief in a "just world." This belief neatly organizes the relationship between people and outcomes: People get what they deserve, and deserve what they get. If something terrible happens to a stranger, our assumption that it was deserved in some way helps us to distance the tragedy and protect ourselves from the possibility of similar harm. However, although this perception may be quite comforting, it falsely denies the unpredictability of life's twists and turns. Bad things *can* happen to good people, much as we may wish otherwise. Because our environment is not entirely controllable, rigid adherence to the belief in a just world can lull us into a false sense of security and control.

In cases of truly undeserved misfortune, a belief in the just world imposes a sense of order on a chaos that is often very threatening or intimidating to us, but at a serious cost. For example, a strong belief in a just world may lead to such harmful misattributions as "blaming the victim" or self-blame. Those who have suffered traumatic life events—such as victims of rape, incest, physical assaults, serious diseases, bereavement, major accidents, or natural disasters—need our empathy and support, not our blame. However, when these events strike seemingly at random, undeserved victimization confronts us with our own vulnerability. One way to minimize the seeming uncontrollability of hazards is to blame victims for their own misfortune. By coming to see the trauma as deserved, we are able to distance ourselves. We can maintain the pretense that because we are undeserving of harm, we are therefore invulnerable to tragedy.

The hindsight bias that was discussed in Chapter 10 also plays an important role in victim-blaming, as social psychologist and trauma expert Ronnie Janoff-Bulman (1992) explains:

> With hindsight, we blame victims for behaviors that they engaged in with only the benefit of foresight. Once we know what happened, we blame victims for what we

believe they, too, should have known. Thus, in a series of studies, my students and I found that a woman who is raped is blamed for prior behaviors, whereas these same behaviors are not regarded as problematic or blameworthy when they are followed by neutral or positive outcomes [Janoff-Bulman, Timko, & Carli, 1985]. Yet the rape victim engaged in these behaviors without knowing that she would be raped. Thus, it is not particularly uncommon for a man to come back to a woman's apartment following a date. If the woman is raped, however, she is apt to be blamed for allowing him to come back to her apartment. Common behaviors can suddenly look very different in hindsight, particularly when it includes awareness of victimization. (p. 151)

You might think that otherwise intelligent, well-meaning people would not be so foolish as to needlessly blame victims for their own misfortunes, but it is surprising how often this dubious reasoning is observed. Consider this extremely distressing instance:

Eileen Gardner, who served for a brief period in the Reagan administration as an aide to Education Secretary William Bennett, once wrote that handicapped individuals "falsely assume that the lottery of life has penalized them at random. This is not so. Nothing comes to an individual that he has not, at some point in his development, summoned." She also claimed that, "As unfair as it may seem, a person's external circumstances do fit his level of inner spiritual development." This is not exactly the philosophy that one would want in the upper reaches of the Department of Education. (Gilovich, 1991, p. 143)

Self-Blame

Similarly problematic reasoning can cloud our judgment when we attempt to make sense of our own misfortune. When we are victimized by unpredictable events, it may be tempting to blame ourselves. Despite the distress that may arise from deciding that we deserved to be victimized, this decision helps by providing a sense of future safety: If we change our ways we will not be victimized again. A rape victim, for example, might blame herself for her experience and scrupulously avoid situations and behaviors like those that led to her victimization. Although such avoidance may be justified, it may produce a false sense of security. It is important to recognize that, despite our best intentions, there remains an element of unpredictability in the world. If we merely change our behavior without this recognition, we may prompt a renewed feeling of invulnerability. As a result, other sensible precautions may be overlooked, and the tragedy may repeat itself.

Stanovich (1998, p. 178) summarizes a story told by Dawes (1991) that describes how this sort of false learning can lead to repeated problems. The story involves

meeting an inmate from a prison education program run by the university for which Dawes was working. The inmate had been a bartender in a tavern and had also had a side job collecting gambling debts (at gunpoint if necessary). One day, he was sent to another state, Oregon, to collect a sum of money. When he got to

Oregon, he cornered the man owing the money and drew out his gun. Just then, the police jumped from hiding and arrested him on the spot. After telling Dawes the story, the inmate declared confidently that he would never go to jail again. When Dawes asked how he knew that he would never go to jail again, the inmate replied, "Because I'll never go to Oregon again!"

Learned Helplessness

In addition to promoting victim-blaming, self-blame, and a false sense of security, illusions of control can also cause misery through what psychologists call "learned helplessness." In a classic experiment, Martin Seligman (1975) first trained dogs to jump from one side of a box to another to escape a painful electric shock. Then, a barrier was installed that prevented the dogs from jumping across to escape the shock. Eventually, the dogs stopped trying. The real surprise came when the researchers eventually removed the barrier: Although the dogs were now free to escape, most of them remained in place, unnecessarily accepting the shocks. They had learned that they were helpless.

The danger inherent in illusions of control lies in the false sense of efficacy that they entail. When people who cling to beliefs that are merely illusions encounter stress or trauma, the fantasy bubble of an illusion of control may burst. That is, they may learn the futility of their actions and enter a state of learned helplessness not unlike that experienced by Seligman's dogs. Seligman draws a link between learned helplessness and depression. When an individual has learned the futility of his or her actions, the ensuing helplessness can create extreme passivity and indifference. As a result, more constructive, adaptive behaviors are not pursued, even when they are available.

THE DOWNSIDE TO MENTAL IMAGERY

Pseudosciences, especially those that fall under the vague heading of "holistic health," are often premised on the notion that we can consciously control the uncontrollable. Recall that Andrew Weil, an outspoken pseudoscientist, suggests that mental telepathy is simply a matter of choice—if we choose to be telepathic, we automatically become so (see Chapter 3). Much of pseudoscience is founded on a mystical "mind over matter" philosophy, and perhaps the greatest belief in the power of the mind in curing disease involves the practice of mental imagery.

Advocates of mental imagery maintain that we can effectively combat disease through thought alone. The idea is that we can accelerate or enhance our body's natural recuperative processes through positive thinking. Not only is there no reliable evidence for this wishful thinking, but it seems that people fail to consider the serious *downside* that would accompany the direct influence of our thoughts on our health. Proponents clearly want to enjoy the alleged benefits of imagery—the ability of positive thinking to alleviate disease—without the obvious risk: that negative thinking might cause or worsen the course of a disease. Gilovich (1991) notes that we can imagine harm at least as easily as we can imagine benefit, and he goes on to discuss the dangers that could therefore result from negative thinking:

> The idea of an immune system that is so responsive to the products of one's mental and emotional life has its troubling aspects. It may be preferable to have a system that hums along just as efficiently regardless of one's mood . . . that does not put one at risk after seeing a sad film, delivering a speech in front of a critical audience, or learning that one's dog has died. Personally, I find it more comforting to believe that whatever crosses my mind will *not* affect my health. Indeed, if you are like me, then the very thought that the products of our imaginations might influence our state of health produces a flood of images of hair loss, cardiac arrhythmia, and advanced carcinomas that, according to many holists, should have dire consequences. The phenomenon is analogous to the results of a simple thought experiment: When asked to imagine that someone can "read your thoughts" or listen in on your internal dialogue, many people report that they cannot avoid thinking of their most humiliating impulses. Similarly, if it were ever conclusively demonstrated that our health conforms to the pictures we have in our minds, I suspect that most of us would have difficulty suppressing images of pathology and decrepitude. (p. 142)

The obvious blindness of holistic health practitioners to the downside of mental imagery is reminiscent of the one-sided attempt to salvage homeopathy through the "water memory" theory (see Chapter 6). Just think how thoroughly terrifying it would be if water did indeed have memory, and if we therefore experienced a potent dose of all substances with which the water had ever come into contact. The same goes for mental telepathy (how frightening it would be for others to be able to read our minds!) and mental imagery (how dangerous it would be to fall prey to every disease or illness whose name passes through our minds!). Advocates of magical beliefs often selectively consider only their positive effects while unrealistically ignoring their unpleasant implications (Radford, 2000).

THE "CHOOSE TO BE HEALTHY" FALLACY

Many so-called holistic health practices are premised on the notion that all that patients need to do is "choose to be healthy." However, although positive thinking has been linked to several short-term changes in immune functioning and in subjective feelings of distress (illness), there is no evidence that positive thinking can cure disease. Moreover, there is an additional downside to this fallacy: It implies that those who are diseased have *chosen* to be sick. This is the vicious victim-blaming aspect of pseudoscience that is seldom advertised.

One of the most fundamental tenets of holistic health practices is that practitioners must consider "what sort of patient has the disease, not what sort of disease the patient has." This statement positively reeks of victim-blaming! Conceptualizing the issue in terms of "what sort of patient has the disease" supposes that something about the patient's thoughts or behavior has brought about the disease. Gilovich (1991) provides some telling examples of this cruel mentality:

- The author of an influential "holistic nursing" textbook stated that "illness occurs when people don't grow and develop their potentials."
- New Age faith healer Elizabeth Stratton claims that "disease is merely a symptom of a deep psychological problem that the person probably isn't even aware of . . . . What I look for is why they created the illness and why they're hanging on to it."

What should we make of these assertions? Let's think holistically for a moment. Consider a woman who develops breast cancer. What sort of patient has this disease? Someone at fault, someone who hasn't grown and developed her full potential. She must have a deep psychological problem that is the *real* root of the breast cancer. Presumably one must "fix" this woman to cure her breast cancer. In contrast, consider the perspective of scientific health care. Although individuals may inherit risk factors or engage in risky behaviors, most diseases still strike in an unpredictable manner. Thus, this woman surely did not seek to become afflicted. This view removes the stigma of blame from the patient and focuses attention on the actual problem, the disease itself. From this perspective, we *should* think in terms of "what sort of disease the patient has." Not only is this approach in sync with evidence-based treatments; it is also more humane.

It is not hard to see how a preoccupation with "treating the whole person" can lead to the assignment of blame to the patient. It is very hard, however, to see how this style of thinking might be constructive or helpful in any way. Moreover, some patients not only fail to speak out against treatments that fail them, but follow a path of self-blame induced by the insistence of their practitioner that they can take personal control of diseases that are in fact uncontrollable. Gilovich (1991) cites the sad case of Carl and Stephanie Simonton, pioneers in advocating mental imagery as a treatment for cancer. The Simontons themselves do not appear troubled by the self-blaming outlook adopted by a number of their own dying patients:

> Some of our early patients felt we had given them the key to certain recovery, and thought, "Yes! I can do it!"—and then, as we discovered later, felt guilty if they failed to recover . . . . Eventually, their families brought us [the patients'] last words: "Tell Carl and Stephanie that the method still works," or "Tell them it isn't their fault." (Simonton, Matthews-Simonton, & Creighton, 1978, p. 220)

It is difficult to conceive of a more disheartening end to a human life. Foregoing scientific medicine that may send their cancers into remission or at least grant them some precious time, patients are somehow deceived into trying an imagery treatment without demonstrated efficacy. The treatment, surely enough, fails. The patients blame themselves. It is a testament to the human need for control that the last words of these patients offered support for those who provided the worthless imagery scheme.

PRAYER AND RELIGION-MOTIVATED MEDICAL NEGLECT

Perhaps the gravest tragedy in all of medicine is the religion-motivated medical neglect of children. What motivates this neglect is the steadfast belief, despite a complete lack of evidence, that devout religious faith—especially *prayer*—is sufficient to maintain optimal health. When a religious group proclaims the efficacy of prayer in curing disease, it makes an empirical claim that is testable through the scientific method. To begin with, how plausible is this claim?

> There's a category of prayer in which God is begged to intervene in human history or just to right some real or imagined injustice or natural calamity—for example, when a bishop from the American West prays for God to intervene and end a devastating dry spell. Why is the prayer needed? Didn't God know of the drought? Was He unaware that it threatened the bishop's parishioners? What is implied here about the limitations of a supposedly omnipotent and omniscient deity? The bishop asked his followers to pray as well. Is God more likely to intervene when many pray for mercy or justice than when only a few do? (Sagan, 1995, p. 276)

It seems to me that the notion of a God who counts prayers is demeaning to religion, likening it to a vast voting booth. Perhaps even more troubling is the staggering diversity of religions around the world that maintain radically different—often completely incompatible—beliefs regarding such profound issues as these:

- The afterlife (e.g., eternal bliss in Heaven or damnation to Hell vs. reincarnation)
- The creation of the universe (e.g., the special creation of Genesis vs. creation from an egg as believed by the Chinese, Finns, Greeks, Hindus, Japanese, Persians, and Samoans)
- The recording and explanation of historical events (e.g., cultures that border rivers or experience flash floods contain stories like the Noachian flood, whereas other cultures do not)
- Morality and societal taboos (e.g., prescribing monogamy vs. polygamy)
- The dutiful practice of religious worship (e.g., is animal sacrifice required?)
- The existence of one or more gods (e.g., monotheistic Judeo-Christian religions vs. pantheistic religions)

Just how does one determine the proper manner in which to pray? What is allowable and what is prohibited? To whom should the prayer be directed? Along with a host of other difficult questions, these are not mere semantic obstacles but serious challenges to the internal logic of belief in the efficacy of prayer. And what is the empirical evidence regarding its alleged healing effects? Sagan (1995) notes:

> The Victorian statistician Francis Galton argued that—other things being equal—British monarchs ought to be very long-lived, because millions of people all over the world daily intoned the heartfelt mantra "God Save the Queen" (or King). Yet, he showed, if anything, they don't live as long as other members of the wealthy and pampered aristocratic class. Tens of millions of people in concert publicly wished (although they did not exactly pray) that Mao Zedong would live "for ten thousand years." Nearly everyone in ancient Egypt exhorted the gods to let the Pharoah live "forever." These collective prayers failed. Their failure constitutes data. (pp. 276–277)

Are there more systematic studies of the effects of prayer on health? Certainly. As described when evaluating the quality of sources, Harris et al. (1999) studied 990 patients in a coronary care unit, finding results *worse* than one would expect by chance. Prayer improved only the "Swan-Ganz catheter" ratings of patients, not the 34 other outcomes that were studied, such as pneumonia, major surgery, cardiac arrest, and death. This well-controlled experiment provides the most reliable results in the history of research on prayer. When believers in the healing effect of prayer cite this study as *supportive* evidence, it shows just how weak their case is.

Despite their inability to argue from evidence that prayer is effective, many religious groups prefer prayer to science-based health care for their children. Asser and Swan (1998) investigated the deaths of 172 children whose parents refused medical care because it conflicted with their religious beliefs. Among the fundamentalist sects that preach faith healing and refuse medicine, the Christian Science and Faith Assembly denominations had more child deaths than any others in the study. Based on a careful review of the causes of death, it was determined that 140 of the 172 children (81%) would have had at least a 90% chance of survival if treated medically; 18 more children died of conditions with a 50% or better chance of survival with treatment. These tragic losses occur because some states exempt parents from legal accountability for medical neglect for religious reasons. The March/April 1998 National Council Against Health Fraud newsletter had this to say:

> Curiously, despite the sympathy that Americans normally exhibit to the plights of children, very few cases of death due to religion-motivated medical neglect have received national press coverage, and reports in the medical literature are also rare.
>
> The authors [Asser and Swan] have shown by their investigation that child deaths due to religion-motivated neglect are not only preventable, *they are predictable and they will continue to occur* as long as good people do nothing to stop

them. The U.S. Supreme Court is clear on whether or not requiring parents to obtain medical care for children is constitutional. It has stated:

"The right to practice religion freely does not include the liberty to expose the community or child to communicable disease, or the latter to ill health or death . . . . Parents may be free to become martyrs themselves. But it does not follow they are free, in identical circumstances, to make martyrs of their children before they have reached the age of full and legal discretion." (*Prince* v. *Massachusetts*, 321 U.S. 158, 1944)

Perhaps the only thing sadder than the victims of pseudoscientific practices who blame themselves for their own victimization is the fate of innocent children at the hands of those who, for religious reasons, cling tenaciously to illusions of control. As has been emphasized throughout this book, the best antidote to the toxicity of pseudoscience is to form your beliefs by drawing on empirical evidence and ground your judgments and decisions in scientific reasoning. An open-minded skepticism is the surest way to dispel illusions.

INFOTRAC COLLEGE EDITION

To learn more about topics included in this chapter, enter the following search terms:

illusion and control
just world
learned helplessness
mental imagery
prayer and health
victim and blame

four

DECISION MAKING AND ETHICS

ASSESSMENT

Classical Decision Theory

Take a look at the portions of three symptom checklists in Figure 4 that are drawn from popular sources. Can you relate to any of these characteristics? If so, what do you suppose that means? Many of the characteristics seem quite vague, and it's not always clear whether a positive or negative answer would indicate something problematic. Many questions cover both ends of the spectrum, suggesting problems at either extreme. Most of the characteristics are quite general and might apply to just about everybody. Bearing all of this in mind, the purported use of these checklists might surprise you: According to their creators, if you see signs of yourself on these lists, it means that you may have repressed memories of being sexually abused as a child! And there's no use in denying it. "If you have some of the warning signals, you probably do have repressed memories. You are unlikely to be the exception to the rule, no matter what your denial is telling you" (Fredrickson, 1992, pp. 53–54). Two leaders of the repressed memory movement, Ellen Bass and Laura Davis (1988), add in *The Courage to Heal,* which has sold over 750,000 copies: "If you think you were abused and your life shows the symptoms, then you probably were" (p. 22).

Other therapists who search for memories of child sexual abuse—despite patients' insistence that none occurred—hold extraordinary beliefs in their powers of observation:

> Therapists often portray their ability to see abuse where the client knows of none as an example of brilliant intuition and diagnostic virtuosity of the highest order. Some therapists, for example, brag that they can tell at the very outset of treatment that the patient has a hidden history of trauma. "Within ten minutes, I can spot it as a person walks in the door, often before they even realize it," said family counselor Brenda Wade on CNBC's program "Real Personal" of her ability to identify victims of child abuse. "There's a lack of trust . . . there's a certain way that the person presents themselves [sic], there's a certain body language." (Ofshe & Watters, 1996, p. 68)

1. Do you find many characteristics of yourself on this list? (Blume, 1990)
   - Fear of being alone in the dark . . . nightmares, night terrors
   - Alienation from the body . . . poor body image
   - Gastrointestinal problems, gynecological disorders, headaches, arithritis or joint pain
   - Eating disorders, drug or alcohol abuse (or total abstinence)
   - Phobias
   - Suicidal thoughts, attempts, obsessions
   - Depression; seemingly baseless crying
   - High risk taking ("daring the fates"); inability to take risks
   - Guilt, shame, low self-esteem, feeling worthless; high appreciation of small favors by others
   - Abandonment issues
   - Blocking out some period of early years (especially 1–12), or a specific person or place
   - Feeling crazy; feeling different; feeling oneself to be unreal and everyone else to be real, or vice versa; creating fantasy worlds, relationships, or identities
   - Sexual issues
2. Do any of these "warning signs" feel familiar? (Bass & Davis, 1988)
   - Do you feel different from other people?
   - Are you afraid to succeed?
   - Do you find yourself clinging to people you care about?
   - Do you feel alienated or lonely?
   - Do you have trouble feeling motivated?
   - Do you find that it is hard to trust your intuition?
3. Are any of these statements true of you? (Fredrickson, 1992)
   - I startle easily
   - I do some things to excess
   - I am preoccupied with thoughts about sex
   - I space out or daydream
   - I neglect my teeth
   - I often have nightmares
   - Certain foods or tastes frighten me or nauseate me
   - I feel a sense of doom, as though my life will end in tragedy or disaster

FIGURE **4**

Portions of symptom checklists from three popular sources.

Clearly, it would be wise to question the validity of these types of assessment. We will come back to the subject of repressed memories, but first let's look at how one evaluates the accuracy of judgments such as this, beginning with a screening tool used every day.

MAMMOGRAMS

A public debate has raged for years over the advisability of routinely screening women for breast cancer through the use of mammograms. There are two sides to this issue, each with serious consequences. The early detection of cancerous breast tumors greatly increases the chances of successful treatment and, ultimately, survival, but the false detection of nonexistent tumors leads to considerable anxiety plus painful, unnecessary, and costly biopsies. Although it is beyond the scope of this book to address the many complex ethical, legal, economic, and practical issues involved in this debate, it is undeniably essential for anyone entering the debate to think clearly about the outcomes involved in routine mammogram screening.

Suppose that 1 out of every 100 women in her 40s actually has a breast tumor, be it malignant or benign, and that use of the mammogram results in an 80% level of "sensitivity" and an 80% level of "specificity." That is, among women *known* to have tumors (through biopsy, for example), doctors using the mammogram can correctly detect 80% of the tumors, though they miss the other 20%; the test results are *sensitive* to tumors 80% of the time. Likewise, among women known *not* to have tumors, doctors can correctly identify their absence 80% of the time, though they falsely identify a tumor 20% of the time; the test results are *specific* to tumors 80% of the time.

Suppose that a woman in her 40s undergoes routine screening and her mammogram results come back positive, suggesting that she has a breast tumor. What is the actual probability that she does in fact have a tumor? To many, this problem seems deceptively easy. Take a moment to think about it and determine your best guess before reading on.

If you are like most people, you have seriously overestimated the correct probability, which is just under 4%! That's right: Despite the positive test result, the chance that a tumor is present is still quite low. Your intuition most likely told you something quite different. How is it that a diagnostic test that is 80% accurate under known conditions is much more likely to be wrong than right in this case?

The way to solve this problem is to consider *both* pieces of information that you are given. It is true that the evidence (80% sensitivity and specificity) is fairly strong. However, the "base rate," or frequency of occurrence, of breast tumors is low (1% of all women in their 40s). We have a tendency to ignore base rates, which are highly relevant information for decisions. Fortunately, there is a straightforward method for incorporating base rates into a solution to this problem.

CLASSICAL DECISION THEORY

When the mammogram results are in, there are four possible combinations of test results and reality that may occur. The test results may be either "positive" (suggesting the presence of a tumor) or "negative" (suggesting the absence of a tumor). It is important to keep in mind that the words "positive" and "negative" are not value judgments; they are merely conventional labels assigned to different results. Neither result is necessarily desirable or correct. Now, in reality, the test results may turn out to be either "true" (correct) or "false" (incorrect). Combining the positive/negative and true/false distinctions yields four possibilities. If the mammogram suggests a tumor (a "positive" result), the test result may be correct (a "true positive") or incorrect (a "false positive"). If the mammogram suggests no tumor (a "negative" result), it may be correct (a "true negative") or incorrect (a "false negative"). These possibilities can be organized into a 2×2 table:

		Reality	
		Tumor	No Tumor
Mammogram	Positive	True Positive	False Positive
	Negative	False Negative	True Negative

Whenever the mammogram result comes back positive, it may be either a true or false positive. This much can be seen by looking across the first row in the table. The question therefore involves determining the relative likelihoods of true and false positive identifications. To calculate these, let's see what would happen if, say, 1,000 women in their 40s were screened using the mammogram.

First, recall that 1% of these women will have tumors, which equals 10 out of our 1,000 total. Of those 10 tumors, how many will the mammogram correctly detect? Well, we know that the sensitivity of the test is 80%, so 10 × .80 = 8 true positives. By subtraction, this means that 10–8 = 2 tumors will be missed. These are false negatives.

Second, we need to repeat this procedure for the women without tumors. By subtraction, we know that 1,000–10 = 990 women will not have tumors. Because the specificity of the mammogram is 80%, this means that 990 ×

.80 = 792 of these women will receive negative test results. These are true negatives. By subtraction, this leaves 990–792 = 198 women without tumors who will nonetheless receive positive test results. These are false positives. We now have all the information we need to fill in the table above with numerical values:

		Reality		
		Tumor	No Tumor	
Mammogram	Positive	8	198	206
	Negative	2	792	794
		10	990	1,000

It is now a simple matter to answer the question with which we began: What is the probability, given that the mammogram came back positive, that this particular woman really had a tumor? We see in the table that for every 206 times the mammogram yields a positive result (8 + 198), it is likely to be correct just 8 times and incorrect 198 times. The probability of a correct identification in this case is therefore 8/206 = .039, or 3.9%.

THE IMPACT OF LOW BASE RATES

The reason for this surprising result is that the base rate of tumors (1%) is more extreme (farther from the midpoint of 50%) than the strength of the evidence (80% sensitivity and specificity). That is, the evidence is not sufficient to overcome the low odds of a breast tumor. This is an instance of a general principle that applies to all decision making: Whenever the base rates are more extreme than the strength of the evidence, you will make a greater number of correct decisions by always choosing the more likely alternative, or "following the base rates" (Meehl & Rosen, 1955). To be more specific, if the base rate is very low, false positives will outnumber true positives. Because many important predictions of interest involve relatively rare events (violent behavior, suicidality, the presence of disease, etc.), we will deal exclusively with low base rates and set aside discussion of high base rates, although the reasoning for both is perfectly symmetrical.

So far, we have noted that extremely strong evidence is needed to predict an especially rare event without tending to reach an erroneous decision. It is also worth noting that comparatively common events can often be predicted with high accuracy. Consider the mammogram again. What if its results had come back negative? Referring back to the table, we see that for every 794 times the test yields negative results, it is correct 792 times and incorrect 2 times, for an accuracy level of 792/794 = .997, or 99.7%. Thus, based on the same test that is too weak to overcome the low base rate of one possible outcome (a relatively rare breast tumor), one can nonetheless have great confidence in predictions of a high base rate outcome (the absence of a tumor). Thus, diagnostic tests can be inaccurate in cases of rare events and accurate in cases of common events.

Many people fail to recognize this fundamental principle of decision theory—that accuracy depends on both the base rate of an event's occurrence *and* the strength of the evidence (Meehl & Rosen, 1955). Only by considering the accuracy of mammograms can a rational debate over mammogram screening take place. Although false positives (198 out of every 1,000) will be quite common, overwhelming true positives (8 out of every 1,000) and resulting in a tremendous amount of needless anxiety and unnecessary surgery, this small handful of true positives represents women for whom early detection will be achieved and a potentially fatal disease will be made more treatable. We are willing to make many mistakes in order to identify women whose lives may be saved. If we were to put greater value on making the fewest possible mistakes, we would simply guess "no tumor" for all women, and we would be correct 99% of the time. To help understand the new terminology introduced in this chapter and review the power of this technique, let's put these new tools to use in another context.

LIE DETECTION

In a brief note on "Problems with the Polygraph" that appeared in *Science,* Phillips (1999) showed that lie detection is a difficult business. Suppose that the polygraph, or "lie detector," is used to screen 1,000 people, only 50 of whom are lying (i.e., the base rate of lying = 5%). Given the documented degree of validity of the polygraph (sensitivity = 76%, specificity = 63%), a 2 × 2 table of decisions would look like this:

		Reality		
		Lie	Truth	
Polygraph	Positive	38	351	389
	Negative	12	599	611
		50	950	1,000

For each of the 389 people accused of lying on the basis of their polygraph test (38 + 351), there is only a 9.8% chance that he or she is *actually* lying (38/389 = .098). However, for each of the 611 people certified as honest on the basis of their polygraph test (12 + 599), there is a 98.0% chance that he or she is honest (599/611 = .980). Thus, the polygraph—like the mammogram—is differentially useful: It provides very weak evidence for a rare event (lying) but a strong case for a common event (honesty).

TWO DIFFERENT PERSPECTIVES ON ACCURACY

Unfortunately, most people—including 95% of all physicians (e.g., Casscells, Schoenberger, & Grayboys, 1978; Eddy, 1982)—fail to recognize that the accuracy of a diagnostic test in practice differs from the sensitivity and specificity levels uncovered in research. Not only are mammograms and lie detectors misunderstood in this way, but so are "do-it-yourself" diagnostic kits available over the counter, such as home pregnancy tests. If you cannot even roughly estimate a relevant base rate to incorporate into these simple calculations, your interpretation of a positive or a negative test result may dramatically miss the mark.

There are two completely different ways of evaluating the "accuracy" of any decision-making procedure, such as a diagnostic test. When the validity of a test is evaluated, sensitivity and specificity are the values of interest. A test must be shown to correctly reveal the existence and nonexistence of a medical condition a large proportion of the time, or else it cannot be of much use. In terms of the 2 × 2 tables shown in this chapter, sensitivity and specificity involve assessing accuracy by looking *down the columns*.

However, once one leaves the research laboratory (in which *known cases* are evaluated) the focus on accuracy shifts. In applied use, a practitioner employing the mammogram is not concerned with the odds of detecting a breast tumor that is known to exist—after all, if the patient is known to have a tumor, no test is required! The doctor wants to know the odds that, *for this patient,* the test result is correct. In this context, two other measures of accuracy are required: "positive predictive power" and "negative predictive power."

Rather than asking, "How many known cases are correctly detected?" the doctor must now ask, "How many decisions yielded by this test are correct?" This involves assessing accuracy by looking *across the rows* in the tables shown in this chapter. Positive predictive power is simply the proportion of all positive identifications that are correct: 3.9% for the mammogram, 9.8% for the polygraph. Negative predictive power is the proportion of all negative identifications that are correct: 99.7% for the mammogram, 98.0% for the polygraph.

As can be seen in each of these cases, low base rate events result in poor positive predictive power and excellent negative predictive power. This is simply another way of stating that rare events cannot be predicted well, whereas common ones can. There remains one final principle of decision theory left to explore.

THE IMPACT OF SELECTION RATIOS

Just as different base rates of occurrence affect the accuracy achieved in practice, so too does the threshold by which decisions are made, or the "selection ratio." By tweaking the threshold that is applied in reaching decisions, the proportions of true and false positives and negatives will be altered in predictable ways. Consider, as an illustrative example, an extremely demanding and competitive graduate program. Given its tough standards, the low base rate of graduation from this program is due to characteristics of the pool of applicants—an admissions committee cannot directly alter the ability and motivation of those who apply to their program. What the committee *can* control, however, is the selection ratio: the proportion of all applicants that are accepted into the program. In a highly competitive program, the selection ratio is quite low. What would happen if the committee increased the selection ratio by admitting more students?

Given a fixed applicant pool from which to choose, the only way to admit more students is to lower the threshold for acceptance: An increase in the selection ratio may be achieved at the cost of a decrease in admissions standards. Although there will be a greater overall number of acceptances, false positives (that is, accepted students who do poorly in the program) will increase more rapidly than true positives (accepted students who succeed). This is because the school, which previously admitted only 5% of all applicants, could carefully select the most promising students. Positive predictive power—the proportion of those accepted who *successfully* complete the program—could be kept relatively high, perhaps at 80%. Increasing the selection ratio to, say, 10% would mean that additional acceptances would have to be offered to less promising students. Positive predictive power would therefore drop a bit, perhaps to 70%. On a related note, decreasing a selection ratio—for example, by admitting only 1% of all applicants—would increase positive predictive power, perhaps to 90%. This demonstrates the impact of selecting a selection ratio.

Thus, there is a trade-off between the number of people accepted and the success among those accepted. Any graduate program must consider the implications of expanding or contracting in size when considering a change in admissions procedures. A larger program will have a higher failure rate among its students—with correspondingly low morale, no doubt—than will a smaller program, which could be more selective and devote more attention to the education of its students. On the other hand, a smaller program with a higher success rate among its students than a larger program will also have fewer human resources (e.g., breadth of faculty expertise) and financial resources (e.g., income from tuition and faculty grants) with which to work.

To review briefly, three factors jointly determine the accuracy of any decision procedure:

1. *Validity.* The greater a procedure's ability to identify known cases, the greater its accuracy will be in practice. The most frequently reported measures of validity—sensitivity and specificity—may be identical, as they were for the mammogram (80% in both cases), or different from one another, as they were for the polygraph (sensitivity = 76%, specificity = 63%).
2. *Base rate.* The lower the frequency with which an event or behavior occurs in the population under consideration, the more difficult it will be to predict. In the laboratory, one can choose an easy base rate (e.g., 50%) for research purposes, but in applied practice the base rate is usually a fixed and immutable characteristic of the population of individuals being served.
3. *Selection ratio.* The threshold used for making decisions also influences the proportions of true and false positives and negatives. Decision makers sometimes have control over the selection ratio, in which case they must carefully consider the pros and cons of setting this ratio at various levels.

Let's see how this framework helps us understand some pseudoscientific practices.

NUTRITIONAL SCAMS

Each of the three factors that affect the accuracy of decisions is taken advantage of by those who perpetrate nutritional scams. The net effect is to increase the number of false positives, each of which represents either (a) a nonexistent condition that can be "treated" by dietary supplements or (b) a misdiagnosed condition that can also be "treated" by supplements rather than receiving a much-needed, safe, and effective treatment. Let's see how false positives can be encouraged.

Validity

Because many practitioners of nutritional scams are either unschooled in science, averse to it for some reason, or fond of a particular theory for which there is little or no scientific support, they tend to use tests with unknown or demonstrably poor validity. For example, in a fascinating chapter on "phony tests," Barrett and Herbert (1994) describe several dubious diagnostic tests, including "hair analysis." Hair analysis is offered by many professional laboratories to help diagnose a wide variety of diseases. In 1983 and 1984, Stephen

Barrett sent two hair samples apiece from two healthy teenagers to 18 commercial hair analysis labs. The labs used different thresholds for what they considered "normal" levels of various minerals and gave markedly different results, even for samples from the same girl processed at the same lab. All of the labs that offered "treatment" advice for detected deficiencies recommended "bizarre mixtures of vitamins, minerals, nonessential food substances, enzymes, and extracts of animal organs. One report diagnosed twenty-three 'possible or probable conditions,' including atherosclerosis and kidney failure, and recommended fifty-six supplement doses per day" (Barrett & Herbert, 1994, p. 125).

By definition, using invalid tests inflates the error rate in decision making. Moreover, terms such as "possible or probable conditions"—obviously intended to be interpreted as indications of disease—will greatly increase the false positive rate; that is, the number of people judged to have a medical condition by the test who, in reality, do not. At the same time, such terms allow practitioners to deftly avoid legal trouble by not coming right out and making false diagnoses. Perhaps the most disturbing thing about practitioners who use invalid tests is their shirking of the serious responsibility that comes with making health claims. The May/June 1998 National Council Against Health Fraud newsletter chronicles the case of Edwin E. Kokes, owner and operator of Independent Testing Labs of Grand Island, Nebraska. Kokes had been diagnosing nonexistent conditions and selling unapproved drugs since 1989. A self-proclaimed but unlicensed physician, he took in nearly $1 million in seven years by diagnosing diseases such as AIDS and cancer from hair or fingernail samples. During its investigation, the Food and Drug Administration sent Kokes samples from healthy adults. Kokes, in turn, identified these adults as having allergies, toxic blood levels, and problems with glands, reproductive organs, and the liver and kidneys. He even diagnosed a number of human diseases when sent *guinea pig* hair! As a follow-up to these diagnoses, Kokes prescribed his own unapproved drugs, one of which was found to contain dilute sulfuric acid (a toxin) and was being sold for up to $300 per 4-ounce container. In August, 1997, Kokes was sentenced to two and a half years in prison, fined $5,000, and ordered to pay $80,000 in restitution to his victims.

Base Rates

One easy method for inflating false positive error rates is to focus on extremely rare conditions. As we have seen, low base rate events result in great proportions of false positive decisions. The ultimate low base rate medical condition is one that does not exist at all. For example, "environmental illness"—also known as "multiple chemical sensitivity" or "allergy to everything"—is an alleged hypersensitivity to common foods and chemicals that self-fashioned "clinical ecologists" claim results from an overload of physical and psychological stress.

However, there is simply no evidence that this hypothetical malady exists. Moreover, this is the only diagnosis that clinical ecologists have to offer, which brings to mind the old saying: "When the only tool you have is a hammer, everything looks like a nail." By refusing to speak the language of valid medical diagnoses, perpetrators of nutritional scams are able to more easily diagnose fictitious disorders.

Selection Ratio

Many questionnaires that allegedly assess nutritional deficiencies have thresholds set at zero: They are specifically designed to suggest that *everyone* should purchase dietary supplements. This effectively sets the selection ratio at 100%. Barrett and Herbert (1994, p. 46) reprinted the following questionnaire from a Neiman-Marcus brochure:

1. Do you work under high pressure conditions?
2. Are you under physical or emotional strain?
3. Do you travel frequently?
4. Are you often frustrated, tense, or anxious?
5. Do you become tired, upset, or depressed easily?
6. Do you abuse your health with too much coffee, alcohol, drugs, or cigarettes?
7. Are you physically active or do you exercise often?
8. Have there been major changes in your life recently?
   If you answered "yes" to any of the above, your body may be depleting itself of nutrients vital for good health.

The questions on this "Stress Survey," in fact, have virtually nothing to do with nutrition. The simple truth is that you cannot determine deficits in the body's nutrients without careful laboratory testing. Thus, questionnaires such as this one are invalid. In particular, the decision threshold is intentionally set fantastically low. It is laughable to think that a mere "yes" answer to any one of these questions suggests a nutritive deficiency.

For an even more extreme example, consider the first two questions from a "Free Radicals Questionnaire" distributed by the manufacturers of Maharishi Ayur-Veda Products:

1. Food quality: which do you eat most—
   a. processed, packaged, and leftover foods
   b. mix of a. and c.
   c. organic and fresh foods
2. Meats: which do you eat most—
   a. ground meats, hamburger, sausage, etc.
   b. chicken, fish
   c. vegetarian dishes (no meat)

These two questions come from "Part One: Toxic Chemicals/Radiation." Although the authors of the test are clearly trying to portray certain foods as good and others as evil, your guess is as good as mine as to where "toxic chemicals" or "radiation" fits into this picture. Two other sections of the test cover "Wear and Tear" and "Emotional Stress." A total of 18 questions cover topics that are, at best, only partially relevant to nutrition. And then you come to . . .

HOW TO EVALUATE YOUR SCORE

Each "A" indicates a VERY HIGH risk factor.
Each "B" indicates a SIGNIFICANT risk factor.
Each "C" indicates a MODERATE risk factor.

Thus, no matter what your choices or how conscientious you are about matters of health, you are at risk! The icing on the cake comes in a special note beneath the scoring system:

> In all cases, free radical risk factors are greater today than ever before, because of pollutants, radiation, toxic chemicals in our water and food, and other factors we cannot individually control. *Everyone needs protection against excess free radicals.* [emphasis added]

This last sentence neatly summarizes the desired effect. The only reason anyone would bother to administer a questionnaire if they have decided that everyone needs protection is to persuade potential customers of their vulnerability.

The combined effect of using invalid tests, diagnosing low base rate (or outright nonexistent) diseases, and artificially setting the decision threshold at zero (selection ratio of 100%) is a gross inflation of the false positive diagnostic rate. This serves the interests of those selling supplements by creating a need for them.

PROTECTING AGAINST PROFESSIONAL MISCONDUCT

Not only are most laypersons unaware of the fundamentals of valid psychological assessment, but so are large numbers of professionals. The best way to protect yourself against the danger of an inappropriate decision is to understand the basics of assessment and decision making.

First, you should be wary of invalid tests and other practices that attempt to force square pegs into round holes. Those who practice a "one-size-fits-all" approach to diagnosis and treatment often shield themselves with seemingly objective "checklists" like those included at the beginning of this chapter. *None* of these checklists has been scientifically evaluated. There is *no* evidence linking even a single one of the alleged "symptoms" to repressed memories of any sort, let alone memories of child sexual abuse. Moreover, as noted in Chapter 15, the validity of repressed memories themselves is highly questionable. Pseudoscientists include symptoms with high base rates of occurrence on checklists with high selection ratios to suggest that just about everyone has repressed memories. Because one can only guess at the predictive power of such checklists, ethical guidelines for the responsible use of tests (American Psychological Association, 1992) prohibit their use. Unfortunately, this does not stop those who fervently believe in widespread repression from using them.

Though their patients may never realize this, unscrupulous practitioners can and do abuse assessment devices to reach the same diagnosis or treatment decision for everyone. You should be very careful to avoid pseudoscientists who strongly endorse only one method of diagnosis or treatment, thereby finding that everyone fits the mold. One way to do this is to ask about the number of patients who are referred elsewhere for more appropriate treatment. Any practitioner who does not routinely refer some patients to other specialists is likely offering one treatment well beyond its limited (if not *absent*) range of effectiveness.

Exercise your right to the best available judgment and care by challenging professionals to give you information about the validity of tests, base rates, and selection ratios so that you can do a rough double-check of their decision-making process. Merely raising these issues may be enough to make practitioners aware that you are unwilling to be a square peg forced into a round hole.

INFOTRAC COLLEGE EDITION

To learn more about topics included in this chapter, enter the following search terms:

decision theory
mammogram
repressed memory

DECISIONS

Clinical Versus Statistical Approaches

The last Rorschach ink blot test that Robyn Dawes (1994) administered had a tremendous impact on his career. The 16-year-old girl that he assessed had been hospitalized against her will by her parents because she was dating a man 10 years older than herself. Though naturally upset about being locked away, she was both smart and mature for her age. The girl achieved an IQ score of 126, which is at the 95th percentile, and 40 out of 41 of her Rorschach responses were scored as "good form," meaning that the images she described could be perceived by an observer. The single "bad form" response was to card eight: "It just looks like a bear. That's all. I can't explain." Though I cannot reprint actual Rorschach cards here, suffice it to say that card eight does not look like a bear. When Dawes brought up the test results at a subsequent staff meeting, here is what occurred:

> The head psychologist displayed card number eight to everyone assembled and asked rhetorically: "Does that look like a bear to you?" No one thought it did. He then "explained why" the girl had said it looked like a bear: She had been hallucinating. She was a "pseudo-neurotic schizophrenic" who knew how to appear normal even though she was often hallucinating. . . . Thus, the staff members should ignore the fact that she did not appear to be psychotic . . . . When I protested that 40 good form responses out of 41 was actually a higher percentage than found among most perfectly normal people, the head psychologist replied that while I understood statistics, I failed to understand people. In particular, I failed to understand that "statistics do not apply to the individual." . . . The patient was finally diagnosed as "schizophrenic" and sent home to her parents, because the particular setting where I was employed was not one that could deal with schizophrenia. *The staff—over my objections—further agreed that if her parents were ever to bring her back, she should be sent directly to the nearby state hospital.* For all I know, she may well have been condemned to serve time in that snake pit on the basis of a single Rorschach response. But I don't know for sure. I quit. (Dawes, 1994, pp. 153–154, emphasis in original)

TWO APPROACHES TO DECISION MAKING

There are two alternative ways to make decisions, and these are traditionally referred to as the "clinical" and "statistical" approaches (Meehl, 1954). The clinical approach involves nothing more sophisticated than using unaided human judgment to evaluate available information and arrive at a decision. This technique does not necessarily involve a professional clinician—the term is broadly applied whenever a person makes a prediction. For example, the head psychologist who considered the test results and reached a diagnosis of schizophrenia was following the clinical approach to decision making. The statistical approach, by contrast, involves the use of an equation derived from quantitative information to make decisions. Dawes's suggestion that the staff should consider the percentage of "bad form" responses made by perfectly normal individuals was an attempt to follow the statistical approach to prediction.

In the end, any decision is made using one of these two approaches. Although a common proposition is that any reasonable decision maker uses a combination of these methods (e.g., Kleinmuntz, 1990), there is an important sense in which this cannot literally be true. If both approaches yield the same prediction, this is a nonissue. When decisions recommended by these approaches disagree, however, you have to choose one or the other. One cannot assign two conflicting diagnoses, for example. The most fair and ethically defensible approach to decision making is the one that has demonstrably superior predictive validity. Anything less shortchanges individuals who lives are affected by these decisions.

The clinical approach to prediction has been associated with a desire for causal rather than probabilistic explanations (Dawes, 1991, 1994, 1995) as well as a search for narrative truth—a plausible "good story"—as opposed to a purely factual or historical account (Spence, 1982). Information is combined into a sequence of events that appears coherent and plausible. This has been identified as a more risky approach to prediction, given its practitioners' refusal to accept the error inherent in statistical techniques by aspiring to perfect predictions (Einhorn, 1986). Although there is a long-standing debate regarding the relative efficacy of these two approaches, research spanning more than four decades has consistently indicated that the predictive accuracy of statistical equations is equal or superior to human judgment (Dawes, Faust, & Meehl, 1989; Grove, 2000). This is true in many contexts, including predictions of academic success, business bankruptcy, longevity, military training success, myocardial infarction, neuropsychological diagnosis, parole violation, police officer termination, psychiatric diagnosis, and violence (Dawes, Faust, & Meehl, 1993). Findings indicate that probabilistic relationships between events are more readily obtained and verified than causal understanding, that historical truth is more accurate than narrative truth, and that acceptance of a fixed amount of error leads to a minimum number of incorrect decisions.

One particular review of the evidence is of special importance. Sawyer (1966) compared the clinical and mechanical (statistical) approaches to decision making at the stages of *data collection* and *data combination*. Methods of clinical and mechanical data combination have already been discussed. Clinical data collection, on the other hand, included tests, questionnaires, and interviews that lacked norms against which to compare individual responses (e.g., the Rorschach). In contrast, mechanical data collection included testing and assessment devices that were standardized in their format, administration, and/or scoring (e.g., IQ tests). Sawyer's review examined the validity of four possible prediction strategies: clinical collection and combination; clinical collection and mechanical combination; mechanical collection and clinical combination; and mechanical collection and combination. His results clearly indicated that mechanical procedures were independently superior at both stages of the decision-making process. Regardless of how it is later combined, information collected mechanically is more useful than information collected clinically. And, in line with the thesis of this chapter, regardless of how it was collected, information is *combined* more validly by a mechanical process than by human judgment.

Paul Meehl, an ardent proponent of the statistical approach, has been urging decision makers to pay attention to these findings since his classic review of the controversy in 1954. By 1986, he was able to cite a vast array of research supporting his initial position:

> There is no controversy in social science that shows such a large body of qualitatively diverse studies coming out so uniformly in the same direction as this one. When you are pushing 90 investigations [as of 1992, the number is 175; Meehl, 1992], predicting everything from the outcome of football games to the diagnosis of liver disease and when you can hardly come up with a half dozen studies showing even a weak tendency in favor of the clinician, it is time to draw a practical conclusion. (1986, p. 374)

WHY IS THE STATISTICAL APPROACH SUPERIOR?

The comparatively high predictive validity of statistical decision making has been attributed to two sources: desirable properties of statistical techniques and undesirable cognitive biases of human judgment. Statistical equations possess many advantageous mathematical properties and, in contrast with fallible human reasoning, are extremely effective in detecting relationships between events amid considerable variability. Our mental shortcuts further broaden the gap between statistical and clinical predictions. Goldberg (1991) outlines five illustrative comparisons between the two approaches that help to explain the superiority of statistical decision making.

Validity

Statistical techniques detect and adjust for the value of different types of information (Dawes, 1971, 1979). Information that is in reality related to an important outcome is weighted more heavily than is irrelevant information. By contrast, human judgment not only fails to appropriately weight information in this way, but also brings various biases to the prediction task (Kahneman, Slovic, & Tversky, 1982; Nisbett & Ross, 1980; Turk & Salovey, 1988). In particular, information processing often relies on three judgmental heuristics—anchoring, availability, and representativeness—and is sometimes plagued by problems such as superstitious belief, illusions of control, mistaken perceptions of randomness, and confirmation bias. This is only a partial listing of the many factors that reduce the validity with which decision makers weight information.

As but one example of the more valid weights assigned by statistical procedures than by human judges, consider the important judgments involved in reaching parole decisions. Quinsey and Maguire (1986) found that when rating the dangerousness of men in a maximum security psychiatric institution, experienced forensic clinicians weighted the frequency of aggression within the institution fairly heavily in their decision policy. While this information seems intuitively compelling, institutional aggression was found to be unrelated to recidivism (the repetition of crime by people after they are released from prison) over a period of 11 years or more, rendering the clinicians' dangerousness ratings invalid. In comparison, statistical prediction systems weighted this and other information more appropriately. As a result, their accuracy—though not 100%—surpassed the accuracy of clinical predictions (Quinsey & Maguire, 1986; Wormith & Goldstone, 1984).

Units of Measurement

Statistical techniques can easily combine information that is measured on different scales, a feat that is challenging for human decision makers given the computational limits of their judgment. Human judges have difficulty combining information that is measured in different ways and tend to over-utilize information presented in the same metric as the outcome (Slovic & MacPhillamy, 1974). In one study, for example, participants were presented with one rank-ordered cue (each target individual's standing relative to peers on an ability test) and one categorical cue (a strong versus weak pattern of extracurricular activities for each individual) and asked to predict college admissions decisions in terms of either ranks or categories (Tversky, Sattath, & Slovic, 1988). In another condition, the metrics were reversed: The rank-ordered cue was extracurricular activities and the categorical cue was the ability test. In both conditions, participants asked to predict in terms of ranks weighted the rank-ordered cue significantly higher than did those asked to predict in terms of categories, with the opposite pattern of results obtained for categorical cue weights.

Now consider a more significant, real-world decision scenario: case workers determining the fate of children referred to the state because of allegations of abuse or neglect. The units of measurement of information typically available in child welfare decision making vary widely. Many types of information are strictly categorical in nature (e.g., child sex and race, the relationship of an alleged perpetrator to the child), whereas other types of information are more continuous in nature (e.g., child age, the duration and number of abuse incidents). Without a common metric, it is remarkably difficult for human judges to effectively combine such disparate types of information, and the accuracy of child welfare decisions that are derived from clinical judgments suffers as a result (Ruscio, 1998).

Reliability

People have a certain irreplaceable skill for identifying information that should be considered when making predictions, but they are incapable of consistently applying any one prediction formula (Goldberg, 1986). The consistent application of a decision strategy is what constitutes judgmental reliability. Reliability can be established for one judge by determining how consistently he or she applies a single decision strategy. It can also be computed for several judges by determining their consistency in judgments regarding the same case(s). The validity of decisions is constrained by a lack of either type of reliability.

For example, suppose an individual decides to place a referred child in foster care on one occasion and is then surreptitiously given exactly the same information about the child at a later date. If the individual's decision this second time is to keep the child at home, this indicates a poor level of reliability. Because only one of these decisions can be "correct," the decision maker may as well be flipping a coin to determine the fate of this child. Likewise, if two different decision makers arrive at different decisions regarding this case, at most one of them can be correct. Thus, the validity of the decisions of one or both decision makers is necessarily low.

Poor reliability (both within and between judges) is perhaps the largest problem faced in the domain of child welfare decision making. Researchers have attributed this problem to a lack of well-defined institutional goals as well as the predominantly subjective nature of decisions made in the absence of a theoretical or empirical foundation for prediction (e.g., Alter, 1985; DePanfilis & Scannapieco, 1994; Gleeson, 1987; Schuerman & Vogel, 1986). The result of these limitations is poor within- and between-judge agreement, even among experts in the field (Mandel, Lehman, & Yuille, 1994). Based in part on the low reliability of child welfare decisions, Lindsey (1992) seriously questioned the foundation of the dramatic interventions commonly used today, arguing that such actions lack sufficient scientific basis.

In contrast, statistical techniques generate predictions in a perfectly reliable manner. Given the same data on repeated occasions, statistical equations generate identical decisions. It is precisely this consistency that accounts for the success of "judgmental bootstrapping" techniques, in which equations modeling human judges are used to make predictions (Camerer, 1981; Dawes, 1971, 1979; Dawes & Corrigan, 1974; Goldberg, 1965, 1970). The human judge possesses some skill for selecting the important cues to incorporate into predictions. Statistical models take advantage of this skill while applying it with perfect reliability. As a result of improved reliability, the accuracy of decisions increases.

Redundancy

When a statistical equation is applied, the redundancy among the different pieces of information is taken into account. If a new variable is added that is highly redundant with other variables in the equation, it is given less weight than if it contributed something unique. Not only is it unlikely that people fully consider these interrelationships among available pieces of information, but evidence suggests that we tend to *prefer* redundant information because it bolsters confidence in our decisions (Kahneman & Tversky, 1973; Slovic, 1966).

For example, some educators believe that "multiple intelligences" should be assessed to aid decision making in the classroom (e.g., Chen & Gardner, 1997). But do additional measures of allegedly distinct intelligences contribute new information that improves decisions? Although multiple intelligences can be assessed reliably, their validity has been called into question (Plucker, Callahan, & Tomchin, 1996). Even more important, "full-scale" or total IQ tends to predict meaningful outcomes so well that additional types of IQ (e.g., verbal, mathematical, spatial, etc.) do not significantly increase predictive power (Glutting, Youngstrom, Ward, Ward, & Hale, 1997). Even when predicting something like reading ability, adding a measure of verbal IQ to full-scale IQ does not boost predictions. Thus, even if multiple intelligences exist, they are likely to be so highly redundant with one another that—for practical purposes—a single measure of general intelligence is sufficient (Bray, Kehle, & Hintze, 1998). The addition of multiple intelligences would therefore add no more validity but considerably more time and expense to the assessment and prediction process (Schmidt & Hunter, 1998).

Regression Effects

One final contrast between clinical and statistical approaches involves a more subtle issue known as "regression toward the mean." Suppose a student takes the Graduate Record Examination (GRE) and scores a 1400. Without studying, practicing, or otherwise preparing, this student takes the GRE again one month later. What score should be expected? If you're like most people, you probably guessed something quite close to 1400, perhaps even a bit higher, as an initial score of this magnitude suggests a high level of ability. However, such an expectation is unlikely to be met. This is because test performance is made up of two components: actual ability and random situational factors (luck, fatigue, etc.). What tends to produce a *particularly* high score is the combination of high ability *and* a lucky day. One's ability is stable, but luck is random. Those who have a very lucky day are not likely to have *as* lucky a day the next time around. Therefore, if everyone who scored high took the test again, they would tend to score a bit lower, on average, because they would not tend to be quite as lucky the second time. By the same reasoning, those who score quite poorly on a test are likely to have done so in part because of poor luck, and therefore should do a little better, on average, on a retest.

Whenever any outcome (such as a second test score) can only be imperfectly predicted, there will be some "regression toward the mean." That is, scores that are extreme the first time around tend to be less extreme the second time. Misunderstanding of this principle contributes to many of our unrealistic expectations.

It has been observed that during the week after appearing on the cover of *Sports Illustrated,* athletes seldom perform as well as they did during the week preceding their appearance on the cover. This observation has given rise to a belief in a *"Sports Illustrated* jinx" which has caused several star athletes to refuse to appear on the cover of this magazine. A more careful consideration of the situation reveals the fallacious reasoning. What is it that gets an athlete onto the cover of *Sports Illustrated?* Surely it is outstanding ability, *in part,* but also a bit of good luck. An outstanding athlete is required to perform *exceptionally* well to get on the cover, which means that a combination of high ability and good luck is required. But because the luck component of performance can be expected to vary over time, most athletes will not experience as good a week following their appearance on the cover of *Sports Illustrated* as they did during the week that got them on the cover.

The failure to consider chance-related aspects of performance is a fundamental flaw in human reasoning. The accuracy of our predictions suffers to the extent that our expectations are too extreme. By contrast, statistical equations make perfectly regressive predictions. In fact, the most commonly used type of equation employed to make predictions is called a "regression equation" for this very reason. Consequently, statistical predictions are usually less extreme than clinical predictions, and therefore afford more accurate decisions.

ADHERENCE TO THE CLINICAL APPROACH

Despite the overwhelming preponderance of empirical evidence and theoretical arguments favoring statistical prediction, practitioners in many fields continue to employ the clinical approach to decision making. One survey, for example, found that a majority of neuropsychologists favor clinical prediction of intellectual deficits over the use of statistical equations whose higher validity has repeatedly been demonstrated (Guilmette, Faust, Hart, & Arkes, 1990). Meehl (1986) attributes this unwarranted adherence to the clinical approach to several sources.

Knowledge Deficit

There are at least three common knowledge deficits that prevent some practitioners from utilizing a statistical decision-making strategy. First, people are often unaware of the many biases that can influence human judgment. Anyone even casually familiar with this subject should understand the need for decision aids to supplement clinical judgment (Arkes, 1991; Faust, 1986; Kleinmuntz, 1990; Ruscio, 1998). Second, even if the pitfalls of human judgment are understood, people may be unaware that statistical techniques are available to aid decision making. Third, among those people who do know about the techniques, some may have no idea how to implement them. However, none of these reasons provide a rational justification for clinging to the clinical approach when making important decisions.

Fear of Computers

Because statistical decision making is generally implemented on computers, practitioners who are relatively unfamiliar or inexperienced with computers tend to avoid the statistical approach to prediction. Although the fear of computers was once more widespread, this trend is likely to erode over time and may in fact be reversing. As computers have become more prevalent in the workplace, an understanding of their use has become a prerequisite for many jobs. Indeed, it is difficult to imagine performing many office tasks *without* the use of a computer. Some modern computer programs have become so sophisticated and user-friendly that one now risks the pitfall of relying on them too heavily because of their simplicity. This, too, can be dangerous; relying on user-friendly, computerized statistical decision aids of undemonstrated validity is every bit as foolish as relying on clinical judgment of undemonstrated (or inferior) validity (Matarazzo, 1986). It is important to keep in mind that the demonstrable validity of a decision-making policy, not simply its ease of use, is what ensures its practical utility and ethical acceptability. Choosing an approach to prediction based primarily on your comfort is unfair to those whose lives are influenced by your decisions.

Fear of Unemployment

Many people avoid statistical decision making because they fear the threat of technological unemployment. They worry that an equation performing professional functions may displace professionals, perhaps even themselves. This is a largely unfounded fear, particularly in fields where there are many social constraints detrimental to decision making: a lack of necessary information, administrative pressures such as deadlines or excessive paperwork, high case-loads, fear of legal reprisal, and a lack of necessary training and experience (Murdach, 1994). Although practitioners faced with these extra challenges may be especially reluctant to abandon the clinical approach to prediction, such factors actually argue strongly for a statistical approach. The presence of severe limits on workers' time and energy highlights the critical importance of improving the efficiency of decision making. The employment of a statistical decision-making tool would do precisely this. Less time would be spent on activities at which people are relatively poor—namely, combining information to reach decisions—thereby freeing time for activities at which they are invaluable, such as gathering relevant information and providing actual services. Thus, technological unemployment is hardly an issue.

Belief in the Efficacy of One's Judgment

Another frequent obstacle to the employment of statistical techniques is the steadfast belief of many individuals in the validity of their own judgments. The persistence of a "controversy" over statistical versus clinical prediction is no doubt due partly to people's unwillingness to admit that equations can perform some professional functions better than professionals. In several telling studies, for example, participants were provided with the predictions generated by the statistical equation against which they were competing (e.g., Goldberg, 1968, 1970; Sawyer, 1966). The simplest possible use of that information—copying it—would have resulted in predictions equal in accuracy to those of the equation. However, people seemed compelled to try to "beat the odds," to modify the statistical predictions with which they disagreed in order to achieve more "hits" and fewer "misses" than the equation. Their attempts almost invariably resulted in lower accuracy.

Decision makers commonly point to their training and experience as support for the quality of their decisions. Considerable research has been conducted to determine whether individuals with extensive training and experience with a particular decision-making task can compete favorably on that task with statistical equations. In fact, Meehl (1954, 1959, 1967) proposed that certain task characteristics, most notably complex relationships between variables, would favor the highly trained and experienced clinician. He maintained that complex decision-making tasks required professionals capable of complex thinking. Contrary to these expectations, the search for individuals who can outpredict equations has thus far been in vain (Goldberg, 1991; Slovic & Lichtenstein, 1971; Stewart, 1988). Substantial bodies of research have demonstrated that neither training nor experience significantly influences the quality of clinical judgment (Berman & Norton, 1985; Dawes, 1989, 1994; Faust, 1986; Faust & Ziskin, 1988; Garb, 1989; Goldberg, 1959; Oskamp, 1965; Ziskin & Faust, 1988). Therefore, it seems that appeals to formal training and clinical experience in support of clinical prediction are, as Dawes would say, "arguments from a vacuum."

Theoretical Identifications

A professional who believes strongly in one theoretical approach is likely to dismiss a decision-making strategy based on other theories. This is unwise because the worth of an approach is determined by its observable accuracy, not by whether one happens to agree with its premises. In fact, strong theoretical identifications and beliefs serve to boost confidence, which is itself worthy of careful scrutiny for two reasons (Ruscio, 2000). First, overconfidence can be harmful to the person making the decision, because an overconfident professional is not likely to try to improve his or her performance. If you already believe that you are doing quite well, where is the motivation to do even better? Second, overconfidence can be harmful to others because it is often mistakenly confused with accuracy. For example, research has found that court testimony may have a greater impact on a judge or jury when it is stated confidently, regardless of its actual validity (Faust & Ziskin, 1988; Ziskin & Faust, 1988). A sizable body of research has demonstrated that, in addition to predicting more poorly than statistical equations, people ordinarily hold greater confidence in their judgments than their validity merits (Dawes, Faust, & Meehl, 1989; Faust & Ziskin, 1988; Lichtenstein & Fischhoff, 1977; Lichtenstein, Fischhoff, & Phillips, 1982; Ruscio, 2000; Ziskin & Faust, 1988).

Fischhoff (1988) suggests that one appeal of the clinical approach to decision making is that it appears to be capable of achieving perfect prediction. In order to significantly improve predictive validity by adopting a statistical decision-making policy, one must first accept that a fixed percentage of decisions will necessarily be wrong. Many practitioners seem unwilling to do this, preferring instead the unknown (but larger) degree of error inherent in their own judgment.

In this sense, professionals' overconfidence may arise from nothing more substantial than pure wishful thinking (Dawes, 1991, 1994). People would like outcomes to be predictable, and often prefer to believe that people—especially trained, experienced professionals—can make important decisions well. Unfortunately, "the simplest principle is that past behavior is the best predictor of future behavior and it isn't very good" (Dawes, 1991, p. 259). Wishful thinking may inflate the *perceived* quality of professional decisions, but not their *actual* quality. This only serves to hurt the people whose lives are affected by inferior decision-making practices.

The "Dehumanizing" Feel of Statistical Equations

Many people erroneously believe that the statistical integration of information denies the uniqueness of individuals or treats people as "mere numbers." In reality, statistical equations can use precisely the same information available to a clinical decision maker. Therefore, the difference between the two approaches has nothing to do with the uniqueness of individuals, but a great deal to do with combining information in the most reliable and valid manner possible for each individual. Moreover, a statistical equation is open to public scrutiny and continual revision, refinement, and improvement. In comparison, human judgment is privately held, potentially biased, and—as the research suggests—unlikely to improve much with training or experience. Therefore, the uneasy feeling that validated decision models are somehow "dehumanizing"—a belief closely linked to the mistaken conception of ethics described below—can be most charitably labeled as misinformed.

Mistaken Conception of Ethics

Perhaps because of several factors that have already been discussed, proponents of clinical prediction often argue that statistical decision making is unethical. When examined carefully, this conception of ethics appears to contain a serious logical flaw. Few would disagree, for example, that the most ethically defensible course of action is the one that has the highest demonstrated validity: the best track record of correct decisions, with the fewest mistakes. To utilize a decision-making policy that is known to err systematically more often than a statistical equation is grossly unfair to those individuals being served. Meehl (1986) states:

> If I try to forecast something important about a college student, or a criminal, or a depressed patient by inefficient rather than efficient means, meanwhile charging this person or the taxpayer 10 times as much money as I would need to achieve greater predictive accuracy, that is not a sound ethical practice. That it feels better, warmer, and cuddlier to me as predictor is a shabby excuse indeed. (p. 374)

EMBRACING STATISTICAL DECISIONS

When it comes to decision making, as with most tasks, the goal of perfection is usually unrealistic. There are irreducible uncertainties involved in many of the predictions on which important decisions are based, and—without being omniscient—we cannot beat the best odds provided by statistical predictions. Thus, the quality of our decisions is likely to improve when we accept the reality that we will make some mistakes and concentrate on minimizing them. Despite our computational limitations, we can nonetheless learn to mimic statistical decision making fairly well in our own reasoning. The simplest way that this can be done is to construct "pro/con" lists.

Pro/Con Lists

When faced with a number of options, you can improve decision making by using the old-fashioned method of writing down lists of "pros" and "cons" for each option. One surprising research finding on the accuracy of different prediction strategies is that it makes little difference how much weight you assign to each piece of information (e.g., Dawes & Corrigan, 1974). What this means is that you can simply calculate the *number* of pros minus cons for each option and choose the option with the highest score.

Consider the application of this strategy when in the market for a new car. Suppose you have narrowed down your search to a handful of models but are having a tough time making the final selection. To simulate a statistical decision process, you can make a chart listing each model of car and each attribute that is important to you, such as performance, size, cost, safety features, and fuel economy. Then, simply rate each car positively ("pro") or negatively ("con") on each attribute and choose the car with the most positive ratings. You can make this process more sophisticated, if you like, by using a numerical rating scale rather than the simple positive/negative distinction or by weighting some attributes more heavily than others into the total score for each car, but you will be surprised at how little difference this makes in most cases. The success of statistical decision making lies not in its precise handling of details (though it is impeccable in this regard) but in its consistent focus on the considerations that truly matter. You can easily apply this process through list-making and simple arithmetic to take advantage of its benefits.

Professional Practice

In addition to incorporating statistical decisions into your personal life through simple pro/con lists, you can use similar strategies to substantially improve decisions that you are asked to make in a professional capacity. For example, imagine that you are a graduate admissions officer. You have to decide which applicants to accept into your highly competitive program. Each applicant's folder contains a tremendous amount of information, including grade point average (GPA), Graduate Record Examination (GRE) scores, a personal statement, letters of reference, a complete college transcript, and a list of extracurricular activities. Left to your own devices, this is a formidable task.

It would be tough to know how to weight each of these pieces of information to reach good decisions. You might overweight information that is in fact unrelated to success in graduate school, or underweight information that would have increased predictive accuracy. By adopting a statistical procedure, weighting information according to its known validity, you would boost your accuracy.

Consider how you might combine each applicant's GPA (measured on a scale from 0 to 4) with his or her GRE score (measured on a scale from 400 to 1600) to most fairly compare one applicant with another. All else being equal, which of these students is the most qualified: a student with a 3.20 GPA and a GRE score of 1200, or a student with a 3.40 GPA and a GRE score of 1100? Think how much more difficult this task would be if you were to also consider additional factors. Whereas these tasks are difficult for the human mind, a statistical equation would handle such work with ease.

Suppose someone takes one of the files you have already read and puts it back into your pile. Provided you do not recognize it, how confident can you be that you would reach the same admissions decision? We tend to be plagued by momentary, situational factors like distraction and fatigue, and for a variety of reasons we are not perfectly consistent in our judgments. Because of this, our accuracy suffers a bit. A statistical approach, on the other hand, would make these predictions with perfect reliability.

Having read one letter of reference, you might be tempted to read the remaining letters to see whether they confirm one another. Such letters tend to paint a consistent picture of the applicant. Thus, because they are at least partially redundant with one another, the letters should not be counted as completely separate pieces of information. Each additional letter should be given less weight than the last because it adds less unique information that has not already been gleaned from other sources. Statistical equations automatically make this type of adjustment for redundancies.

Finally, recognizing that extreme scores—whether good or bad—are the product of both ability and luck, you might wisely temper your predictions. Someone who has an impressive GRE score but a modest GPA may not be more qualified than someone who has a somewhat above-average GRE score and GPA. Though your attention can easily be drawn to a single extreme score, taking into account regression toward the mean will likely improve the validity of your decisions. Once again, the use of a statistical decision aid—which automatically adjusts for regression toward the mean—can help you reach more accurate decisions and make fewer admissions mistakes.

Professionals should take advantage of statistical decision making to the greatest extent possible. How can statistical prediction formulas be obtained? A fortunate investigator may hit the jackpot by coming across a validated prediction formula through a careful search of the relevant research literature. Even if the investigator is not so fortunate, this literature search will reveal variables that are—and are not—important to assess and incorporate into the decision process. With this information, a prediction system can be developed fairly easily. In fact, even without any background data on potential variables to assess, you will find that developing a statistical prediction formula starting from scratch is not particularly difficult (see Ruscio, 1998).

Statistics Do Apply to the Individual

Back in Chapter 8, we debunked the "probability is irrelevant to the individual" fallacy. It is disheartening to observe that many people—often those in positions of power—subscribe to this erroneous belief, including the head psychologist in the case that opened this chapter. Would this psychologist have preferred to play Russian roulette with one or with four bullets in the chamber? Keep in mind the important fact that statistics *do* apply to the individual and that denial of this fact, like adherence to the demonstrably inferior clinical approach to decision making, may be positively unethical.

INFOTRAC COLLEGE EDITION

To learn more about topics included in this chapter, enter the following search terms:

child welfare
decision making
multiple intelligence
recidivism
regression effect

ETHICS

The Use and Promotion of Unverified Treatments

Anxiety and depression are the two most common symptoms of the millions of people who seek psychotherapy each year. For a moment, put yourself in the shoes of someone who has become anxious or depressed. Perhaps you have recently been separated or divorced, lost your job, or lost a loved one. Now suppose you decide to enlist the services of a psychotherapist to help you reduce these symptoms and learn to cope better with future stresses. What would you expect an initial meeting to involve? You would no doubt explain what brought you to therapy, describing your problems with the hope that the therapist can provide some mixture of support and sound advice. What if your therapist, however, was not interested in your complaints? What if he or she had all but decided, before even meeting you, that the *true* cause of your problems is that you were sexually abused as a child, ritually abused by a satanic cult, or abducted by aliens? What if your therapist believes that this hypothetical trauma—of which you have not even the faintest recollection—has caused your personality to split such that you are suffering not from anxiety or depression, but from multiple personality disorder?

OVERLOOKING THE OBVIOUS IN FAVOR OF THE UNLIKELY

Although this scenario probably seems unreal to you, it is very real for large numbers of unsuspecting patients. Some therapists *do* choose to look beyond the obvious and discern the fantastic, as this patient's story illustrates:

> My psychologist kept asking me about my childhood and he seemed insistent that I had been sexually abused as a child. I tried to be very cooperative because I wanted out of that hospital. I didn't understand why my therapist was not interested in hearing about the recent causes of my depression—a painful divorce, sexual harassment on the job, stress from a new marriage, and a recent drastic change in lifestyle. I trusted him, however, and if he believed that all of my

problems were due to some traumatic incident in my childhood [that] I apparently had forgotten, I assumed he must be right because he was the psychology expert. (Gavigan, 1992, p. 246)

For this patient—and for Patricia Burgus, whose story opened this book—her presenting symptoms and related stressors were willfully ignored. Bennett Braun and his colleagues eagerly overlooked Patricia's obvious symptoms of depression, along with its clear causes, in an effort to ferret out evidence to support their preferred diagnosis of MPD. Likewise, rather than treat Patricia's depression, they insisted that she recover memories of satanic ritual abuse. One can only guess how her life would be different if she had received a short-term, empirically supported cognitive therapy or appropriate medication for her depression rather than 10 years of an unverified treatment that plunged her into the depths of human misery.

As we explore such questionable therapeutic practices, consider the ethics of the situation. The following discussion of repressed memories and multiple personalities leads to a focused treatment of the ethical issues.

REPRESSED MEMORIES AND MULTIPLE PERSONALITIES

Among the most virulent and destructive mental health pseudosciences of our time are two trauma-related approaches to psychotherapy. First, practitioners who specialize in "memory recovery" argue that when we are confronted with traumatic events, our mind automatically represses the trauma, blocking it from our conscious awareness as an adaptive response to overwhelming circumstances. Years or even decades later, these repressed memories are said to manifest themselves in psychological disturbances and disorders that cannot be alleviated until the underlying memories are addressed. Thus, the task of recovering memories is considered the central component of therapy.

Second, those who specialize in diagnosing and treating multiple personality disorder argue that when we are confronted with traumatic events, our conscious awareness splits, or dissociates, creating "alter personalities" that store the experience of the tramua to protect us. Later, when we show signs of psychological disturbance, it is allegedly the work of our disjointed personalities.

The techniques by which repressed memories are recovered and alter personalities are elicited are quite similar. In both cases, therapists take advantage of the authority of their role, probing the patients' past with highly suggestive and leading questions. They also urge patients—most of whom initially deny the bizarre claims of trauma-related memory and MPD therapists—to suspend their disbelief. Many therapists' practices encourage an active imagination, giving free reign and encouragement to flights of fantasy (Poole, Lindsay, Memon, & Bull, 1995). These therapists advise their patients to keep journals of their thoughts, feelings, and dreams, any of which might later be interpreted as evidence of a "memory" or a "personality" breaking through into awareness. "Truth serum" drugs such as sodium amytal or sodium brevital, as well as hypnosis, are frequently used as well. In the end, therapists often succeed in eliciting memories or personalities that are remarkably consistent with their initial suspicions.

As you may already suspect, there are many logical and empirical challenges facing both of these therapeutic approaches and the beliefs on which they are based. Below, I review some of the major problems facing memory recovery, the diagnosis and treatment of MPD, or both (see Dawes, 1994; Lilienfeld et al., 1999; Loftus, 1997; Ofshe & Watters, 1996; Pendergrast, 1995; Piper, 1997, 1998; Sagan, 1995; Spanos, 1996; for extended discussions).

1. Ever since Freud coined the term "repression" in the 19th century, there has never been any empirical evidence to demonstrate the existence of such a mental mechanism (Ofshe & Watters, 1996). Of course, it is possible to forget information, or even to "suppress" it, *intentionally* blocking it from conscious awareness. However, the brain does not seem to "repress"—or *automatically* block out—information. In his later writing, Freud himself rejected the mechanism of repression, concluding that he had pressured his patients into creating fantasies (Ofshe & Watters, 1996).

2. There is a curious asymmetry in the cases in which repression is said to have occurred: Individuals with *no* recollection or documentation of trauma are said to have repressed it, whereas individuals with *documented* histories of trauma are often unable to forget the painful events.

   A case in point: children who endured unspeakable maltreatment in the ghettoes, boxcars, and concentration camps of Nazi Germany . . . no evidence exists that any developed MPD (Bower, 1994; Des Pres, 1976; Eitinger, 1980; Krystal, 1991; Sofsky, 1997) or that any dissociated or repressed their traumatic memories (Eisen, 1988; Wagenaar & Groeneweg, 1990). Similarly, the same results hold in studies of children who saw a parent murdered (Eth & Pynoos, 1994; Malmquist, 1986); studies of kidnapped children (Terr, 1979, 1983); studies of children known to have been abused (Gold, Hughes, & Hohnecker, 1994); and in several other investigations (Chodoff, 1963; Pynoos & Nader, 1989; Strom, Refsum, & Eitinger, 1962). Victims neither repressed the traumatic events, forgot about them, nor developed MPD. (Piper, 1998, pp. 48–49)

   Indeed, those who have been traumatized tend not to *repress* the memories of their experiences, but to have precisely the opposite problem: intrusive, painful flashbacks and reexperiencing of the trauma. This problem is a cardinal feature of post-traumatic stress disorder (American Psychiatric Association, 1994). Why is it that the only people who have allegedly repressed their trauma are those for whom no trauma has been documented?

3. It is noteworthy that patients undergoing "memory recovery" only recover memories that are consistent with their therapists' beliefs. Memory recovery therapists tend to subscribe to one of three theories regarding the trauma underlying psychological disturbance: child sexual abuse, satanic ritual abuse, or alien abduction. There are therapists who specialize in each of these types of trauma. Isn't it astounding, then, that patients whose therapist happens to believe in satanic ritual abuse only recover memories of being abused by satanic cults? Likewise, therapists who believe in alien abductions elicit memories of alien abduction, and those who believe that child sexual abuse is the cause of most psychological dysfunction elicit memories of child sexual abuse (Sagan, 1995). The uncanny agreement between therapists' beliefs and recovered memories strains the possibility of coincidence.

4. There is no denying that child sexual abuse is a serious problem in all human societies, that it is grossly inappropriate behavior with potentially long-lasting effects. However, there is good reason to doubt that alien abductions and/or satanic ritual abuse are harming anyone at all. Why is this? There is no evidence that either one occurs. The case against alien visitation and the claims of abductees was reviewed in Chapter 6. Moreover, the belief in satanic cults as a grand conspiracy—often said to be international and transgenerational—is dubious at best for all the reasons noted in Chapter 11. Claims of cult activity have appeared in the cultural and historical record chiefly in those times and places in which religious fundamentalism has flourished (Sagan, 1995), perhaps because certain religious beliefs necessitate the existence of the devil. Furthermore, whether law enforcement professionals espouse the penal code or the Ten Commandments (Ofshe & Watters, 1996), they are also prone to the creation of adversaries. However, the implausible allegations are also completely unsubstantiated. Independent reviews of massive investigations into hundreds (Lanning, 1989, 1991) or thousands (Goodman, Qin, Bottoms, & Shaver, 1994) of alleged satanic rituals—including those in which animals or humans (babies or adults) were killed, eaten, or buried—have concluded that there is simply *no* physical evidence of such activities.

5. In contrast to the beliefs of some therapists, our memories are not perfect recollections of the past, but *reconstructions* of our experiences (e.g., Loftus, 1997). We tend to store only "traces" of an event, then fill in the gaps with plausible details when we "remember." Here is a simple demonstration: Picture a scene in which you experienced something pleasurable. It can be anything at all, but it must be something that you are absolutely certain occurred and that you are able to visualize with 100% accuracy. Close your eyes and summon such an image. Once you have done so, answer this question: Did you see yourself in the scene?

Most people do. If you did, then it cannot have been an actual memory, but a reconstruction: You could not have been outside your own body when you stored the original memory. Traces of the memory are no doubt accurate, but you filled in the rest with educated guesses or with information that others have conveyed to you over time. Consequently, those who argue that memory is infallible—and that we should therefore accept all recovered memories as valid—are in error.

6. Disquieting as it may be, there is no infallible way to determine the validity of our memories. Research evidence has demonstrated that neither vivid detail nor emotional power is related to the accuracy of our recall (e.g., Neisser & Harsch, 1992). For example, here is what one freshman wrote of her experience the day after the space shuttle *Challenger* exploded:

   I was in my religion class and some people walked in and started talking about it. I didn't know any details except that it exploded and the schoolteacher's students had all been watching which I thought was so sad.

   As a senior, this same student described her experience quite differently:

   When I first heard about the explosion I was sitting in my freshman dorm room with my roommate and we were watching TV. It came on a news flash and we were both totally shocked. I was really upset and I went upstairs to talk to a friend of mine and then I called my parents.

   This new statement is untrue despite the fact that it contains an impressive amount of detail, compelling emotion, *and* was asserted with the highest level of confidence.

7. Just as there is no such thing as a perfect "lie detector," there is also no such thing as a perfect "truth serum." Drugs such as sodium amytal or sodium brevital merely reduce our inhibitions and place us in a more suggestible state. Thus, memories retrieved under their influence are not necessarily accurate (Ofshe & Watters, 1996).

8. Hypnosis, too, involves strong suggestions. Though we can generally retrieve more memories under the influence of a hypnotic induction procedure, the proportion of true and false memories is unchanged (Orne & Dinges, 1989). Moreover, the hypnotic "age regression" technique—in which patients are asked to reexperience an episode from earlier in life—used by some therapists merely encourage patients to engage in role-playing. It is just as easy to use hypnotic suggestions to regress people all the way back to *past lives* or, alternately, to *future lives* ("age progression"), than to their childhoods, and all of these "memories" are held with a certainty equivalent to those obtained through age regression. Because neither the existence of past lives nor the ability to see into the future has been convincingly demonstrated, the degree of confidence held in these "memories" calls the validity of

all hypnotically induced memories into question (Spanos, Weekes, Menary, & Bertrand, 1986; Spanos, Menary, Gabora, DuBreuil, & Dewhirst, 1991).

9. As was shown in Chapter 2, false memories can be implanted through a brief series of suggestive and leading questions, especially when combined with the questionable techniques described above (Loftus, 1997). These memories are compelling, but false. Ceci and Bruck (1995) have documented the increased risk of false memories when respected, high-status individuals conduct repeated interviews under the influence of a powerful confirmation bias. Over the course of many weeks, months, or even years, it should not be surprising that therapists can exert a dramatic influence over patients who eagerly trust their wisdom in the quest for relief.

10. The enactment of multiple personalities has also been observed in laboratory settings. Perfectly normal, healthy individuals have been shown to understand the social cues used to elicit "alter" personalities and tend to respond accordingly when the situation calls for such play-acting (Spanos, Weekes, & Bertrand, 1985).

11. Multiple identity enactments are common across the diverse cultures of the world (Spanos, 1996). Throughout history, for example, individuals acting out demonic possession or mass hysteria have tended to behave in ways consistent with the cultural expectations of their societies. So do the MPD patients of today. Multiple identity enactments that match cultural expectations can be elicited in a variety of ways—including the rituals and traditions of many cultural groups as well as the simple laboratory inductions of psychological researchers—and are not necessarily related to trauma, alter personalities, or any psychological disturbance at all.

12. As noted in Chapter 7, there is no evidence that documented trauma is associated with a diagnosis of MPD, let alone that it is a causal factor (Lilienfeld et al., 1999; Ofshe & Watters, 1996; Piper, 1997). Unfortunately, due to the popularization of two cases with questionable authenticity—*Sybil* and *The Three Faces of Eve*—the "argument from a vacuum" that trauma causes MPD is widely believed.

13. The rate of MPD diagnoses has exploded in the past two decades. As noted in Chapter 9, the 200 or so cases present in the world literature before the media popularization of MPD (Bliss, 1980) have grown to estimates that as many as 5 to 10% of all adults suffer from MPD (Ross, 1991). Is it at all plausible that the disorder has suddenly become so common? Why haven't more of us noticed this?

14. What should we make of the observation that MPD has been seen almost exclusively in America and Europe, and by relatively few clinicians (Thigpen & Cleckley, 1984)? In a telling study of all

psychiatrists in Switzerland, 90% had never seen a case of MPD, whereas three psychiatrists had diagnosed more than 20 MPD patients each. In fact, 1% of psychiatrists (6 of 655) made two-thirds of all MPD diagnoses in the country (Modestin, 1992). The most reasonable explanation for this pattern of data seems to be that a handful of trauma-focused therapists, acting on a strong confirmation bias, presume unsubstantiated traumas and overlook their own role in creating their patients' multiple identities.

15. The average age at which patients' first "alter" personality is alleged to have formed—that is, the age at which the first dissociative "split" was said to occur within the individual—has been decreasing. During the last century, it dropped from 22 to 11 years (Goff & Simms, 1993); Coons, Bowman, & Milstein (1988) estimated it at just 7 years. Why, then, are there no cases of children who exhibit multiple personalities? Given the outlandish behaviors indicative of MPD, it would surely not be a difficult condition to recognize—particularly in children, who are supervised and observed by many adults.

16. Multiple personality disorder is virtually never observed before therapy has begun. Rather, it tends to emerge only after many months or years of therapy with a trauma-focued practitioner (Ofshe & Watters, 1996; Piper, 1997). In fact, the diagnosis of MPD is not made until an average of *six to seven years* into therapy (Piper, 1997)! How could even the most naïve observer among all of the therapists, family members, friends, co-workers, and others with whom MPD patients interact fail to notice something so dramatic as MPD for so long? Why do alter personalities and eccentric behaviors typically emerge only years after therapy has begun?

All of this evidence points clearly to one conclusion: Repressed memories and alter personalities are created by therapists and suggested—using persuasive and leading tactics—to patients who have entrusted these people with their mental health. Spanos (1994) summarizes the socially constructed nature of MPD: "It is context bounded, goal-directed, social behavior geared to the expectations of significant others, and its characteristics have changed over time to meet changing expectations" (p. 143). Much the same is true of memory recovery. Therefore, the most generous assessment of these therapeutic practices is that they are "unverified treatments," whereas the most critical assessment is that they represent blatant professional misconduct.

The popularity of pseudoscientific therapy, despite its lack of demonstrated safety and efficacy, indicates that many people have incredibly lax standards of evidence. Although all of us are free to believe as we wish, when it comes to health care, universally accepted ethical principles must be followed. Two particular principles will be explored here. First, the requirement that a treatment has a net benefit—that it essentially does more good than harm—is what ethicists often call a favorable "cost-benefit ratio." Second, the closely related issues of "informed consent" and "patient autonomy" will be evaluated. Based on these analyses, I will argue that it is unethical not only to administer unverified treatments, but even to merely promote or endorse them.

COST-BENEFIT RATIO

Proponents of pseudosciences advocate treatments without providing sufficient empirical support. When considering the ethics of any such unverified treatment, one must ask whether the benefits outweigh the costs. Often, though, pseudoscientists attempt to bypass the estimation of a cost-benefit ratio by suggesting that their treatments are harmless, but might help, so therefore patients have nothing to lose. In other words, "Why not try it?" There is a certain "who knows, anything could happen" attitude underlying this carefree query. However, there are three questionable premises underlying this hand-waving approach to ethics: Proponents simultaneously overestimate the likelihood of benefit, underestimate the potential for harm, and altogether fail to consider the cost of foregoing evidence-based medical treatments.

Skewed Projections of Benefit and Harm

The benefits of trauma-focused therapy—if any—are often overstated by its practitioners. As noted earlier, there is no evidence for the benefits of either memory recovery or MPD-related treatments. Testimonials abound on *both* sides of this controversy, yet not a shred of scientific data suggests that these techniques offer any therapeutic value (Lilienfeld et al., 1999; Ofshe & Watters, 1996; Piper, 1997).

At the same time, the possibility of harm is generally understated, despite evidence that these therapies may in fact involve serious risk to patients. Loftus (1997) cites a study (Parr, 1996a, 1996b) that followed up 30 patients who recovered traumatic memories in therapy:

> Before the memories, only 3 (10%) had thought about or attempted suicide; after memories, 20 (67%) had. Before memories, only 2 (7%) had been hospitalized (presumably for psychiatric reasons); after memories, 11 (37%) had. Before memories, only one woman had engaged in self-mutilation; after memories 8 (27%) had. . . . Before entering therapy, the majority (25/30 = 83%) of the patients had been employed, but after three years of therapy, only 3 of 30 (10%) were still employed. Before therapy, 23 of the 30 (77%) were married; within three years of this time, 11/23 (48%) were either separated or divorced. Of the 21 patients who had children, one third lost custody. All 30 were estranged from their extended families. (p. 186)

Although it would be useful to compare these patients to a group of patients with similar symptoms who had instead been given empirically supported treatments, these are nevertheless not the kinds of outcomes that most people hope for when entering therapy. Better-controlled studies are needed to determine whether recovered memory therapy is as hazardous as this study suggests.

What about individuals who are diagnosed with and treated for MPD? Piper (1998) summarizes the available data pertaining to MPD therapy:

> MPD patients often significantly deteriorate during treatment (Kluft, 1984; Ofshe & Watters, 1996, Ch. 10; Pendergrast, 1995, Ch. 6). One of the disorder's leading adherents acknowledges that MPD psychotherapy "causes significant disruption in a patient's life outside the treatment setting" and that suicide attempts may occur in the weeks following the diagnosis (Putnam, 1989, pp. 98, 299). As MPD psychotherapy progresses, patients may become more dissociative, more anxious, or more depressed (Braun, 1989); the longer they remain in treatment, the more florid, elaborate, and unlikely their stories about their alleged childhood maltreatment tend to become (Ganaway, 1995; Spanos, 1996, Ch. 20). This worsening contributes to the lengthy hospitalizations—some costing millions of dollars (*Frontline*, 1995; Piper, 1994)—that often occur when MPD patients who are well-insured are treated by the disorder's enthusiasts. Hospitalizations occur more frequently after the MPD diagnosis is made (Piper, 1994; Ross & Dua, 1993). (pp. 47–48)

The Overlooked Opportunity Costs

In addition to overestimating benefit and underestimating harm, proponents of pseudoscientific treatments completely ignore what economists refer to as the "opportunity cost" of a decision. Under this principle, by choosing any one option, we miss what might have been gained through a different choice. When an unverified treatment is the chosen "opportunity," the resulting costs may include the lost benefits of science-based treatment, unchecked worsening of the condition, or aggravation of the condition by the treatment.

For example, in the *New England Journal of Medicine,* Coppes et al. (1998) presented the case of a 15-year-old boy with Hodgkin's disease who chose to take an herbal remedy rather than the chemotherapy recommended by his doctors. For two weeks, the disease progressed. By the time the boy changed his mind, the cancer had advanced to the point that more intensive chemotherapy was required. The opportunity cost of the herb was the progression of disease.

When it comes to recovered memory therapy or the diagnosis and treatment of MPD, there are substantial opportunity costs associated with forgoing empirically supported treatments for the problems that actually bring patients to therapy. As noted earlier in this chapter, the two most common presenting symptoms of mental health patients are anxiety and depression, and there are several effective treatments available for each (Chambless et al., 1996; Dobson & Craig, 1998).

Perhaps the gravest opportunity cost of all was the one discussed in Chapter 12: the religion-motivated medical neglect of children. Each year, innocent children die because their parents forgo medical treatment in lieu of religious faith alone.

When one combines the improbability of benefit, the possibility of harm, and the various opportunity costs associated with unverified treatments, the cost-benefit ratio of these treatments comes out negative. This means that pseudoscience, on the whole, is likely to do more harm than good. Moreover, anyone who *promotes* pseudoscience steers others toward a path in which they are more likely to be harmed than helped. By all standards, these practices are clearly unethical.

TRULY INFORMED CONSENT AND PATIENT AUTONOMY

Another important ethical principle involves the necessity of obtaining a patient's informed consent prior to treatment. This is done to ensure patients' autonomy and avoid paternalism. To violate someone's autonomy is to reduce his or her personal freedom. It is the professional responsibility of all health practitioners to fully inform their patients of the potential benefits and risks—and the likelihood of each—associated with each available type of treatment. A patient can make a truly informed choice *only* when provided with all of this information.

A difficult ethical dilemma arises when seriously ill patients become desperate. Cancer patients in particular are known for seeking bizarre treatments when hope is running out. We can only imagine the grief and anxiety of a terminally ill individual who is told that medical science has no effective treatment left to offer. Surely there must be *something* that can be done. Some have identified the very success of science as a cause of this failure to accept the unavailability of an effective remedy: We have become so accustomed to astonishing breakthroughs, to diseases being wiped out, to suffering being alleviated that we cannot believe there is no hope for our own return to health. Nevertheless, there remain many conditions for which there are not yet successful treatments. To pretend otherwise is to take advantage of a vulnerable human being.

Consider these two cancer treatments:

- Donald MacNay charged patients $12,000 for a cancer treatment neither approved by the FDA nor endorsed by the National Cancer Institute: administering aloe vera intravenously. After three cancer patients died following this treatment, MacNay's license was suspended by the Virginia Board of Medicine.

- Sandor Olah injected Essiac herb tea into 54-year-old Petra Hall's veins as a treatment for cancer, and she "began to experience shortness of breath and other symptoms following the treatment. Nevertheless, Olah sent Hall home. Later that day she checked into Hackley Hospital in Muskegon [Michigan] where she experienced multiple organ failure, dying 11 days later. Cause of death was listed as respiratory distress syndrome due to vitamin therapy" (May/June 1997 National Council Against Health Fraud newsletter).

All of the above-mentioned patients gave their "informed consent" prior to receiving these treatments. This demonstrates the importance of providing complete information on all likely benefits and foreseeable risks about the treatment for consent to be meaningful.

In therapy that aims to recover repressed memories or elicit multiple personalities, patient autonomy is often violated. For example, there is no allowance for patients to disagree with their therapists' judgments. One of the alleged "symptoms" of repressed memories is the absence of memories of abuse, and leaders of the MPD movement (e.g., Putnam, 1989) argue that even if patients deny having MPD and exhibit no symptoms of the disorder, they should still be treated for it! Kluft (1983) goes even further by implying that the patient's permission is not always necessary to begin treatment: "Hypnotic work should await the obtaining of informed consent, *whenever practical*" (p. 77, emphasis added). As Piper (1997) comments, "One wonders if Putnam and Kluft are aware that ethical and legal authorities take an exceedingly jaundiced view of physicians who trouble themselves so little with the bothersome trifles of informed consent" (p. 79).

How different are these attitudes from those of the clergy and judiciary who organized medieval witch hunts? Some therapists certainly possess the conviction and presumed infallibility of these priests, asserting that patients should be treated for their repressed memories or MPD whether they like it or not. Accused witches were thrown into a lake: If they sank, they were innocent; if they floated, they were guilty (and burned). Neither alternative is particularly attractive! The same is true for those who find themselves in therapy with a practitioner who targets memories of trauma or the presence of alter personalities to the exclusion of all other causal explanations.

When practitioners of unverified treatments mislead their patients by offering false hope, this clearly violates the principle of informed consent. If evidence in support of a treatment cannot be offered to a patient, if other available treatments that *are* backed by research are not described to the patient, or if any known risks of the proposed treatment are not adequately explained to the patient, then truly informed consent cannot be obtained. Pseudoscientists routinely violate this ethical principle in their advertisements and in their professional practices. This dangerous state of affairs is reminiscent of the free-for-all "dietary supplement" market described in Chapter 4. The concluding portion of the present chapter will consider proposed legislation that threatens to make the situation much, much worse.

THE "HEALTH FREEDOM" FALLACY

The Access to Medical Treatment Act is similar in many regards to DSHEA, which has thwarted consumer protection in the drug marketplace. This new proposal is a more generalized and potent threat to consumers, allowing practitioners to use *any* unverified treatment if they can obtain patients' consent. To do this, there is no obligation to communicate the probabilities of benefit or harm, but merely to provide a dubious warning: "This food, drug, or device has not been declared safe and effective by the Federal Government, and any individual who uses such food, drug, or device, does so at his or her own risk." This legitimizes unethical treatments by disguising them as a "freedom of choice" for consumers. The September/October 1997 National Center Against Health Fraud newsletter explains:

> It is obvious that the only freedom that this act would confer is to health care providers who traffic in dubious alternative/complementary medicine. In the first place, people do not want to be cheated, nor do they want to be harmed. The only reason an individual would want to be treated by an unapproved procedure is that someone has convinced them that it *IS safe and effective.* Desperate patients are willing to try most anything that a health care provider suggests *might help.*
>
> Alienation also plays a powerful role in patient behavior. Deviant providers often convince their patients that an oppressive and corrupted bureaucracy is keeping the treatment off the market. Even the language "declared . . . by the Federal Government" rather than "determined on the basis of evidence" is prejudicial. This bill is a charlatan's dream because it entices patients to sign away their rights.

If something like the Access to Medical Treatments Act is passed into law, not only would you and I be responsible for researching the safety and effectiveness of all over-the-counter drugs (including herbal and homeopathic remedies), but we would also personally have to determine the safety and efficacy of every treatment proposed by our health care providers. This presumes that we can obtain access to all health-related scientific journals, read the literature without years of specialized training, and synthesize disparate or contradictory results for ourselves. Moreover, the impossibly time-consuming task of reviewing scientific studies presumes that there *are* relevant studies out there, which certainly would not be encouraged by the new system. If research evidence were no longer the currency of the health profession—the standard by which treatments were judged appropriate by providers, insurers, and the law—what impact do you think this would have on the quantity and quality of research, not to mention the quality of health care?

Any attempt to free practitioners from the need to base their treatments on evidence is dangerous. Only a pseudoscientist requires such liberties to thrive. The Access to Medical Treatment Act would strike a major blow to the edifice of science that we have labored so hard to build. It would pry open even further the floodgates of unethical health practices. Aren't informed choices about our health difficult enough already? Once we have given informed consent under a system that openly condones health fraud, we become easy targets for malpractice. The responsibility will be solely *ours* as we take a perilous leap with our health and our lives, without the safety nets of consumer protection that any civilized society owes its citizens. Is this the future that we desire?

InfoTrac College Edition

To learn more about topics included in this chapter, enter the following search terms:

Bennett Braun
false memory/false memories
hypnosis
informed consent
multiple personality disorder/dissociative identity disorder
opportunity cost
patient autonomy

TOOLS

Suggestions for Clear Thinking

As Patricia Burgus distanced herself from the therapy directed by Bennett Braun, the High Priestess's memories of satanic cult activities began to fade. The fantastic world of her therapy began to seem less and less real; her faith in it wavered and eventually crumbled altogether. Years after seeking therapy for depression stemming from clear—though by no means simple or easily solved—problems, her life in utter disarray, and justifiably outraged at the mistreatment to which she and her two sons were subjected, Patricia filed a civil suit against Braun and his colleagues. In October 1998, the case was settled out of court for $10.6 million. Although no amount of money can repair the damage done to Patricia and her family, the settlement did bring closure to the dreadful chapter of their lives that began back in 1982.

In August 1998, shortly before the civil settlement was reached, the Illinois Department of Professional Regulation filed complaints against Bennett Braun and two of his colleagues, psychologist Roberta Sachs and child psychiatrist Elva Poznanski. The 23-page complaint about Braun included allegations of "Gross Negligence," "Dishonorable, Unethical, and Unprofessional Conduct," "Making a False or Misleading Statement Regarding the Skill or Efficacy or Value of the Medicine, Treatment, or Remedy Prescribed By Him at His Discretion in the Treatment of Any Disease or Other Condition of the Body or Mind," and "A Pattern of Practice or Other Behavior Which Demonstrates Incapacity or Incompetence to Practice." Bloomberg (1999) cites some of the charges made in the "Gross Negligence" section of the complaint (note that "P. B." represents Patricia Burgus):

- Established an unorthodox treatment regimen in assigning P. B. various "personalities."
- Improperly implemented the aforesaid treatment regimen, encouraging and assisting P. B. in developing "personalities" which the Respondent [Braun] represented were "alter" personalities within P. B., when no such personalities existed.

- Improperly implemented the aforesaid treatment regimen using suggestive and coercive techniques to encourage and assist P. B. to "remember" episodes of abuse.
- Advised P. B. and her husband that "repressed memories" being uncovered during the course of her treatment and her children's treatment represented real memories of actual historical events.
- Advised P. B. and her husband that organized, world-wide transgenerational satanic cults which engaged in mass murder, torture, satanic ritual abuse, human sacrifices, and similar activities did in fact exist and that their existence and activities were well-known.
- Repeatedly advised and convinced P. B. and her husband, when either or both expressed doubt as to the existence of satanic ritual abuse or the memories of such abuse, that they were the only people questioning such concepts and beliefs.
- Advised P. B. that she had sexually abused her minor children.
- Advised P. B. and her husband that P. B. had caused their minor children to participate in various satanic ritual activities including human and animal sacrifice, cannibalism, and various acts of human torture.
- Failed to adequately inform P. B. and her husband of the risk that the techniques used in treatment were capable of causing false memories of events which never occurred but which nevertheless seem real to the patient.

Other allegations more specifically targeted the questionable beliefs and practices of therapists who recover repressed memories and elicit personalities:

- Failed to inform P. B. and her husband that the theory of repression lacked scientific validity and was not generally accepted in the scientific community.
- Failed to adequately inform P. B. and her husband of the risk that the diagnosis of multiple personality disorder was controversial and that the diagnosis was not widely accepted within the mental health community.
- Failed to inform P. B. and her husband that there was further controversy in the mental health community as to whether or not multiple personality disorder was being overdiagnosed and often found in people who did not in fact have that disorder.
- Failed to inform P. B. and her husband of the risk that "multiple personality disorder" can be caused by improper therapy.

Similar complaints were filed against Sachs and Poznanski. The case against Poznanski was settled without action when she agreed to testify against Braun, who had overseen all of the defendants' work. Perhaps due in part to this turn of events, Braun settled his case shortly before the trial was scheduled to take place. His medical license was revoked, he was fined, and additional medical education was ordered. Combined with the $10.6 million settlement of the civil suit, as well as many other civil suits in which patients have successfully sued their former therapists for similar practices (Ofshe & Watters, 1996), the actions taken against Braun send a powerful cautionary message to other therapists who utilize these questionable techniques. By 1996, Ofshe and Watters were able to write:

> The tide, we are glad to report, has turned. The theories and practices which were on the verge of being institutionalized when we began writing about recovered memory therapy in 1991 are now, just a few years later, routinely challenged and rapidly being dispensed with. By early 1996 many recovered memory promoters are back-pedaling on their "discovery" of an international satanic cult ring that was supposedly abusing and "programming" masses of children. The public's belief in memories uncovered during therapy has shifted from acceptance, to uncertainty, to skepticism, and is finally settling on disbelief. The army of therapists who rushed forward to practice, market, and write about this revolutionary step in therapy is now a demoralized group in retreat. (p. 306)

THE DANGERS OF A PSEUDOSCIENTIFIC APPROACH TO HEALTH CARE

Although we can all feel safer knowing that these therapies are on their way out of practice, it is important to remember the lesson that this disastrous episode teaches. Health care practitioners—and those aspiring to become practitioners—should pay particular attention to the perils of abandoning scientific reasoning. There is a pervasive and dangerous tendency for many who wish to "practice" a health science focused on either physical or mental health to view it more as an art than a science. When students and professionals avoid the tough work of thinking scientifically and instead indulge in the comparatively easy pursuit of all that sounds nice and feels good, questionable therapeutic practices can gain a foothold in the profession.

Health sciences are often divided into two broad segments that reflect different approaches to practice: "research-oriented" and "non-research-oriented." Those who emphasize research base their therapeutic interventions on empirical evidence, whereas those who ignore research operate on the basis of anecdotes, testimonials, and—above all—personal experience. The dangers of such an orientation have been a primary focus of this book. Whereas research-oriented practitioners seldom endorse pseudoscientific claims, dubious "discoveries" are aggressively promoted within the non-research-oriented community.

For example, Gaudiano and Herbert (2000) and Swenson (1999) discuss the alarming popularity of "thought field therapy," a "miraculous" body-tapping treatment for psychological problems. Rhythmic tapping is hypothesized to influence a human energy field in some manner. As noted in Chapter 3, the rationale for any such energy-based treatment is implausible in the extreme. Moreover, there is no reliable evidence that it benefits patients, and curiously, its creators will only reveal their methods to interested practitioners who enroll in workshops (which cost up to $100,000!) and promise not to speak about it to others. Likewise, Lilienfeld (1996) challenges the practice of "eye movement desensitization and reprocessing" therapy (EMDR), in which practitioners redirect patients' gaze to somehow relieve psychological disorders. This bizarre practice has gained a substantial following for the treatment of trauma despite evidence that is flimsy, at best. Only time will tell whether these unverified treatments will come to replace repressed memory therapy and the diagnosis and treatment of multiple personality disorder as the premier pseudosciences of psychotherapy.

There is no end to the succession of pseudoscientific fads that attempt to cash in on practitioners' credulity. By ignoring research evidence and failing to conduct carefully controlled research of their own, relying on anecdotal evidence, falling prey to cognitive biases, and so forth, practitioners become convinced that pseudoscientific techniques are effective and apply them without a second thought. The expense is borne by patients, who will receive treatments that are only as good as the evidence demanded by their therapists.

Thinking Clearly

Patricia Burgus was clearly the victim of therapy gone wrong, and the abuses perpetrated against her and her family were unethical and inexcusable. If Patricia is guilty of anything at all, however, it may be her failure to engage in skeptical thinking. Scientific psychology offers suggestions for ways of thinking that balance our natural inclination toward wonder with a healthy mix of skepticism. Although it takes some practice to incorporate critical thinking skills into our reasoning repertoire, the payoff is a more rational belief system and a reduced risk of being duped. Here, then, are some strategies for overcoming many of the common biases present in our judgment and decision making.

Reconceptualize Issues in Multiple Ways

Many issues can be framed as either gains, in which case we tend to be risk-averse, or losses, in which case we tend to be risk-seeking. To avoid being influenced by the framing of an issue, try thinking about it using your own frames. For example, when a wondrous "tax cut" is proposed or a dreaded "tax hike" is criticized, ask yourself what the implications are for the balance of payments and services. Moreover, don't let others influence you through deceptive language. Try to see beyond "weasel words" such as "pro life" or "pro choice" by considering the underlying issues without getting wrapped up in buzzwords and other linguistic tricks.

Beware of Wishful Thinking

There are at least two ways to deal with the unknown. One is simply to imagine how you would like the world to work and presume that whatever you find most pleasing or comforting is true. Such wishful thinking, however, provides only a false sense of understanding and impedes the growth of knowledge. Once you have an "explanation" in your mind, no matter how untrue it may be, you are unlikely to seek new information actively or to be eager to revise your beliefs. Wishful thinking is therefore reckless, and you would be well advised to avoid it. Instead, you can follow a different approach: Recognize the limitations of current knowledge. It is more appropriate, even valuable, to formulate theories or hypotheses that go beyond the data. However, be sure to carefully distinguish your untested hypotheses from evidence-based beliefs.

Consider the Legitimacy of Authorities

We could not survive in our complex and rapidly changing world without relying on legitimate experts to inform us. However, our tendency toward obedience to authority is strong, and some self-proclaimed "authorities" are not the neutral experts they seem. Thus, it is important to consider carefully the qualifications of authorities. Try to weigh an expert's true knowledge and experience against his or her self-interest. You should be particularly cautious with anyone who has a clear motive to take advantage of you.

Seek Risky Tests, Not Weak Confirmation

We tend to seek information that is consistent with our existing beliefs and to preferentially interpret ambiguous information as supportive of our beliefs. This style of thinking provides only very weak, uninformative confirmation of our ideas that fails to provide opportunities to examine and change mistaken beliefs. It is only by subjecting our ideas to genuine tests in which they run a real risk of being disproved that we can judge whether they are in fact worth keeping. Beliefs that survive even risky tests are valuable, whereas those that fail should be scrapped.

Don't Be Misled by Testimonials

When a large number of competing explanations are offered for an observed behavior or event, knowing which one is correct is often impossible. This is the most basic problem with testimonials, case studies, and anecdotes. One possibility is that someone may be fabricating or exaggerating a story to suit his or her own purposes. Another is that an honest, well-intentioned individual may simply be wrong. For example, in the case of a testimonial involving the alleviation of illness, there are at least 10 explanations competing with the possibility that a disease has really been cured. More important, there is simply no way to know which of these explanations is correct. Furthermore, testimonials may actually represent unusual counterexamples to a probabilistic general principle that truly exists. Thus, overgeneralizing from a testimonial may cause us to formulate a belief that squarely contradicts reality. Although they may suggest interesting leads to pursue, testimonials, case studies, and anecdotes are simply incapable of testing a hypothesis or providing good evidence in support of a belief or theory. Treat them with extreme caution.

Keep in Touch with Reality

Remember that the plausibility of a claim to knowledge is one useful indication of its truth. A claim that contradicts conceptualizations of reality that are well supported by scientific research is probably undeserving of your attention, much less your belief.

Remember That Correlation Does Not Imply Causation

This powerful principle is remarkably easy to overlook. We are bombarded with correlational data, particularly in the field of health. For example, we are told that people who choose a certain diet or choose a certain type of exercise are more or less healthy than others. This evidence cannot establish that there is any *effect* on health, because the people who choose particular diets or exercise programs are self-selected groups whose lifestyles may differ in countless other ways from those of other individuals. It is easy—but foolhardy—to slip into causal language on the basis of correlational evidence. If only correlational data are available, insist on seeing a coherent pattern of correlations pointing toward the same conclusion before turning over your money, vote, or belief.

Beware the Media Paradox

Avoid being overly influenced by what you see, hear, and read through the popular media. Keep in mind that news and entertainment outlets carefully select *unusual* events to spark the interest of their audience and then present them in a compelling manner. This is risky because vivid portrayals—often mere testimonials—are likely to be more readily available in our memory, leading us to mistake the true prevalence of an event, the true degree of danger in a hazard, or the true legitimacy of a claim to knowledge. Whereas scientific sources such as peer-reviewed journals generally provide trustworthy information, the more you rely on the popular media, the more likely you may be to misplace your fears.

Formulate Multiple Working Hypotheses

One of the best ways to avoid the premature acceptance of a false idea is to consider as many possible alternatives as you can. In particular, an effective way to avoid a wide range of reasoning pitfalls is to routinely *ask yourself why you might be wrong.* This will enable you to more clearly identify weaknesses in a belief and encourage you to consider other ideas that may be better.

Ask What Can Be Predicted

We are all adept at "explaining" past events, but many of our explanations are really nothing more than nice stories. To avoid hindsight biases, post-hockery, and overconfidence, demand and test predictions of future events. This is a sure-fire way to determine whether a claim represents a true understanding of reality or merely a tall tale about the past.

Challenge Conspiracy Theories

Conspiracy theories sometimes contain only a thin veneer of plausibility, and scratching this surface will often reveal the emptiness that lies beneath. Particularly in the case of grand conspiracy theories, consider whether the alleged conspirators have enough common interests to provide a motive for collusion. Also, consider whether the logistics of the conspiracy—for example, the sheer number of people involved over the proposed time span—are feasible, or whether they are more likely to represent a flight of fancy. Very few, if any, conspiracy theories continue to seem plausible in light of a few simple questions along these lines.

Watch Out for Illusions of Control

In order to reduce the threat of uncertainty, we tend to perceive a sense of control even when this perception is only illusory. Moreover, we often underestimate the role of chance in observed events or confuse chance-determined with skill-determined situations. The result can be an illusion of control that holds certain risks for ourselves and for others, including the development of learned helplessness if we repeatedly fail to achieve a goal. When trying to make sense of the world, remember Abelson's advice: "Give chance a chance."

Be Careful Not to Blame Victims

Another way we maintain a feeling of security is to believe that people get what they deserve and deserve what they get. This belief can be carried too far, however, when we impose it on the victims of unpredictable disasters and infer that they must have done something to bring about their own suffering. When you find yourself blaming people for playing a part in their own victimization, be wary of hindsight bias. Would you have judged a certain behavior to be blameworthy had you not already known that the person was later victimized in some way? Keep in mind that the world is not as predictable or controllable as we often wish to believe.

Consider Both Positive and Negative Consequences of a Claim

There is a very real danger in considering only the positive side of any theory. For example, some people who believe that the mind controls health point to the beneficial effects of positive thinking, neglecting to mention the implied harmful effects of negative thinking. Likewise, believers of "water memory" fail to acknowledge just how terrifying it would be if water had a memory for the dangerous (and filthy) as well as the beneficial materials with which it came into contact. Remember that the full consequences of wishful thinking are often not as desirable as they appear when their positive features are selectively presented. Thus, be sure to evaluate the negative as well as the positive implications of any theory.

Pay Attention to Base Rates

The simple frequency with which certain events occur is a tremendously valuable (and often underutilized) type of information. We tend to consider only the strength of evidence in a single instance, ignoring the baseline probabilities of different outcomes. For example, recall that even a highly valid test makes a large proportion of errors when used to diagnose or predict a relatively rare condition or event. There is a simple phrase that may help you remember to pay attention to base rates: "When you hear hoofbeats, think horses, not zebras."

Accept Some Mistakes in Order to Minimize Error

The unrealistic goal of perfection is often an obstacle to improving our decisions. Striving for the perfect prediction of human behavior is foolish because all behavior contains elements of uncertainty. By contrast, the realization that every plan is likely to have some flaw—and that the optimal solution is the one with the most strengths and the fewest weaknesses—may simplify the decision process immensely. The preference for clinical, or intuitive, decision making is partly based on the unattainable goal of perfect prediction and results in decisions of demonstrably poorer quality than those yielded by statistical decision making. The superior statistical method rests on the acceptance that there will be a certain number of mistakes, that there is no way to beat the best available odds.

Take Advantage of the Power of Statistical Decision Making

Statistical decision making is a remarkably simple and effective technique. It is simple because, fundamentally, it involves nothing more than counting. To take advantage of this technique in your own thinking, use simple lists of pros and cons when you are confronted with difficult choices. The weight that you attach to the attributes of each option makes little difference, as the process usually reveals your true preference fairly clearly even without this information. Professionals should use not only this technique but also prediction formulas when they are available. A search of the research literature will indicate at least what the relevant variables are for a particular decision-making task, and perhaps it will even uncover an existing prediction formula.

Don't Misinterpret Regression Toward the Mean

Remember that extreme events tend to be followed by less extreme events. We are apt to forget that truly exceptional performance results from a rare combination of both outstanding ability and unusually good luck. Because luck is unlikely to be unusually good at all times, less impressive performance will tend to follow performance that is truly exceptional. Bear in mind the unfounded "*Sports Illustrated* jinx" when you find yourself trying to understand why repeated events produce increasingly average results. Even those with the greatest ability are not equally lucky all the time.

Consider Both Costs and Benefits

In order to reach ethical decisions, you must weigh fairly all costs and benefits. An easy error to commit is overestimating the probability of benefits and underestimating the probability of harm. Even easier is overlooking the "opportunity costs" of choosing any particular course of action, forgetting that following one path means forgoing others. For example, the opportunity cost of keeping your money in your mattress is the interest you could earn if you put it into a savings account. Considerations of opportunity cost become increasingly important as the consequences of your choices become more serious. The decisions most consistent with your own values will result from a fair weighing of all relevant costs and benefits, including the less obvious opportunity costs involved.

Practice Scientific Reasoning

The skepticism of scientific reasoning promotes a general approach to thinking that provides the greatest protection against unwarranted beliefs and shields you from the persuasion of those who do not share your best interests. In addition to the suggestions described earlier in this chapter, perfectly consistent with sound scientific reasoning, the six criteria of "FiLCHeRS" provide further guidelines for skeptical thought:

- Verify that a claim to knowledge is potentially *falsifiable*, that there is some way for it to be proven false if indeed it is. A claim that is not falsifiable is untestable and therefore worthless.
- Examine the *logic* of a claim, including both the truth of each of its premises and the validity of the conclusion based on these premises.
- Check to see that a claim is *comprehensive*, that it accounts for all available evidence rather than just a selected assortment of supportive statements.
- Evaluate claims with *honesty*, subjecting even cherished beliefs to the same risky tests—involving the same rigorous standards of evidence— that you would require for any other claims.
- Insist that a claim be based on *replicable* evidence, that there is support from independent tests. This allows you to rule out the possibility that the claim is based on a fluke or chance result.
- Demand *sufficient* evidence before believing a claim. Remember that the burden of proof lies with the person making the claim (it is not your job to disprove it), that extraordinary claims require extraordinary evidence, and that arguments based on someone's say-so—or on mere authority—are not good enough to warrant your belief.

A CLOSING THOUGHT ON WISHFUL THINKING

My sincere hope is that our exploration of the psychology of human reasoning in this book will enable you to make smarter choices in all areas of your life. The most remarkable powers of the mind lie not in an ability to communicate telepathically, bend spoons, or consciously control our health, but in the ability to reason intelligently, to make accurate judgments, and ultimately to reach personally satisfying decisions. We are born with an astounding capacity for complex thought, but it takes effort to achieve our full potential. Millions of people spend considerable time exercising their bodies, but how many rigorously exercise their minds?

The first step to expanding the powers of your mind is to learn about reasoning. This includes becoming aware of the commonly used mental shortcuts that lead us to predictable mistakes, many of which have been outlined here. The next step is to work actively toward clearer thinking by knowing when and how to override these shortcuts. The tools of clear thinking are freely available to anyone who is willing to practice them. As you gain experience with these tools, you will find that foolish arguments and attempts to persuade you on superficial grounds will become easier to spot, allowing you to enjoy a quick laugh rather than succumb to nonsense. In addition, clearer thinking will carry over into all aspects of your life. You will become better able to express yourself clearly and concisely, to organize a presentation based on the natural flow of rational ideas, and to construct arguments that are persuasive on logical grounds.

Clear thinking is empowering and addictive. Once you begin to spot fallacious reasoning—both in yourself and in others—you will increasingly come to enjoy the powers of your mind. And when you see the value of just a few of the principles of scientific reasoning, the rest quickly sell themselves. It may be only wishful thinking on my part, but my deepest wish in writing this book is to have given away a few general-purpose tools that will serve you well in any walk of life and last you a lifetime.

References

Abelson, R. P. (1995). *Statistics as principled argument.* Mahwah, NJ: Erlbaum.

Adams, R. M. (1992). The "hot hand" revisited: Successful basketball shooting as a function of intershot interval. *Perceptual and Motor Skills, 74,* 934.

Alpert, M., & Raiffa, H. (1982). A progress report on the training of probability assessors. In D. Kahneman, P. Slovic, & A. Tversky (Eds.), *Judgment under uncertainty: Heuristics and biases* (pp. 294–305). New York: Cambridge University Press.

Alter, C. F. (1985). Decision-making factors in cases of child neglect. *Child Welfare, 64,* 99–111.

American Psychiatric Association. (1994). *Diagnostic and statistical manual of mental disorders* (4th ed.). Washington, DC: Author.

American Psychological Association. (1992). Ethical principles of psychologists and code of conduct. *American Psychologist, 47,* 1597–1611.

Angell, M., & Kassirer, J. P. (1998). Alternative medicine: The risks of untested and unregulated remedies. *New England Journal of Medicine, 339,* 839–841.

Arkes, H. R. (1991). Costs and benefits of judgment errors: Implications for debiasing. *Psychological Bulletin, 110,* 486–498.

Asser, S. M., & Swan, R. (1998). Child fatalities from religion-motivated medical neglect. *Pediatrics, 101,* 625–629.

Atlas, D. H. (1978). Longevity of orchestra conductors. *Forum on Medicine, 1,* 50–51.

Ausubel, N. (Ed.). (1948). *A treasury of Jewish folklore: Stories, traditions, legends, humor, wisdom and folk songs of the Jewish people.* New York: Crown.

Bach, R. (1973). Nothing by chance. *The American Way, 6,* 32–38.

Bar-Hillel, M., & Ben-Shakhar, G. (1986). The a priori case against graphology: Methodological and conceptual issues. In B. Nevo (Ed.), *Scientific aspects of graphology* (pp. 263–279). Springfield, IL: Charles C. Thomas.

Barrett, S., & Herbert, V. (1994). *The vitamin pushers: How the "health food" industry is selling America a bill of goods.* Amherst, NY: Prometheus Books.

Bass, E., & Davis, L. (1988). *The courage to heal.* New York: Harper & Row.

Beck, A. J., & Shipley, B. E. (1989). *Recidivism of prisoners released in 1983* (U.S. Bureau of Justice Statistics Special Report). Washington, DC: U.S. Department of Justice.

Ben-Shakhar, G. (1991). Clinical judgment and decision-making in CQT-polygraphy: A comparison with other pseudoscientific applications in psychology. *Integrative Physiological and Behavioral Science, 26,* 232–240.

Berman, J. S., & Norton, N. C. (1985). Does professional training make a therapist more effective? *Psychological Bulletin, 98,* 401–407.

Beyerstein, B. L. (1997). Why bogus therapies seem to work. *Skeptical Inquirer, 21,* 29–34.

Blackmore, S. (1998). Abduction by aliens or sleep paralysis? *Skeptical Inquirer, 22,* 23–28.

Bliss, E. L. (1980). Multiple personalities: A report of 14 cases with implications for schizophrenia and hysteria. *Archives of General Psychiatry, 37,* 138–139.

Bloomberg, D. (1999). Illinois files complaint against repressed memory doctors. *Skeptical Inquirer, 23,* 6–7.

Blume, S. E. (1990). *Secret survivors.* New York: Ballantine.

Borgida, E., & Nisbett, R. E. (1977). The differential impact of abstract vs. concrete information on decisions. *Journal of Applied Social Psychology, 7,* 258–271.

Bower, H. (1994). The concentration camp syndrome. *Australian and New Zealand Journal of Psychiatry, 28,* 391–397.

Bransford, J. D., & Franks, J. J. (1971). The abstraction of linguistic ideas. *Cognitive Psychology, 2,* 331–350.

Braun, B. G. (1989). Psychotherapy of the survivor of incest with a dissociative disorder. *Psychiatric Clinics of North America, 12,* 307–324.

Bray, M. A., Kehle, T. J., & Hintze, J. M. (1998). Profile analysis with the Wechsler scales: Why does it persist? *School Psychology International, 19,* 209–220.

Breland, K., & Breland, M. (1961). The misbehavior of organisms. *American Psychologist, 16,* 681–684.

Breland, K., & Breland, M. (1966). *Animal behavior.* New York: Macmillan.

Brooks, J. (1985). Polygraph testing: Thoughts of a skeptical legislator. *American Psychologist, 40,* 348–354.

Camerer, C. (1981). General conditions for the success of bootstrapping models. *Organizational Behavior and Human Performance, 27,* 411–422.

Casscells, W., Schoenberger, A., & Grayboys, T. (1978). Interpretation by physicians of clinical laboratory results. *New England Journal of Medicine, 299,* 999–1000.

Ceci, S. J., & Bruck, M. (1995). *Jeopardy in the courtroom: A scientific analysis of children's testimony.* Washington, DC: American Psychological Association.

Ceci, S. J., Huffman, M. L. C., Smith, E., & Loftus, E. F. (1994). Repeatedly thinking about a non-event: Source misattributions among preschoolers. *Consciousness and Cognition, 3,* 388–407.

Chambless, D. L., Sanderson, W. C., Shoham, V., Johnson, S. B., Pope, K. S., Crits-Christoph, P., Baker, M., Johnson, B., Woody, S. R., Sue, S., Beutler, L., Williams, D. A., & McCurry, S. (1996). An update on empirically validated therapies. *Clinical Psychologist, 49,* 5–18.

Chapman, L. J., & Chapman, J. (1967). Genesis of popular but erroneous diagnostic observations. *Journal of Abnormal Psychology, 72,* 193–204.

Chapman, L. J., & Chapman, J. (1982). Test results are what you think they are. In D. Kahneman, P. Slovic, & A. Tversky (Eds.), *Judgment under uncertainty: Heuristics and biases* (pp. 239–248). New York: Cambridge University Press.

Chen, J., & Gardner, H. (1997). Alternative assessment from a multiple intelligences theoretical perspective. In D. P. Flanagan, J. L. Genshaft, & P. L. Harrison (Eds.), *Contemporary intellectual assessment: Theories, tests, and issues.* New York: Guilford.

Chodoff, P. (1963). Late effects of the concentration camp syndrome. *Archives of General Psychiatry, 8,* 323–333.

Christy, M. M. (1994). *Your own perfect medicine: The incredible proven natural miracle cure that medical science has never revealed!* Scottsdale, AZ: Wishland.

Cialdini. R. (1993). *Influence: The psychology of persuasion.* New York: Quill.

Cohen, M., & Davis, N. (1981). *Medication errors: Causes and prevention.* Philadelphia: G. F. Strickley.

Combs, B., & Slovic, P. (1979). Causes of death: Biased newspaper coverage and biased judgments. *Journalism Quarterly, 56,* 837–843.

Coons, P. M. (1986). *Newsletter for the International Society for the Study of Multiple Personality and Dissociation, 4,* 6–7.

Coons, P. M., Bowman, E. S., & Milstein, V. (1988). Multiple personality disorder: A clinical investigation of fifty cases. *Journal of Nervous and Mental Disease, 176,* 519–527.

Coppes, M. J., Anderson, R. A., Egeler, R. M., & Wolff, J. E. (1998). Alternative therapies for the treatment of childhood cancer. *New England Journal of Medicine, 339,* 846–847.

Davenas, E., Beauvais, F., Amara, J., Oberbaum, M., Robinzon, B., Miadonna, A., Tedeschi, A., Pomeranz, B., Fortner, P., Belon, P., et al. (1988). Human basophil degranulation triggered by very dilute antiserum against IgE. *Nature, 333,* 816–818.

Dawes, R. M. (1971). A case study of graduate admissions: Application of three principles of human decision making. *American Psychologist, 26,* 180–188.

Dawes, R. M. (1979). The robust beauty of improper linear models in decision making. *American Psychologist, 34,* 571–582.

Dawes, R. M. (1989). Experience and validity of clinical judgment: The illusory correlation. *Behavioral Sciences and the Law, 7,* 457–467.

Dawes, R. M. (1991). Probabilistic versus causal thinking. In D. Cicchetti & W. M. Grove (Eds.), *Thinking clearly about psychology* (Vol. 1, pp. 235–264). Minneapolis: University of Minnesota Press.

Dawes, R. M. (1994). *House of cards: Psychology and psychotherapy built on myth.* New York: Free Press.

Dawes, R. M. (1995). The nature of human nature: An empirical case for withholding judgment—perhaps indefinitely. *Political Psychology, 16,* 81–97.

Dawes, R. M., & Corrigan, B. (1974). Linear models in decision making. *Psychological Bulletin, 81,* 95–106.

Dawes, R. M., Faust, D., & Meehl, P. E. (1989). Clinical versus actuarial judgment. *Science, 243,* 1668–1674.

Dawes, R. M., Faust, D., & Meehl, P. E. (1993). Statistical prediction versus clinical prediction: Improving what works. In G. Keren & C. Lewis (Eds.), *Handbook for data analysis in the behavioral sciences: Methodological issues* (pp. 351–367). Hillsdale, NJ: Erlbaum.

Dean, G., Mather, A., & Kelly, I. W. (1996). Astrology. In G. Stein (Ed.), *Encyclopedia of the paranormal* (pp. 47–99). Buffalo, NY: Prometheus.

"Death Odds." (1990, September 24). *Newsweek*, p. 10.

DePanfilis, D., & Scannapieco, M. (1994). Assessing the safety of children at risk of maltreatment: Decision-making models. *Child Welfare, 73*, 229–245.

Des Pres, T. (1976). *The survivor: An anatomy of life in the death camps.* New York: Washington Square Press.

Dickson, D. H., & Kelly, I. W. (1985). The "Barnum effect" in personality assessment: A review of the literature. *Psychological Reports, 57*, 367–382.

Doane, D. C. (1956). *Astrology: 30 years research.* Hollywood, CA: Professional Astrologers, Inc.

Dobson, K. S., & Craig, K. D. (Eds.). (1998). *Empirically supported therapies: Best practice in professional psychology.* Thousand Oaks, CA: Sage.

Drosnin, M. (1997). *The Bible Code.* New York: Simon & Schuster.

Eddy, D. M. (1982). Probabilistic reasoning in clinical medicine: Problems and opportunities. In D. Kahneman, P. Slovic, & A. Tversky (Eds.), *Judgment under uncertainty: Heuristics and biases* (pp. 249–267). New York: Cambridge University Press.

Einhorn, H. J. (1986). Accepting error to make less error. *Journal of Personality Assessment, 50*, 387–395.

Eisen, G. (1988). *Children and play in the Holocaust: Games among the shadows.* Amherst, MA: University of Massachusetts Press.

Eisenberg, D. M., Kessler, R. C., Foster, C., Norlock, F. E., Calkins, D. R., & Delbanco, T. L. (1993). Unconventional medicine in the United States—prevalence, costs, and patterns of use. *New England Journal of Medicine, 328*, 246–252.

Eitinger, L. (1980). The concentration camp syndrome and its late sequelae. In J. E. Dimsdale (Ed.), *Survivors, victims, and perpetrators: Essays on the Nazi Holocaust.* Washington, DC: Hemisphere Press.

Englebretson, G. (1997). The filling of scholarly vacuums. *Skeptical Inquirer, 21*, 57–59.

Eth, S., & Pynoos, R. S. (1994). Children who witness the homicide of a parent. *Psychiatry, 57*, 287–306.

Faust, D. (1986). Research on human judgment and its application to clinical practice. *Professional Psychology: Research and Practice, 17*, 420–430.

Faust, D., & Ziskin, J. (1988). The expert witness in psychology and psychiatry. *Science, 241*, 31–35.

Festinger, L. (1957). *A theory of cognitive dissonance.* Stanford: Stanford University Press.

Fischhoff, B. (1975). Hindsight ≠ foresight: The effect of outcome knowledge on judgment under uncertainty. *Journal of Experimental Psychology: Human Perception and Performance, 1*, 288–299.

Fischhoff, B. (1982). For those condemned to study the past: Heuristics and biases in hindsight. In D. Kahneman, P. Slovic, & A. Tversky (Eds.), *Judgment under uncertainty: Heuristics and biases* (pp. 335–351). New York: Cambridge University Press.

Fischhoff, B. (1988). Judgment and decision making. In R. J. Sternberg & E. E. Smith (Eds.), *The psychology of human thought* (pp. 153–187). Cambridge: Cambridge University Press.

Forer, B. R. (1949). The fallacy of personal validation: A classroom demonstration of gullibility. *Journal of Abnormal and Social Psychology, 44,* 118–123.

Fredrickson, R. (1992). *Repressed memories.* New York: Simon & Schuster.

Frontline. (1995). *Searching for satan.* Videotape shown on October 24. PBS.

Ganaway, G. K. (1995). Hypnosis, childhood trauma, and dissociative identity disorder: Toward an integrative theory. *International Journal of Clinical and Experimental Hypnosis, 43,* 127–144.

Garb, H. N. (1989). Clinical judgment, clinical training, and professional experience. *Psychological Bulletin, 105,* 387–396.

Garb, H. N. (1999). *Studying the clinician: Judgment research and psychological assessment.* Washington, DC: American Psychological Association.

Gardner, M. (1952). *Fads and fallacies in the name of science.* New York: Dover.

Gardner, M. (1999). Urine therapy. *Skeptical Inquirer, 23,* 13–15.

Garry, M., Manning, C., Loftus, E. F., & Sherman, S. J. (1996). Imagination inflation. *Psychonomic Bulletin and Review, 3,* 208–214.

Gaudiano, B. A., & Herbert, J. D. (2000). Can we really tap our problems away? A critical analysis of thought field therapy. *Skeptical Inquirer, 24,* 29–33, 36.

Gavigan, M. (1992). False memories of sexual abuse: A personal account. *Issues in Child Abuse Accusations, 4,* 246–247.

Gergen, K. J., Hepburn, A., & Fisher, D. C. (1986). Hermeneutics of personality description. *Journal of Personality and Social Psychology, 50,* 1261–1270.

Gilovich, T. (1991). *How we know what isn't so: The fallibility of human reason in everyday life.* New York: Free Press.

Gilovich, T., & Savitsky, K. (1996). Like goes with like: The role of representativeness in erroneous and pseudoscientific beliefs. *Skeptical Inquirer, 20,* 34–40.

Gilovich, T., Vallone, R., & Tversky, A. (1985). The hot hand in basketball: On the misperception of random sequences. *Cognitive Psychology, 17,* 295–314.

Gleeson, J. P. (1987). Implementing structured decision-making procedures at child welfare intake. *Child Welfare, 66,* 101–112.

Glutting, J. J., Youngstrom, E. A., Ward, T., Ward, S., & Hale, R. L. (1997). Incremental efficacy of WISC-III factor scores in predicting achievement: What do they tell us? *Psychological Assessment, 9,* 295–301.

Goff, D. C., & Simms, C. A. (1993). Has multiple personality disorder remained consistent over time? A comparison of past and recent cases. *Journal of Nervous and Mental Disease, 181,* 595–600.

Goffman, E. (1967). *Interaction ritual.* New York: Anchor.

Gold, S. N., Hughes, D., & Hohnecker, L. (1994). Degrees of repression of sexual abuse memories. *American Psychologist, 49,* 441–442.

Goldberg, L. R. (1959). The effectiveness of clinicians' judgments: The diagnosis of organic brain damage from the Bender-Gestalt test. *Journal of Consulting Psychology, 23,* 25–33.

Goldberg, L. R. (1965). Diagnosticians vs. diagnostic signs: The diagnosis of psychosis vs. neurosis from the MMPI. *Psychological Monographs, 79,* 1–28.

Goldberg, L. R. (1968). Simple models or simple processes? Some research on clinical judgments. *American Psychologist, 23,* 483–496.

Goldberg, L. R. (1970). Man versus model of man: A rationale, plus some evidence, for a method of improving on clinical inferences. *Psychological Bulletin, 73,* 422–432.

Goldberg, L. R. (1986). Some informal explorations and ruminations about graphology. In B. Nevo (Ed.), *Scientific aspects of graphology* (pp. 281–293). Springfield, IL: Charles C. Thomas.

Goldberg, L. R. (1991). Human mind versus regression equation: Five contrasts. In D. Cicchetti & W. M. Grove (Eds.), *Thinking clearly about psychology* (Vol. 1, pp. 173–184). Minneapolis: University of Minnesota Press.

Goodman, G., Qin, J., Bottoms, B., & Shaver, P. (1994). *Characteristics of allegations of ritual satanic abuse.* Final report to the National Center on Child Abuse and Neglect, Washington, DC.

Greenberg, R. P., Bornstein, R. F., Zborowski, M. J., Fisher, S., & Greenberg, M. D. (1994). A meta-analysis of fluoxetine outcome in the treatment of depression. *Journal of Nervous and Mental Disease, 182,* 547–551.

Greenberg, R. P., & Fisher, S. (1997). Mood-mending medicines: Probing drug, psychotherapy, and placebo solutions. In S. Fisher & R. P. Greenberg (Eds.), *From placebo to panacea: Putting psychiatric drugs to the test.* New York: Wiley.

Grice, H. P. (1975). Logic and conversation. In P. Cole & J. L. Morgan (Eds.), *Syntax and semantics. Vol. 3: Speech acts* (pp. 41–58). New York: Academic Press.

Grove, W. M. (2000). Clinical versus mechanical prediction: A meta-analysis. *Psychological Assessment, 12,* 19–30.

Guilmette, T. J., Faust, D., Hart, K., & Arkes, H. R. (1990). A national survey of psychologists who offer neurological services. *Archives of Clinical Neuropsychology, 5,* 373–392.

Harris, W. S., Gowda, M., Kolb, J. W., Strychacz, C. P., Vacek, J. L., Jones, P. G., Forker, A., O'Keefe, J. H., & McCallister, B. D. (1999). A randomized, controlled trial of the effects of remote, intercessory prayer on outcomes in patients admitted to the coronary care unit. *Archives of Internal Medicine, 159,* 2273–2278.

Hill, A. B. (1965). The environment and disease: Association or causation? *Proceedings of the Royal Society of Medicine, 58,* 295–300.

Hofling, C. K., Brotzman, E., Dairymple, S., Graves, N., & Pierce, C. M. (1966). An experimental study in nurse-physician relationships. *Journal of Nervous and Mental Disease, 143,* 171–180.

Hu, F. B., Stampfer, M. J., Rimm, E. B., Manson, J. E., Ascherio, A., Colditz, G. A., Rosner, B. A., Spiegelman, D., Speizer, F. E., Sacks, F. M., Hennekens, C. H., & Willett, W. C. (1999). A prospective study of egg consumption and risk of cardiovascular disease in men and women. *Journal of the American Medical Association, 281,* 1387–1394.

Hunsley, J., & Bailey, J. M. (1999). The clinical utility of the Rorschach: Unfulfilled promises and an uncertain future. *Psychological Assessment, 11*, 266–277.

Hyman, I. E., & Billings, F. J. (1995). *Individual differences and the creation of false childhood memories.* Unpublished manuscript, Western Washington University.

Hyman, I. E., Husband, T. H., & Billings, F. J. (1995). False memories of childhood experiences. *Applied Cognitive Psychology, 9*, 181–197.

Janoff-Bulman, R. (1992). *Shattered assumptions: Toward a new psychology of trauma.* New York: Free Press.

Janoff-Bulman, R., Timko, C., & Carli, L. L. (1985). Cognitive biases in blaming the victim. *Journal of Experimental Social Psychology, 21*, 161–177.

Jensen, A. R. (1965). Review of the Rorschach Inkblot Test. In O. K. Burros (Ed.) *Sixth Measurements Yearbook* (pp. 501–509). Highland Park, N. J.: Gryphon Press.

Kahneman, D., Slovic, P., & Tversky, A. (Eds.). (1982). *Judgment under uncertainty: Heuristics and biases.* New York: Cambridge University Press.

Kahneman, D., & Tversky, A. (1972). Subjective probability: A judgment of representativeness. *Cognitive Psychology, 3*, 430–454.

Kahneman, D., & Tversky, A. (1973). On the psychology of prediction. *Psychological Review, 80*, 237–251.

Kahneman, D., & Tversky, A. (1979). Prospect theory. *Econometrica, 47*, 263–292.

Kelly, I. W. (1997). Modern astrology: A critique. *Psychological Reports, 81*, 1035–1066.

Kelly, I. W. (1998). Why astrology doesn't work. *Psychological Reports, 82*, 527–546.

Kern, F. (1991). Normal plasma cholesterol in an 88-year-old man who eats 25 eggs a day. *New England Journal of Medicine, 324*, 896–899.

Kirsch, I., & Sapirstein, G. (1998). Listening to Prozac but hearing placebo: A meta-analysis of antidepressant medication. *Prevention and Treatment, 1*, Article 0002a. Available on the World Wide Web: http://journals.apa.org/treatment/volume1/pre0010002a.html.

Klass, P. J. (1983). *UFOs: The public deceived.* Buffalo, NY: Prometheus.

Klass, P. J. (1997a). *Bringing UFOs down to Earth.* Buffalo, NY: Prometheus.

Klass, P. J. (1997b). *The real Roswell crashed saucer coverup.* Buffalo, NY: Prometheus.

Klass, P. J. (2000). The new bogus Majestic-12 documents. *Skeptical Inquirer, 24*, 44–46.

Kleinmuntz, B. (1990). Why we still use our heads instead of the formulas: Toward an integrative approach. *Psychological Bulletin, 107*, 296–310.

Kluft, R. P. (1983). Hypnotherapeutic crisis intervention in multiple personality. *American Journal of Clinical Hypnosis, 26*, 73–83.

Kluft, R. P. (1984). Treatment of multiple personality disorder: A study of 33 cases. *Psychiatric Clinics of North America, 7*, 9–29.

Knox, R. E., & Inkster, J. A. (1968). Postdecision dissonance at post time. *Journal of Personality and Social Psychology, 8*, 319–323.

Ko, R. J. (1998). Adulterants in Asian patent medicines. *New England Journal of Medicine, 339*, 847.

Krystal, H. (1991). Integration and self-healing in post-traumatic states: A ten-year retrospective. *American Imago, 48*, 93–118.

Langer, E. J. (1975). The illusion of control. *Journal of Personality and Social Psychology, 32,* 311–328.

Lanning, K. V. (1989). Satanic, occult, ritualistic crime: A law enforcement perspective. *The Police Chief, 56,* 62–85.

Lanning, K. V. (1991). Ritual abuse: A law enforcement view or perspective. *Child Abuse and Neglect, 15,* 171–173.

Lazarus, A. A. (1971). *Behavior therapy and beyond.* New York: McGraw-Hill.

Lerner, M. J. (1980). *The belief in a just world: A fundamental delusion.* New York: Plenum.

Lett, J. (1990). A field guide to critical thinking. *Skeptical Inquirer, 14,* 153–160.

Levi, R. (2000). Assessing the quality of medical web sites. *Skeptical Inquirer, 24,* 41–45.

Lichtenstein, S., & Fischhoff, B. (1977). Do those who know more also know more about how much they know? *Organizational Behavior and Human Performance, 26,* 149–171.

Lichtenstein, S., Fischhoff, B., & Phillips, L. D. (1982). Calibration of probabilities: The state of the art to 1980. In D. Kahneman, P. Slovic, & A. Tversky (Eds.), *Judgment under uncertainty: Heuristics and biases* (pp. 306–334). New York: Cambridge University Press.

Lichtenstein, S., Slovic, P., Fischhoff, B., Layman, M., & Combs, B. (1978). Judged frequency of lethal events. *Journal of Experimental Psychology: Human Learning and Memory, 4,* 551–578.

Lilienfeld, S. O. (1996). EMDR treatment: Less than meets the eye? *Skeptical Inquirer, 20,* 25–31.

Lilienfeld, S. O., Lynn, S. J., Kirsch, I., Chaves, J. F., Sarbin, T. R., Ganaway, G. K., & Powell, R. A. (1999). Dissociative identity disorder and the sociocognitive model: Recalling the lessons of the past. *Psychological Bulletin, 125,* 507–523.

Lindsey, D. (1992). Reliability of the foster care placement decision: A review. *Research on Social Work Practice, 2,* 65–80.

Livingston, J. D. (1998). Magnetic therapy: Plausible attraction? *Skeptical Inquirer, 22,* 25–30, 58.

Loftus, E. F. (1997). Dispatch from the (un)civil memory wars. In J. D. Read & D. S. Lindsay (Eds.), *Recollections of trauma: Scientific evidence and clinical practice* (pp. 171–198).

Loftus, E. F., & Palmer, J. C. (1974). Reconstruction of automobile destruction: An example of the interaction between language and memory. *Journal of Verbal Learning and Verbal Behavior, 13,* 585–589.

Loftus, E. F., & Pickrell, J. (1995). The formation of false memories. *Psychiatric Annals, 25,* 720–724.

Malmquist, C. P. (1986). Children who witness parental murder: Post-traumatic aspects. *Journal of the Academy of Child and Adolescent Psychiatry, 25,* 320–325.

Mandel, D. R., Lehman, D. R., & Yuille, J. C. (1994). Should this child be removed from home? Hypothesis generation and information seeking as predictors of case decisions. *Child Abuse and Neglect, 18,* 1051–1062.

Matarazzo, J. D. (1986). Computerized clinical psychological test interpretations: Unvalidated plus all mean and no sigma. *American Psychologist, 41,* 14–24.

McKelvie, S. J. (1990). Student acceptance of a generalized personality description: Forer's graphologist revisited. *Journal of Social Behavior and Personality, 5,* 91–95.

Meehl, P. E. (1954). *Clinical vs. statistical prediction: A theoretical analysis and a review of the evidence.* Minneapolis: University of Minnesota Press.

Meehl, P. E. (1959). A comparison of clinicians with five statistical methods of identifying psychotic MMPI profiles. *Journal of Counseling Psychology, 6,* 102–109.

Meehl, P. E. (1967). What can the clinician do well? In D. N. Jackson & S. Messick (Eds.), *Problems in human assessment* (pp. 594–599). New York: McGraw-Hill.

Meehl, P. E. (1986). Causes and effects of my disturbing little book. *Journal of Personality Assessment, 50,* 370–375.

Meehl, P. E. (1992). Cliometric metatheory: The actuarial approach to empirical, history-based philosophy of science. *Psychological Reports, 71,* 339–467.

Meehl, P. E., & Rosen, A. (1955). Antecedent probability and the efficiency of psychometric signs, patterns, or cutting scores. *Psychological Bulletin, 52,* 194–216.

Milgram, S. (1974). *Obedience to authority.* New York: Harper & Row.

Modestin, J. (1992). Multiple personality disorder in Switzerland. *American Journal of Psychiatry, 149,* 88–92.

Murdach, A. D. (1994). Avoiding errors in clinical prediction. *Social Work, 39,* 381–386.

Neisser, U., & Harsch, N. (1992). Phantom flashbulbs: False recollections of hearing news about *Challenger.* In E. Winograd & U. Neisser (Eds.), *Affect and accuracy in recall: Studies of "flashbulb" memories.* New York: Cambridge University Press.

Neter, E., & Ben-Shakhar, G. (1989). The predictive validity of graphological inferences: A meta-analytic approach. *Personality and Individual Differences, 10,* 737–745.

Nisbett, R. E., Borgida, E., Crandall, R., & Reed, H. (1976). Popular induction: Information is not necessarily informative. In J. S. Carroll and J. W. Payne (Eds.), *Cognition and social behavior* (Vol. 2, pp. 227–236). Hillsdale, NJ: Erlbaum.

Nisbett, R. E., & Ross, L. 1980. *Human inference: Strategies and shortcomings of social judgment.* Englewood Cliffs, NJ: Prentice-Hall.

Norris, C. (1993). *The truth about postmodernism.* Cambridge, MA: Blackwell.

Ofshe, R., & Watters, E. (1996). *Making monsters: False memories, psychotherapy, and sexual hysteria.* Berkeley, CA: University of California Press.

Orne, M. T., & Dinges, D. F. (1989). Hypnosis. In H. I. Kaplan & B. J. Sadock (Eds.), *Comprehensive textbook of psychiatry* (Vol. 2). Baltimore: Williams & Wilkins.

Oskamp, S. (1965). Overconfidence in case-study judgments. *Journal of Consulting Psychology, 29,* 261–265.

Park, R. L. (1997). Alternative medicine and the laws of physics. *Skeptical Inquirer, 21,* 24–28.

Parr, L. E. (1996a). *Repressed memory claim referrals to the nurse consultant.* Department of Labor & Industries. Crime Victims Compensation Program. State of Washington. Unpublished manuscript submitted to Mental Health Subcommittee. (CVC Program, PO Box 44520, Olympia, Washington, 98504-4520. Tel: (360) 902-4945).

Parr, L. E. (1996b). *Repressed memory claims in the crime victims compensation program.* Department of Labor & Industries. Crime Victims Compensation

Program. State of Washington. Unpublished manuscript (with contributions from B. Huseby and R. Brown).

Pendergrast, M. (1995). *Victims of memory: Incest accusations and shattered lives.* Hinesburg, VT: Upper Access.

Phillips, M. (1999). Problems with the polygraph. *Science, 286,* 413.

Piper, A. (1994). Treatment for multiple personality disorder: At what cost? *American Journal of Psychotherapy, 48,* 392–400.

Piper, A. (1997). *Hoax and reality: The bizarre world of multiple personality disorder.* Northvale, NJ: Jason Aronson.

Piper, A. (1998). Multiple personality disorder: Witchcraft survives in the twentieth century. *Skeptical Inquirer, 22,* 44–50.

Plous, S. (1993). *The psychology of judgment and decision making.* Philadelphia: Temple University Press.

Plucker, J. A., Callahan, C. M., & Tomchin, E. M. (1996). Wherefore art thou, multiple intelligences? Alternative assessments for identifying talent in ethnically diverse and low income students. *Gifted Child Quarterly, 40,* 81–92.

Poole, D. A., Lindsay, D., Memon, A., & Bull, R. (1995). Psychotherapy and the recovery of memories of childhood sexual abuse: U.S. and British practitioners' opinions, practices, and experiences. *Journal of Consulting and Clinical Psychology, 63,* 426–437.

Potter, C. (1983). *Knock on wood.* New York: Beaufort Books.

Putnam, F. W. (1989). *Diagnosis and treatment of multiple personality disorder.* New York: Guilford.

Pynoos, R. S., & Nader, K. (1989). Children's memory and proximity to violence. *Journal of the American Academy of Child Psychiatry, 28,* 236–241.

Quinsey, V. L., & Maguire, A. (1986). Maximum security psychiatric patients: Actuarial and clinical prediction of dangerousness. *Journal of Interpersonal Violence, 1,* 143–171.

Radford, B. (2000). Worlds in collision: Applying reality to the paranormal. *Skeptical Inquirer, 24,* 37–39, 61.

Renaud, H., & Estess, F. (1961). Life history interviews with one hundred normal American males: "Pathogenicity" of childhood. *American Journal of Orthopsychiatry, 31,* 786–802.

Rosa, L., Rosa, E., Sarner, L., & Barrett, S. (1998). A close look at therapeutic touch. *Journal of the American Medical Association, 279,* 1005–1010.

Rosenhan, D. L. (1973). On being sane in insane places. *Science, 179,* 250–258.

Ross, C. A. (1991). Epidemiology of multiple personality disorder and dissociation. *Psychiatric Clinics of North America, 14,* 503–517.

Ross, C. A., & Dua, V. (1993). Psychiatric health care costs of multiple personality disorder. *American Journal of Psychotherapy, 47,* 103–112.

Ross, J. F. (1995). Risk: Where do real dangers lie? *Smithsonian, 26,* 42–53.

Rugg, D. (1941). Experiments in wording questions: II. *Public Opinion Quarterly, 5,* 91–92.

Ruscio, J. (1998). Information integration in child welfare cases: An introduction to statistical decision making. *Child Maltreatment, 3,* 143–156.

Ruscio, J. (2000). The role of complex thought in clinical prediction: Social accountability and the need for cognition. *Journal of Consulting and Clinical Psychology, 68,* 145–154.

Russo, J. E., & Shoemaker, P. J. H. (1989). *Decision traps: Ten barriers to brilliant decision making and how to overcome them.* New York: Simon & Schuster.

Sabadell, M. A. (1998). Biomagnetic pseudoscience and nonsense claims. *Skeptical Inquirer, 22,* 28.

Sagan, C. (1995). *The demon-haunted world: Science as a candle in the dark.* New York: Random House.

Sagan, C. (1997). *Billions and billions: Thoughts on life and death at the brink of the millenium.* New York: Random House.

Saravi, F. D. (1999). Energy and the brain: Facts and fantasies. In S. Della Sala (Ed.), *Mind myths: Exploring popular assumptions about the mind and brain* (pp. 43–58). New York: Wiley.

Sawyer, J. (1966). Measurement and prediction, clinical and statistical. *Psychological Bulletin, 66,* 178–200.

Saxe, L., Dougherty, D., & Cross, T. (1985). The validity of polygraph testing: Scientific analysis and public controversy. *American Psychologist, 40,* 355–366.

Scheiber, B., & Selby, C. (Eds.). (2000). *Therapeutic touch.* Amherst, NY: Prometheus.

Schmidt, F. L., & Hunter, J. E. (1998). The validity and utility of selection methods in personnel psychology: Practical and theoretical implications of 85 years of research findings. *Psychological Bulletin, 124,* 262–274.

Schnabel, J. (1994). *Round in circles.* New York: Penguin Books.

Schreiber, F. R. (1973). *Sybil.* Chicago: Henry Regnery.

Schuerman, J. R., & Vogel, L. H. (1986). Computer support of placement planning: The use of expert systems in child welfare. *Child Welfare, 65,* 531–543.

Search engines fall short. (1999, July 16). *Science, 285,* 295.

Seligman, M. E. P. (1975). *Helplessness: On depression, development, and death.* San Francisco: Freeman.

Sheaffer, R. (1997). The truth is, they never were 'saucers.' *Skeptical Inquirer, 21,* 22–23.

Simonton, O. C., Matthews-Simonton, S., & Creighton, J. (1978). *Getting well again.* Boston: J. P. Tarcher.

Skinner, B. F. (1948). *Walden two.* New York: Macmillan.

Skinner, B. F. (1953). *Science and human behavior.* New York: Macmillan.

Slovic, P. (1966). Cue-consistency and cue-utilization in judgment. *American Journal of Psychology, 79,* 427–434.

Slovic, P., Fischhoff, B., & Lichtenstein, S. (1979, April). Rating the risks. *Environment, 21,* 14–20, 36–39.

Slovic, P., & Lichtenstein, S. (1971). Comparison of Bayesian and regression approaches to the study of information processing in judgment. *Organizational Behavior and Human Performance, 6,* 649–744.

Slovic, P., & MacPhillamy, D. (1974). Dimensional commensurability and cue utilization in comparative judgment. *Organizational Behavior and Human Performance, 11,* 172–194.

Sofsky, W. (1997). *The order of terror: The concentration camp.* Princeton: Princeton University Press.

Sokal, A. D. (1996). Transgressing the boundaries: Toward a transformative hermeneutics of quantum gravity. *Social Text, 46/47,* 217–252.

Sokal, A. D., & Bricmont, J. (1998). *Fashionable nonsense: Postmodern intellectuals' abuse of science.* New York: Picador.

Spanos, N. P. (1994). Multiple identity enactments and multiple personality disorder: A sociocognitive perspective. *Psychological Bulletin, 116,* 143–165.

Spanos, N. P. (1996). *Multiple identities and false memories: A sociocognitive perspective.* Washington, DC: American Psychological Association.

Spanos, N. P., Menary, E., Gabora, N. J., DuBreuil, S. C., & Dewhirst, B. (1991). Secondary identity enactments during hypnotic past-life recognition. *Journal of Personality and Social Psychology, 61,* 308–320.

Spanos, N. P., Weekes, J. R., & Bertrand, L. D. (1985). Multiple personality: A social psychological perspective. *Journal of Abnormal Psychology, 94,* 362–376.

Spanos, N. P., Weekes, J. R., Menary, E., & Bertrand, L. D. (1986). Hypnotic interview and age regression procedures in the elicitation of multiple personality symptoms. *Psychiatry, 49,* 298–311.

Spence, D. P. (1982). *Narrative truth and historical truth.* New York: W. W. Norton.

Spitzer, R. L. (1976). More on pseudoscience in science and the case for psychiatric diagnosis. *Archives of General Psychology, 33,* 459–470.

Standing, L., & Keays, G. (1986). Computer assessment of personality: A demonstration of gullibility. *Social Behavior and Personality, 14,* 197–202.

Stanovich, K. E. (1998). *How to think straight about psychology* (5th ed.). New York: Longman.

Stewart, T. R. (1988). Judgment analysis: Procedures. In B. Brehmer & C. R. B. Joyce (Eds.), *Human judgment: The SJT view* (pp. 41–74). Amsterdam: North-Holland Elsevier.

Strom, A., Refsum, S. B., & Eitinger, L. (1962). Examination of Norwegian ex-concentration camp prisoners. *Journal of Neuropsychiatry, 4,* 43–62.

Swenson, D. X. (1999). Thought field therapy: Still searching for the quick fix. *Skeptic, 7,* 60–65.

Sykes, C. J. (1995). *Dumbing down our kids: Why America's children feel good about themselves but can't read, write, or add.* New York: St. Martin's Press.

Terr, L. C. (1979). Children of Chowchilla. *Psychoanalytic Study of the Child, 34,* 547–623.

Terr, L. C. (1983). Chowchilla revisited: The effects of psychic trauma four years after a school-bus kidnapping. *American Journal of Psychiatry, 140,* 1543–1550.

Thaler, R. (1980). Toward a positive theory of consumer choice. *Journal of Economic Behavior and Organization, 1,* 39–60.

Thigpen, C. H., & Cleckley, H. M. (1957). *The three faces of Eve.* New York: Fawcett.

Thigpen, C. H., & Cleckley, H. M. (1984). On the incidence of multiple personality disorder: A brief communication. *International Journal of Clinical and Experimental Hypnosis, 32,* 63–66.

Thomas, D. E. (1997). Hidden messages and the Bible Code. *Skeptical Inquirer, 21,* 30–36.

Thomas, D. E. (1998). Bible Code developments. *Skeptical Inquirer, 22,* 57–58.

Turk, D. C., & Salovey, P. (Eds.). (1988). *Reasoning, inference, and judgment in clinical psychology.* New York: Free Press.

Tversky, A., & Kahneman, D. (1973). Availability: A heuristic for judging frequency and probability. *Cognitive Psychology, 4,* 207–232.

Tversky, A., & Kahneman, D. (1974). Judgment under uncertainty: Heuristics and biases. *Science, 185,* 1124–1131.

Tversky, A., & Kahneman, D. (1981). The framing of decisions and the psychology of choice. *Science, 211,* 453–458.

Tversky, A., Sattath, S., & Slovic, P. (1988). Contingent weighting in judgment and choice. *Psychological Review, 95,* 371–384.

U. S. Surgeon General. (1964). Smoking and health. *Report of the Advisory Committee to the Surgeon General of the Public Health Service.* Washington, DC: U.S. Government Printing Office.

Vandell, D. L., & Corasantini, M. A. (1991). Child care and the family: Complex contributors to child development. *New Directions for Child Development, 49,* 23–37.

Van Rooij, J. (1994). The whole chart and nothing but the whole chart. *Correlation, 13,* 54–56.

Vaupel, J. W., & Graham, J. D. (1980). Egg in your bier? *The Public Interest, 58,* 3–17.

Wagenaar, W. A., & Groeneweg, J. (1990). The memory of concentration camp survivors. *Applied Cognitive Psychology, 4,* 77–87.

Weil, A. J. (1972). *The natural mind: A new way of looking at drugs and the higher consciousness.* Boston: Houghton Mifflin.

Weil, A. J. (1998). *Ask Dr. Weil.* New York: Fawcett Columbine

Wormith, J. S., & Goldstone, C. S. (1984). The clinical and statistical prediction of recidivism. *Criminal Justice and Behavior, 11,* 3–34.

Ziskin, J., & Faust, D. (1988). *Coping with psychiatric and psychological testimony.* Venice, CA: Law and Psychology Press.

Index

TO THE OWNER OF THIS BOOK:

We hope that you have found *Clear Thinking with Psychology* useful. So that this book can be improved in a future edition, would you take the time to complete this sheet and return it? Thank you.

School and address: _____

Department: _____

Instructor's name: _____

1. What I like most about this book is: _____

_____

_____

2. What I like least about this book is: _____

_____

_____

3. My general reaction to this book is: _____

_____

4. The name of the course in which I used this book is: _____

_____

5. Were all of the chapters of the book assigned for you to read? _____

   If not, which ones weren't? _____

6. In the space below, or on a separate sheet of paper, please write specific suggestions for improving this book and anything else you'd care to share about your experience in using the book.

_____

_____

_____

_____

Optional:

Your name: _____ Date: _____

May Brooks/Cole quote you, either in promotion for *Clear Thinking with Psychology* or in future publishing ventures?

Yes: _____ No: _____

Sincerely,

John Ruscio

FOLD HERE

- -

FOLD HERE